Japanese
Phrasebook

LAROUSSE

Editors
Tessa Carroll, Harumi Currie

with

Valerie Grundy, Christy Johnson, Donald Watt

Supplement on Japanese language and culture
Tessa Carroll

Publishing manager
Janice McNeillie

Design and typesetting
Sharon McTeir

© Larousse 2007
21, rue du Montparnasse
75283 Paris Cedex 06

ISBN: 978-2-0354-2156-2

Sales: Houghton Mifflin Company, Boston

Achevé d'imprimer en Janvier 2007 sur les presses de «La Tipografica Varese S.p.A.» (Italie

Introduction

This phrasebook is the ideal companion for your trip. It gets straight to the point, helping you to understand and make yourself understood so that you don't miss a thing. Use it like a dictionary to find the exact word you're looking for right away. And at each word we've provided a selection of key phrases that will help you in any situation, no matter how tricky things may have gotten.

The English–Japanese section contains all those essential expressions that you'll need to get by in Japan. And because you need to be able to pronounce the words you see on the page properly, we've provided a simple and straightforward standardized phonetic transcription that will enable you to make yourself understood with ease.

The Japanese–English section provides all the most important words and expressions that you might read or hear while on vacation. It's arranged by subject for ease of look-up.

And that's not all: we've added practical and cultural tips for getting by, a supplement on Japanese language, life and culture – everything, in fact, to make your trip go as smoothly as possible.

Pronunciation

So that you can say what you want to say in Japanese without running any risk of being misunderstood, we have devised a simple and straightforward phonetic transcription to show how every Japanese word or phrase used in this guide is pronounced. This phonetic transcription, which is shown in brackets after each Japanese word or phrase, uses standard English sounds, so that it is virtually self-explanatory.

Japanese works in syllables rather than individual vowels and consonants. Syllables consist of one of the following: 1) a vowel alone (e.g. "a"); 2) a consonant followed by a vowel (e.g. "ka"); 3) "n," which counts as a syllable in its own right; 4) a consonant followed by "y" followed by vowel (e.g. "kya"). When different vowels follow each other, each individual vowel is clearly pronounced: for example, *aoi* (blue) is pronounced *a-o-i*. Nor do the vowel sounds change when combined with different consonants; for example, *kane* (money) is pronounced *ka-ne*. It is important to note that there is no stress on a particular syllable of a word as there is in English.

Vowels

a	as in "c**ar**," but shorter
e	as in "b**e**d," but shorter
i	as in "f**ee**t," but shorter
o	as in "**oh**," but shorter and with the lips slightly more rounded
u	as in "b**oo**k," but shorter and with the lips less rounded

Consonants

b	as in "**b**ed"
ch	as in "**ch**at"
d	as in "**d**ay"

f	pronounced without the upper teeth touching the lower lip, so between the English sounds "f" and "h"
g	as in "**g**o" (*g* is sometimes nasalized, like the "ng" in "si**ng**," particularly in the Tokyo area)
h	as in "**h**ot"
j	as in "**j**ob"
k	as in "**k**ill"
m	as in "**m**an"
n	as in "**n**ot," except at the end of words, when it is a syllable in its own right and is pronounced as in "si**ng**"
n'	as in "si**ng**" (used to distinguish pronunciation from 'n' mid-word)
p	as in "**p**ay"
r	the *r* sound is between the English sounds "r" and "l"
s	as in "**s**it"
sh	as in "**sh**ow"
t	as in "**t**ake"
tsu	as in "ba**ts**"
w	as in "**w**alk," but with the lips less rounded
y	as in "**y**es"
z	as in "**z**oo"

If *i* or *u* occurs between any of the consonants *k*, *s*, *t*, *h* and *p*, they are usually whispered so they are barely heard; for example, the name *Yamashita* sounds like *Yamashta*. This also happens at the end of words, particularly verbs ending in *su*; for example, *ikimasu* (go) is often pronounced *ikimas*.

Each of the vowels can be lengthened. This is shown by a circumflex over the vowel: *â, î, û, ê, ô*. The vowel sounds are the same as described above – just hold the sound for twice as long. It is important to distinguish between short and long vowels, as some words are identical apart from this difference; for example *shujin* (husband, landlord) and *shûjin* (prisoner).

In double consonants (*kk, nn, pp, ss,* and *tt*) too, the sound is lengthened. For example, *kk* in *gakkô* is pronounced as in "bla**ck** **c**at." Note that when *ch* is doubled, it is written as *tch*.

Writing system

The Japanese writing system combines Chinese characters (*kanji*), which include an element of meaning, and two phonetic syllabaries, *hiragana* and *katakana*, which represent only sounds. Words can be written using either of these scripts. Any Japanese words can be written in *hiragana*, but this script is mainly used to write grammatical words and endings of words where the main part that conveys the concept is written in *kanji*. The *katakana* script is used mainly for loanwords of foreign origin. Japanese was traditionally written vertically, right to left, but is now also written horizontally, left to right, and there are no breaks between words.

English–Japanese phrasebook

able
- to be able to... ...ことができる [...koto ga dekiru]
- I'm not able to come tonight 今夜は行くことができません [kon ya wa iku koto ga dekimasen]

about ...について [...ni tsuite] ◆ 約 [yaku]
- I think I'll stay for about an hour 約一時間いるつもりです [yaku ichi jikan iru tsumori desu]

abroad *(live, travel)* 海外に [kaigai ni]
- I've never been abroad before 海外に行ったことはありません [kaigai ni itta koto wa arimasen]

absolutely 絶対的に [zettaiteki ni]
- you're absolutely right 絶対的に正しいです [zettaiteki ni tadashî desu]

accept 受け取る [uketoru]
- do you accept traveler's checks? トラベラーズチェックは受け取りますか [toraberâzu chekku wa uketorimasu ka]

access 通路 [tsûro]
- is there disabled access? 身障者用の通路はありますか [shinshôsha yô no tsûro wa arimasu ka]

accident 事故 [jiko]
- there's been an accident 事故がありました [jiko ga arimashita]

according to ...によれば [...ni yoreba]
- it's well worth seeing, according to the guidebook ガイドブックによれば、見る価値があるそうです [gaidobukku ni yoreba, miru kachi ga aru sô desu]

address *(details of place)* 住所 [jûsho] ◆ *(speak to)* 演説する [enzetsu suru]
- could you write down the address for me? 住所を書いてくれませんか [jûsho o kaite kuremasen ka]
- here is my address and phone number, if you're ever in the US もしアメリカに来ることがあれば、これが私の住所と電話番号です [moshi amerika ni kuru koto ga areba, kore ga watashi no jûsho to denwa bangô desu]

adult 大人 [otona]
- two adults and one student, please 大人二人と学生一人、お願いします [otona futari to gakusê hitori, onegai shimasu]

advance *(money)* 前払い [mae barai] ◆ **in advance** *(pay, reserve)* 前もって [mae motte]

> do you have to book in advance? 前もって予約しなければなりませんか
> [mae motte yoyaku shinakereba narimasen ka]

after の後 [...no ato]

> it's twenty after eight 8時20分です [hachi ji nijippun desu]
> the stadium is just after the traffic lights スタジアムは信号のすぐ後です
> [sutajiamu wa shingô no sugu ato desu]

afternoon 午後 [gogo]

> is the museum open in the afternoons? 博物館は午後開いていますか
> [hakubutsukan wa gogo aite imasu ka]

aftershave シェーブローション [shêbu rôshon]

> a bottle of aftershave, please シェーブローションを一本、ください
> [shêbu rôshon o ippon kudasai]

afterwards あとで [ato de]

> join us afterwards あとでまた会いましょう [ato de mata aimashô]

again また [mata]

> the plane is late again 飛行機はまた遅れています [hikôki wa mata okurete
> imasu]

age 年齢 [nenrê], 年 [toshi] ◆ **ages** 長い間 [nagai aida]

> what ages are your children? お子さんの年はいくつですか [okosan no
> toshi wa ikutsu desu ka]
> we've been waiting for ages! 長い間待っています [nagai aida matte imasu]

agency 代理店 [dairiten]

> what is the contact number for the agency? 代理店の電話番号は何番で
> すか [dairiten no denwa bangô wa namban desu ka]

ago 前に [mae ni]

> I've been before, several years ago 何年か前に行ったことがあります
> [nan nen ka mae ni itta koto ga arimasu]

---

agreement/disagreement

> absolutely! もちろん！ [mochiron]
> that's fine by me 私はそれでいいですよ [watashi wa sore de î desu yo]
> you're right そのとおり [sono tôri]
> go on, then それなら、やったら [sore nara, yattara]
> I'm not at all convinced 納得できません [nattoku dekimasen]
> I disagree ちょっと違うと思いますが [chotto chigau to omoimasu ga]

airlines

JAL (Japan Airlines) and ANA (All Nippon Airways) operate international and domestic flights, and JAS (Japan Air System) and other smaller carriers offer domestic flights. Both JAL and ANA offer special discounts for domestic airfares bought outside Japan together with an international ticket to Japan.

---

agreement 意見の一致 [iken no itchi]
- we need to come to some agreement about where we're going next 次はどこに行くか、意見の一致が必要です [tsugi wa doko ni iku ka, iken no itchi ga hitsuyô desu]

ahead 先の [saki no]
- is the road ahead clear? この先の道は空いていますか [kono saki no michi wa aite imasu ka]

air *(wind)* 空気 [kûki]
- the air is much fresher in the mountains 山の空気はもっと新鮮です [yama no kûki wa motto shinsen desu]

air-conditioning エアコン [eakon]
- do you have air-conditioning? エアコンはありますか [eakon wa arimasu ka]

airline 航空会社 [kôkû gaisha]
- no, we're traveling with a different airline いいえ、別の航空会社の便で旅行しています [îe, betsu no kôkû gaisha no bin de ryokô shite imasu]

airmail 航空便 [kôkûbin]
- I'd like to send it airmail 航空便で出したいんですが [kôkûbin de dashitai n desu ga]

airport 空港 [kûkô]
- how long does it take to get to the airport? 空港までどれぐらいかかりますか [kûkô made dore gurai kakarimasu ka]

---

at the airport

- where is gate number 2? 二番ゲートはどこですか [ni ban gêto wa doko desu ka]
- where is the check-in desk? チェックインカウンターはどこですか [chekku-in kauntâ wa doko desu ka]
- I'd like an aisle seat 通路側の席をお願いします [tsûro gawa no seki o onegai shimasu]
- where is the baggage claim? 荷物はどこで受け取りますか [nimotsu wa doko de uketorimasu ka]

alcohol

Rice wine (酒 [sake]) is well-known as the traditional Japanese alcoholic drink. However, the word also refers to alcohol in general, so 日本酒 [nihonshu] is also used to refer specifically to rice wine. It comes in two broad varieties: sweet (甘口 [amakuchi]) and dry (辛口 [karakuchi]). There are over 2,500 types available, of varying quality and strength. It can be drunk cold (冷や [hiya]) or hot (熱燗 [atsukan]), and is always served in tiny cups called (杯 [sakazuki]), meaning frequent refills are required! It is not considered polite to pour your own drink when you are in company; if you pour a drink for someone else, he or she will return the favor. Everyone clinks glasses and says 乾杯 [kampai] (cheers) when they start drinking.

airport shuttle シャトルバスや電車 [shatoru basu ya densha]
▸ is there an airport shuttle? 空港へのシャトルバスや電車はありますか [kûkô e no shatoru basu ya densha wa arimasu ka]

air pressure 空気圧 [kûki atsu]
▸ could you check the air pressure in the tires? タイヤの空気圧を調べてくれませんか [taiya no kûki atsu o shirabete kuremasen ka]

airsick 飛行機酔い [hikôki yoi]
▸ can I have an airsick bag? 飛行機酔いの衛生袋をもらえますか [hikôki yoi no êsêbukuro o moraemasu ka]

aisle *(between plane seats)* 通路 [tsûro]; *(plane seat)* 通路側の席 [tsûro gawa no seki]
▸ two seats, please: one window and one aisle 席を二つお願いします。一つは窓側、一つは通路側です [seki o futatsu onegai shimasu. hitotsu wa mado gawa, hitotsu wa tsûro gawa desu]

aisle seat 通路側の席 [tsûro gawa no seki]
▸ I'd like an aisle seat 通路側の席をお願いします [tsûro gawa no seki o onegai shimasu]

alarm (clock) 目覚まし（時計）[mezamashi (dokê)]
▸ I set the alarm for nine o'clock 目覚ましを九時にかけました [mezamashi o ku ji ni kakemashita]

alcohol *(for drinking)* 酒 [sake]; *(for medicinal use)* 消毒用アルコール [shôdoku yô arukôru]
▸ I don't drink alcohol お酒は飲みません [osake wa nomimasen]

alcohol-free ソフトドリンク [sofuto dorinku]
▸ what kind of alcohol-free drinks do you have? ソフトドリンクはどんなものがありますか [sofuto dorinku wa donna mono ga arimasu ka]

all 全ての [subete no] ◆ *(the whole amount)* 全部 [zembu]; *(everybody)* みんな [minna]
- all the time いつも [itsumo]
- all English people イギリス人みんな [igirisujin minna]
- not at all 全然 [zenzen]

allergic アレルギーの [arerugî no]
- I'm allergic to aspirin/nuts/wheat/dairy products アスピリン/ナッツ/小麦/乳製品にアレルギーがあります [asupirin/nattsu/komugi/nyûsêhin ni arerugî ga arimasu]

allow 大丈夫だ [daijôbu da]
- how much luggage are you allowed? 荷物はどれだけ大丈夫ですか [nimotsu wa dore dake daijôbu desu ka]
- are you allowed to smoke here? ここでタバコを吸っても大丈夫ですか [koko de tabako o sutte mo daijôbu desu ka]

almost ほとんど [hotondo]
- it's almost one o'clock ほとんど一時です [hotondo ichi ji desu]

alone 一人で [hitori de]
- I'm traveling alone 一人で旅行しています [hitori de ryokô shite imasu]

along に沿って [ni sotte]
- along the river 川に沿って [kawa ni sotte]

altogether *(in total)* 全部で [zembu de]
- how much does it cost altogether? 全部でいくらですか [zembu de ikura desu ka]

always いつも [itsumo]
- I always stay in the same hotel when I come to Kyoto 京都に来る時はいつも同じホテルに泊まります [kyôto ni kuru toki wa itsumo onaji hoteru ni tomarimasu]

ambulance 救急車 [kyûkyûsha]
- could you send an ambulance right away to...? ...に救急車を至急お願いします [...ni kyûkyûsha o shikyû onegai shimasu]

America アメリカ [amerika]
- I'm from America アメリカから来ました [amerika kara kimashita]
- I live in America アメリカに住んでいます [amerika ni sunde imasu]
- have you ever been to America? アメリカに行ったことがありますか [amerika ni itta koto ga arimasu ka]

American アメリカの [amerika no] ◆ アメリカ人 [amerikajin]
- I'm/we are American(s) アメリカ人です [amerikajin desu]

ankle 足首 [ashikubi]
- I've sprained my ankle 足首をくじきました [ashikubi o kujikimashita]

announcement 放送 [hôsô]
- was that an announcement about the Tokaido line train? 今のは東海道線についての放送でしたか [ima no wa tôkaidô sen ni tsuite no hôsô deshita ka]

another *(additional)* もうひとつ [mô hitotsu]; *(different)* 違う [chigau]
- another coffee, please コーヒーをもう一杯お願いします [kôhî o mô ippai onegai shimasu]
- (would you like) another drink? もう一杯いかがですか [mô ippai ikaga desu ka]

answer 答え [kotae] ◆ 答える [kotaeru]
- there's no answer 誰も出ません [dare mo demasen]
- I phoned earlier but nobody answered 前に電話しましたが、誰も出ませんでした [mae ni denwa shimashita ga, dare mo demasen deshita]

answering machine 留守番電話 [rusuban denwa]
- I left a message on your answering machine 留守番電話にメッセージを残しました [rusuban denwa ni messêji o nokoshimashita]

anti-dandruff shampoo ふけ取りシャンプー [fuketori shampû]
- do you have anti-dandruff shampoo? ふけ取りシャンプーはありますか [fuketori shampû wa arimasu ka]

anybody, anyone 誰か [dare ka]
- is there anybody there? 誰かいますか [dare ka imasu ka]

anything 何か [nani ka]
- is there anything I can do? 何か私にできることはありますか [nani ka watashi ni dekiru koto wa arimasu ka]

anywhere どこか [doko ka]
- I can't find my room key anywhere 部屋の鍵がどこにもありません [heya no kagi ga doko ni mo arimasen]
- do you live anywhere near here? どこかこの近くに住んでいますか [doko ka kono chikaku ni sunde imasu ka]

apartment アパート [apâto]
- we'd like to rent an apartment for one year アパートを一年借りたいんですが [apâto o ichi nen karitai n desu ga]

apologizing

- excuse me! すみません [sumimasen]
- I'm sorry, I can't come on Saturday すみません、土曜日は行けません [sumimasen, doyôbi wa ikemasen]
- that's OK/it doesn't matter/don't mention it いいですよ [î desu yo]

apologize 謝る [ayamaru]
- there's no need to apologize 謝る必要はありません [ayamaru hitsuyô wa arimasen]

appetizer アペタイザー [apetaizâ]
- which of the appetizers would you recommend? どのアペタイザーがお勧めですか [dono apetaizâ ga osusume desu ka]

apple りんご [ringo]
- could I have five apples, please? りんごを五つください [ringo o itsutsu kudasai]

apple juice アップルジュース [appuru jûsu]
- I'd like some apple juice アップルジュースがほしいんですが [appuru jûsu ga hoshî n desu ga]

appointment 面会の予約 [menkai no yoyaku]
- could I get an appointment for tomorrow morning? 明日の朝に面会の予約ができるでしょうか [ashita no asa ni menkai no yoyaku ga dekiru deshô ka]
- I have an appointment with Doctor... ...先生に予約してあります [...sensê ni yoyaku shite arimasu]

April 四月 [shigatsu]
- April 6th 4月6日 [shigatsu muika]

area *(region)* 地方 [chihô]; *(small)* 部分 [bubun]; *(of town)* 地域 [chi-iki]
- I'm visiting the Nara area for a few days 奈良地方に数日来ています [nara chihô ni sû nichi kite imasu]
- what walks can you recommend in the area? この地域で散歩にいいところを教えてください [kono chi-iki de sampo ni î tokoro o oshiete kudasai]

area code *(for telephoning)* 市外局番 [shigai kyokuban]
- what's the area code for Nagoya? 名古屋の市外局番は何番ですか [nagoya no shigai kyokuban wa namban desu ka]

arm 腕 [ude]
- I can't move my arm 腕が動きません [ude ga ugokimasen]

around *(in all directions)* まわり [mawari]; *(nearby)* 近く [chikaku]; *(here and there)* あちこち [achikochi] ◆ *(encircling)* 回って [mawatte]; *(through)* あちこちに [achikochi ni]; *(approximately – amount)* ぐらい [gurai]; *(approximately – point in time)* 頃 [goro]
- we've been traveling around Japan 日本のあちこちを旅行しています [nihon no achikochi o ryokô shite imasu]
- I don't know my way around yet まだ地理がよく分かりません [mada chiri ga yoku wakarimasen]
- I arrived around two o'clock 二時頃、着きました [ni ji goro tsukimashita]
- I'd like something for around 1000 yen 1000円ぐらいのものがほしいです [sen en gurai no mono ga hoshî desu]

arrive 着く [tsuku]
- my luggage hasn't arrived 荷物がまだ着きません [nimotsu ga mada tsukimasen]
- we arrived late 遅く着きました [osoku tsukimashita]
- we just arrived 着いたばかりです [tsuita bakari desu]

art 芸術 [gêjutsu]
- I'm not really interested in art 芸術にはあまり興味がありません [gêjutsu ni wa amari kyômi ga arimasen]

as *(while)* 時 [toki]; *(like)* ように [yô ni]; *(since)* ので [node] ◆ *(in comparisons)* ぐらい [gurai]
- the lights went out just as we were about to eat ちょうど食事をしようとした時に電気が消えました [chôdo shokuji o shiyô to shita toki ni denki ga kiemashita]
- as I said before 前にも言ったように [mae ni mo itta yô ni]
- leave it as it is そのままにしておいてください [sono mama ni shite oite kudasai]
- as... as ...と同じぐらい [...to onaji gurai...]
- this building is as old as the imperial palace この建物は皇居と同じぐらい古いです [kono tatemono wa kôkyo to onaji gurai furui desu]

ashtray 灰皿 [haizara]
- could you bring us an ashtray? 灰皿を持って来てくれませんか [haizara o motte kite kuremasen ka]

ask *(question)* 質問する [shitsumon suru]; *(direction, time)* 聞く [kiku]
- can I ask you a question? 質問してもいいですか [shitsumon shite mo î desu ka]

aspirin アスピリン [arupirin]
- I'd like some aspirin アスピリンがほしいんですが [asupirin ga hoshî n desu ga]

asking questions

- is this seat free? この席は空いていますか [kono seki wa aite imasu ka]
- where is the railway station? 駅はどこですか [eki wa doko desu ka]
- could you help me get my suitcase down, please? スーツケースを下ろすのを手伝ってもらえませんか [sûtsukêsu o orosu no o tetsudatte moraemasen ka]
- could you give me a hand? 手伝ってもらえませんか [tetsudatte moraemasen ka]
- could you lend me an umbrella? 傘を貸してくれませんか [kasa o kashite kuremasen ka]

ATMs

Few ATMs take international Visa® cards or MasterCard®, even in Tokyo, except those of the Sumitomo-Mitsui bank (the sign has a green flag divided into three) or Citibank (a white star on a blue circle). Even these usually have limited business hours. However, over 21,000 post offices now have ATMs that accept foreign credit, debit and cash cards. Business hours of ATMs at large branches are 7 a.m. to 11 p.m. on weekdays and 9 a.m. to 7 p.m. on weekends and on national holidays, but are more restricted in smaller branches.

asthma 喘息 [zensoku]
  ▸ I have asthma 喘息持ちです [zensoku mochi desu]

at ...に [...ni]
  ▸ our bags are still at the hotel かばんはまだホテルにあります [kaban wa mada hoteru ni arimasu]
  ▸ we arrive at midnight 深夜に着きます [shin ya ni tsukimasu]

ATM 現金自動支払機 [genkin jidô shiharaiki], ATM [êtîemu]
  ▸ I'm looking for an ATM ATMを探しています [êtîemu o sagashite imasu]
  ▸ the ATM has eaten my card ATMからカードが出てきません [êtîemu kara kâdo ga dete kimasen]

attack (of illness) 発作 [hossa] ◆ (person) 襲う [osou]
  ▸ he had a heart attack 心臓発作に襲われました [shinzô hossa ni osowaremashita]
  ▸ I've been attacked 襲われました [osowaremashita]

attention 注意 [chûi]
  ▸ may I have your attention for a moment? しばらく注意してお聞きいただけますか [shibaraku chûi shite okiki itadakemasu ka]

attractive 魅力的な [miryokuteki na]
  ▸ I find you very attractive あなたはとても魅力的です [anata wa totemo miryokuteki desu]

August 八月 [hachigatsu]
  ▸ we're arriving on August 29th 8月29日に着きます [hachigatsu nijûku nichi ni tsukimasu]

automatic 自動の [jidô no] ◆ (car) オートマチック車 [ôtomachikku sha]
  ▸ I want a car with automatic transmission オートマチック車がいいんですが [ôtomachikku sha ga î n desu ga]
  ▸ is it a manual or an automatic? マニュアルですか、オートマチックですか [manyuaru desu ka, ôtomachikku desu ka]

available ある [aru]
- you don't have a table available before then? それより前に空いている席はありませんか [sore yori mae ni aite iru seki wa arimasen ka]

average 平均的な [hēkinteki na]
- what's the average price of a meal there? 平均的な食事の値段はどれくらいですか [hēkinteki na shokuji no nedan wa dore gurai desu ka]

avoid 避ける [sakeru]
- is there a route that would help us avoid the traffic? 渋滞を避けられる道はありますか [jūtai o sakerareru michi wa arimasu ka]

away *(indicating movement)* 向こうへ [mukō e]; *(indicating position)* 離れて [hanarete] ◆ **away from** ...から離れた [...kara hanareta]
- the village is 10 km away 村は１０キロ離れています [mura wa jikkiro hanarete imasu]
- we're looking for a cottage far away from the town 町から離れた小ロッジを探しています [machi kara hanareta shōrojji o sagashite imasu]
- do you have any rooms away from the main road? 大きな道から離れた部屋はありますか [ōki na michi kara hanareta heya wa arimasu ka]

b

baby bottle 哺乳瓶 [honyūbin]
- I need to sterilize a baby bottle 哺乳瓶の消毒をしなければなりません [honyūbin no shōdoku o shinakereba narimasen]

back 後の [ushiro no] ◆ *(part of body)* 背中 [senaka]; *(of room)* 後ろ [ushiro]
- I'll be back in 5 minutes 5分後に戻って来ます [go fun go ni modotte kimasu]
- I've got a bad back 背中が悪いです [senaka ga warui desu]
- I prefer to sit at the back 後ろに座る方がいいです [ushiro ni suwaru hō ga ī desu]

backache 腰痛 [yōtsū]
- I've got a backache 腰が痛いです [koshi ga itai desu]

backpack バックパック [bakkupakku]
- my passport's in my backpack パスポートはバックパックの中にあります [pasupōto wa bakkupakku no naka ni arimasu]

back up 戻る [modoru]
- I think we have to back up and turn right 戻って右に曲がったほうがいいと思います [modotte migi ni magatta hō ga ī to omoimasu]

bad 悪い [warui]

> the weather's bad today 今日は天気が悪いです [kyô wa tenki ga warui desu]

bag 袋 [fukuro]; *(suitcase)* かばん [kaban], バッグ [baggu]; *(purse)* ハンドバッグ [handobaggu]

> are these the bags from flight 502? これは５０２便のバッグですか [kore wa gohyakuni bin no baggu desu ka]

> can someone take our bags up to the room, please? かばんを部屋まで運んでもらえませんか [kaban o heya made hakonde moraemasen ka]

baggage 荷物 [nimotsu]

> my baggage hasn't arrived 荷物がまだ着いていません [nimotsu ga mada tsuite imasen]

> I'd like to report the loss of my baggage 荷物の紛失を届けたいんですが [nimotsu no funshitsu o todoketai n desu ga]

baggage cart カート [kâto]

> I'm looking for a baggage cart カートを探しています [kâto o sagashite imasu]

bakery パン屋 [pan ya]

> is there a bakery nearby? 近くにパン屋はありますか [chikaku ni pan ya wa arimasu ka]

bamboo 竹 [take]

> is that bamboo over there? あれは竹ですか [are wa take desu ka]

banana バナナ [banana]

> eight bananas, please バナナを八本ください [banana o happon kudasai]

bandage 包帯 [hôtai]

> I need a bandage for my ankle 足首に包帯がいります [ashikubi ni hôtai ga irimasu]

---

at the bank

> I'd like to change 200 dollars into yen ２００ドルを円に換えたいんですが [nihyaku doru o en ni kaetai n desu ga]

> in small bills, please 小額の紙幣をください [shôgaku no shihê o kudasai]

> what is the exchange rate for the dollar? ドルの交換率はいくらですか [doru no kôkan ritsu wa ikura desu ka]

> how much is that in dollars? ドルでいくらですか [doru de ikura desu ka]

> do you take traveler's checks? トラベラーズチェックを受け取りますか [toraberâzu chekku o uketorimasu ka]

> do you charge a commission? 手数料がかかりますか [tesûryô ga kakarimasu ka]

Band-Aid® バンドエイド® [bando-êdo]
▸ can I have a Band-Aid® for my cut? 切ったのでバンドエイド®をもらえますか [kitta node bando-êdo o moraemasu ka]

bank *(finance)* 銀行 [ginkô]
▸ is there a bank nearby? 近くに銀行はありますか [chikaku ni ginkô wa arimasu ka]
▸ are banks open on Saturdays? 銀行は土曜日も開いていますか [ginkô wa doyôbi mo aite imasu ka]; see box on p. 11

bank card 銀行のカード [ginkô no kâdo]
▸ I've lost my bank card 銀行のカードを失くしました [ginkô no kâdo o nakushimashita]

bar *(establishment serving alcohol)* バー [bâ]; *(counter)* カウンター [kauntâ]
▸ are there any good bars around here? この辺にいいバーはありますか [kono hen ni î bâ wa arimasu ka]

base *(bottom,)* 底 [soko]; *(starting point)* 拠点 [kyoten]
▸ the base of the lamp got broken 電気スタンドの底が壊れました [denki sutando no soko ga kowaremashita]
▸ we're going to use the village as our base to explore the area そのあたりを見て回る拠点として、その村を使うことにします [sono atari o mite mawaru kyoten toshite, sono mura o tsukau koto ni shimasu]

basic 基本的な [kihonteki na] ◆ **basics** 基本的なもの [kihonteki na mono]
▸ do the staff all have a basic knowledge of English? スタッフはみんな基本的な英語を知っていますか [sutaffu wa minna kihonteki na êgo o shitte imasu ka]
▸ I know the basics, but no more than that 基本的なことは知っていますが、それだけです [kihonteki na koto wa shitte imasu ga, sore dake desu]

bat *(for table tennis)* ラケット [raketto]
▸ can you rent bats? ラケットは借りられますか [raketto wa kariraremasu ka]

bath 風呂 [furo]
▸ to take a bath 風呂に入る [furo ni hairu]

bathroom *(with bathtub and/or shower)* 風呂場 [furoba]; *(with toilet)* トイレ [toire], お手洗い [otearai]
▸ where's the bathroom? *(with bathtub)* 風呂場はどこですか [furoba wa doko desu ka]; *(toilet)* トイレはどこですか [toire wa doko desu ka]

bathtub 風呂 [furo]
▸ there's no plug for the bathtub 風呂の栓がありません [furo no sen ga arimasen]

battery *(for radio, flashlight)* 電池 [denchi]; *(in car)* バッテリー [batterî]
▸ I need new batteries 新しい電池が必要です [atarashî denchi ga hitsuyô desu]

bathing

Bathing is almost a ritual and a source of great pleasure in Japan, used for relaxation even more than for cleansing. The traditional bathroom is a 'wet room,' with low faucets and a shower fitting, and there is a low stool to sit on. You wash and rinse yourself thoroughly outside the bathtub so you are clean before getting in for a good soak. Everyone uses the same bathwater, so it is very important to keep it clean. A Japanese bathtub is deep enough to sit in with the water up to your chest or neck, and those in homes are square in shape. The water is kept very hot, these days with a gas heater, and there is usually a lid to keep the heat in. In Japanese-style inns and guesthouses, there will be a large communal bath, used by men and women at different times. There are still public baths (銭湯 [sentô]) in many areas, and these too are segregated by sex inside. For the ultimate Japanese bathing experience, visit a natural hot spring (温泉 [onsen]). These are very popular for day and weekend trips. They range from beautiful old bathhouses to large modern complexes, and many have outdoor pools (露天風呂 [rotemburo]) so you can relax in the midst of nature. Bathrooms in hotels are western-style, with a shower over the bathtub.

▸ the battery needs to be recharged 電池を充電しなければなりません [denchi o jûden shinakereba narimasen]
▸ the battery's dead *(radio, camera)* 電池が切れました [denchi ga kiremashita]; *(car)* バッテリーがあがってしまいました [batterî ga agatte shimaimashita]

be

▸ where are you from? どこからですか [doko kara desu ka]
▸ I'm a teacher 教師です [kyôshi desu]
▸ I'm happy うれしいです [ureshî desu]
▸ how are you? お元気ですか [ogenki desu ka]
▸ I'm fine はい、元気です [hai, genki desu]
▸ where is terminal 1? 第一ターミナルはどこですか [dai ichi tâminaru wa doko desu ka]
▸ could you show me where I am on the map? 今、どこにいるか、この地図で教えてくれませんか [ima doko ni iru ka, kono chizu de oshiete kuremasen ka]
▸ have you ever been to the United States? アメリカに行ったことはありますか [amerika ni itta koto wa arimasu ka]
▸ it's the first time I've been here ここに来たのは初めてです [koko ni kita no wa hajimete desu]
▸ how old are you? おいくつですか [oikutsu desu ka]

beer

Beer has been popular in Japan since the end of World War II, and the three main brands are Asahi, Sapporo and Kirin.

- I'm 18 (years old) １８歳です [jûhassai desu]
- it was over 35 degrees ３５度以上ありました [sanjûgo do ijô arimashita]
- it's cold in the evenings 夕方は寒いです [yûgata wa samui desu]
- how much is it? いくらですか [ikura desu ka]
- I'm 1.68 meters tall 身長は１メートル６８センチです [shinchô wa ichi mêtoru rokujûhassenchi desu]

beach 浜（辺） [hama (be)]
- it's a sandy beach 砂浜です [suna hama desu]
- is it a quiet beach? 静かな浜辺ですか [shizuka na hamabe desu ka]

beach umbrella ビーチパラソル [bîchi parasoru]
- can you rent beach umbrellas? ビーチパラソルを貸してもらえますか [bîchi parasoru o kashite moraemasu ka]

beautiful 美しい [utsukushî]、きれいな [kirê na]
- it's a beautiful park きれいな公園です [kirê na kôen desu]

bed ベッド [beddo]
- is it possible to add an extra bed? ベッドを追加してもらえますか [beddo o tsuika shite moraemasu ka]
- do you have a children's bed? 子供用のベッドはありますか [kodomo yô no beddo wa arimasu ka]
- to go to bed 寝る [neru]
- I went to bed late 遅く寝ました [osoku nemashita]
- I need to put my children to bed now もう子供を寝かさなければなりません [mô kodomo o nekasanakereba narimasen]

bedroom 寝室 [shinshitsu]
- how many bedrooms does the apartment have? アパートに寝室はいくつありますか [apâto ni shinshitsu wa ikutsu arimasu ka]

bedside lamp ベッドの電気スタンド [beddo no denki sutando]
- the bedside lamp doesn't work ベッドの電気スタンドが壊れています [beddo no denki sutando ga kowarete imasu]

beef ビーフ [bîfu]、牛肉 [gyûniku]
- I don't eat beef ビーフは食べません [bîfu wa tabemasen]

beer ビール [bîru]
- two beers, please ビールを二本、お願いします [bîru o ni hon, onegai shimasu]

before ...の前 [... no mae]
▸ before breakfast 朝ごはんの前に [asagohan no mae ni]
▸ before I go 行く前に [iku mae ni]

begin *(start)* 始まる [hajimaru]
▸ when does the concert begin? 何時からコンサートは始まりますか [nan ji kara konsâto wa hajimarimasu ka]

beginner 初心者 [shoshinsha]
▸ I'm a complete beginner 全くの初心者です [mattaku no shoshinsha desu]

behind 後ろの [ushiro no]
▸ from behind 後ろから [ushiro kara]
▸ the rest of the family was in the car behind 家族の他の者は後ろの車にいました [kazoku no hoka no mono wa ushiro no kuruma ni imashita]

berth *(on ship)* 船室 [senshitsu]; *(on sleeper train)* 寝台 [shindai]
▸ I'd prefer the upper berth *(on ship)* 上の船室のほうがいいです [ue no senshitsu no hô ga î desu]; *(on sleeper train)* 上の寝台のほうがいいです [ue no shindai no hô ga î desu]

beside 隣の [tonari no]
▸ is there anyone sitting beside you? 隣は空いていますか [tonari wa aite imasu ka]

best 一番いい [ichi ban î]
▸ what's the best restaurant in town? 町で一番いいレストランはどれですか [machi de ichi ban î resutoran wa dore desu ka]

better よい [yoi] ◆ よく [yoku]
▸ I've been on antibiotics for a week and I'm not any better 抗生物質を一週間使っていますが、全然よくなりません [kôsêbushitsu o isshû kan tsukatte imasu ga, zenzen yoku narimasen]
▸ the better situated of the two hotels 二つのホテルの中では位置がよい [futatsu no hoteru no naka de wa ichi ga yoi]

between の間 [...no aida]
▸ a bus runs between the airport and the hotel バスが空港とホテルの間を通っています [basu ga kûkô to hoteru no aida o tôtte imasu]

bicycle 自転車 [jitensha]
▸ is there a place to leave bicycles? 自転車を置くところはありますか [jitensha o oku tokoro wa arimasu ka]; see box on p. 16

bicycle pump 空気入れ [kûki ire]
▸ do you have a bicycle pump? 空気入れはありますか [kûki ire wa arimasu ka]

big 大きい [ôkî]
▸ do you have it in a bigger size? もっと大きいサイズはありますか [motto ôkî saizu wa arimasu ka]
▸ it's too big 大きすぎます [ôkisugimasu]

bicycles

Bicycles are widely used in Japanese cities. People generally ride on the sidewalk and are skilled at avoiding pedestrians, who legally have right of way. They also often ride across crosswalks, even though this is officially illegal. It is easy to hire bicycles in tourist areas.

bike オートバイ [ôtobai]
> ▸ I'd like to rent a bike for an hour オートバイを一時間借りたいんですが [ôtobai o ichi jikan karitai n desu ga]
> ▸ I'd like to do a bike tour オートバイ旅行をしたいんですが [ôtobai ryokô o shitai n desu ga]

bill 請求書 [sêkyûsho], 勘定 [kanjô]; *(paper money)* 紙幣 [shihê], お札 [osatsu]
> ▸ I think there's a mistake with the bill 勘定に間違いがあるんじゃないかと思うんですが [kanjô ni machigai ga aru n ja nai ka to omou n desu ga]
> ▸ put it on my bill 請求書につけておいてください [sêkyûsho ni tsukete oite kudasai]
> ▸ can you send the bill to my company, please? 請求書は会社に送ってもらえますか [sêkyûsho wa kaisha ni okutte moraemasu ka]

birthday 誕生日 [tanjôbi]
> ▸ happy birthday! 誕生日おめでとう！ [tanjôbi omedetô]

bite *(animal)* かみ傷 [kami kizu]; *(insect)* 虫刺され [mushi sasare] ◆ *(animal)* かむ [kamu]; *(insect)* 刺す [sasu]
> ▸ do you have a cream for mosquito bites? 虫刺されのクリームはありますか [mushi sasare no kurîmu wa arimasu ka]
> ▸ I've been bitten by a mosquito 蚊に刺されました [ka ni sasaremashita]

black 黒い [kuroi]; *(coffee)* ブラック [burakku]
> ▸ I'm looking for a black bag 黒いかばんを探しています [kuroi kaban o sagashite imasu]

black-and-white 白黒 [shiro kuro]
> ▸ I like black-and-white movies 白黒映画が好きです [shiro kuro êga ga suki desu]

blanket 毛布 [môfu]
> ▸ I'd like an extra blanket 毛布をもう一枚ください [môfu o mô ichi mai kudasai]

bleed 出血する [shukketsu suru]
> ▸ it won't stop bleeding 出血が止まりません [shukketsu ga tomarimasen]

blood type

Many young Japanese believe that blood type indicate different personalities, so don't be surprised if you are asked what your blood type is.

blind *(on window)* ブラインド [buraindo]
▸ can we pull down the blinds? ブラインドを下ろしてもいいですか [buraindo o oroshite mo î desu ka]

blister まめ [mame]
▸ I got a blister まめができました [mame ga dekimashita]

block *(pipe, sink)* 詰まる [tsumaru]; *(road)* ふさぐ [fusagu]
▸ the toilet's blocked トイレが詰まりました [toire ga tsumarimashita]
▸ my ears are completely blocked 耳が完全にふさがっています [mimi ga kanzen ni fusagatte imasu]

blond 金髪の [kimpatsu no]
▸ I have blond hair 金髪です [kimpatsu desu]

blood 血 [chi]
▸ traces of blood 血の跡 [chi no ato]

blood pressure 血圧 [ketsu atsu]
▸ I have high blood pressure 高血圧です [kô ketsu atsu desu]

blood type 血液型 [ketsueki gata]
▸ my blood type is A positive 血液型はA型のプラスです [ketsueki gata wa ê gata no purasu desu]

blue 青い [aoi]
▸ the blue one 青いの [aoi no]

board *(plane)* 搭乗する [tôjô suru] ◆ *(stay somewhere)* 下宿する [geshuku suru]
▸ what time will the plane be boarding? 飛行機の搭乗は何時ですか [hikôki no tôjô wa nan ji desu ka]
▸ where is the flight to Fukuoka boarding? 福岡行きの飛行機の搭乗はどこですか [fukuoka yuki no hikôki no tôjô wa doko desu ka]

boarding pass 搭乗券 [tôjô ken]
▸ I can't find my boarding pass 搭乗券が見つかりません [tôjô ken ga mitsukarimasen]

boat 船 [fune]
▸ can we get there by boat? 船でそこに行けますか [fune de soko ni ikemasu ka]

boat trip 遊覧船 [yûransen]
> are there boat trips on the river? 川に遊覧船はありますか [kawa ni yûransen wa arimasu ka]

book *(for reading)* 本 [hon]; *(of tickets)* 回数券 [kaisûken] ◆ *(ticket, room)* 予約する [yoyaku suru]
> do you sell English–language books? 英語の本はありますか [êgo no hon wa arimasu ka]
> is it more economical to buy a book of tickets? 回数券を買うほうが安いですか [kaisûken o kau hô ga yasui desu ka]
> I'd like to book a ticket チケットの予約をしたいんですが [chiketto no yoyaku o shitai n desu ga]
> do you need to book in advance? 前もって予約しなければなりませんか [mae motte yoyaku shinakereba narimasen ka]

born
> to be born 生まれる [umareru]
> I was born on March 3rd, 1985 １９８５年3月3日生まれです [sen kyûhyaku hachijûgo nen sangatsu mikka umare desu]

bottle びん [bin]
> a bottle of red wine, please 赤ワインを一本、お願いします [aka wain o ippon, onegai shimasu]

bottle opener 栓抜き [sennuki]
> can you pass me the bottle opener? 栓抜きをまわしてくれますか [sennuki o mawashite kuremasu ka]

bottom *(of a well, of a box)* 底 [soko]
> my passport's at the bottom of my suitcase パスポートはスーツケースの底に入っています [pasupôto wa sûtsukêsu no soko ni haitte imasu]

box 箱 [hako]
> could I have a box of matches, please? マッチを一箱ください [matchi o hito hako kudasai]

boy *(young male)* 男の子 [otoko no ko]; *(son)* 息子 [musuko]
> he seems like a nice boy あの男の子はいい子のようです [ano otoko no ko wa î ko no yô desu]
> she has two boys 息子さんが二人います [musuko-san ga futari imasu]

boyfriend ボーイフレンド [bôifurendo]
> my boyfriend is a biologist ボーイフレンドは生物学者です [bôifurendo wa sêbutsugakusha desu]

brake ブレーキ [burêki]
> the brakes aren't working properly ブレーキがちゃんとききません [burêki ga chanto kikimasen]

brake fluid ブレーキ液 [burêki eki]
- could you check the brake fluid? ブレーキ液を点検してくれませんか [burêki eki o tenken shite kuremasen ka]

branch (of bank) 支店 [shiten]
- which branch should I visit to get the replacement traveler's checks? トラベラーズチェックの再発行にはどの支店に行けばいいですか [toraberâzu chekku no saihakkô ni wa dono shiten ni ikeba î desu ka]

bread パン [pan]
- do you have any bread? パンはありますか [pan wa arimasu ka]
- could we have some more bread? パンをもう少しもらえませんか [pan o mô sukoshi moraemasen ka]

break (pause) 休み [yasumi] ◆ (object) 壊す [kowasu]; (part of the body) 折る [oru]
- should we take a break? ちょっと休みましょうか [chotto yasumimashô ka]
- be careful you don't break it 壊さないように気をつけてください [kowasanai yô ni ki o tsukete kudasai]
- I think I've broken my ankle 足首を折ったようです [ashikubi o otta yô desu]

break down 故障する [koshô suru]
- my car has broken down 車が故障しました [kuruma ga koshô shimashita]

breakdown 故障 [koshô]
- we had a breakdown on the freeway 高速道路で故障しました [kôsoku dôro de koshô shimashita]

breakfast 朝食 [chôshoku], 朝ごはん [asagohan]
- to have breakfast 朝食を食べる [chôshoku o taberu]
- what time is breakfast served? 朝食は何時ですか [chôshoku wa nan ji desu ka]

bridge 橋 [hashi]
- do you have to pay a toll to use the bridge? 橋を渡るのに料金がかかりますか [hashi o wataru no ni ryôkin ga kakarimasu ka]

bring 持って行く [motte iku]
- what should we bring to drink? 飲み物は何を持って行きましょうか [nomimono wa nani o motte ikimashô ka]

bring down (bags, luggage) 下ろす [orosu]
- could you get someone to bring down our luggage, please? 誰か荷物を下ろしてくれませんか [dare ka nimotsu o oroshite kuremasen ka]

bring in (bags, luggage) 運び込む [hakobikomu]
- can you bring in my bags, please? かばんを運び込んでくれませんか [kaban o hakobikonde kuremasen ka]

Britain イギリス [igirisu], 英国 [êkoku]
- I lived in Britain for a year 一年間イギリスに住んでいました [ichi nen kan igirisu ni sunde imashita]

British *(country)* イギリスの [igirisu no]; *(person)* イギリス人 [igirisujin]
- I have many British friends イギリス人の友達がたくさんいます [igirisujin no tomodachi ga takusan imasu]

broken *(equipment)* 壊れた [kowareta]; *(part of the body)* 骨折した [kossetsu shita]
- the lock is broken 鍵が壊れています [kagi ga kowarete imasu]
- I think I've got a broken leg 足を骨折したようです [ashi o kossetsu shita yô desu]

bronchitis 気管支炎 [kikanshien]
- do you have anything for bronchitis? 気管支炎に利くものはありませんか [kikanshien ni kiku mono wa arimasen ka]

brother *(general)* 兄弟 [kyôdai]; *(one's own elder)* 兄 [ani]; *(someone else's elder)* お兄さん [onî-san]; *(one's own younger)* 弟 [otôto]; *(someone else's younger)* 弟さん [otôto-san]
- I don't have any brothers or sisters 兄弟姉妹はありません [kyôdai shimai wa arimasen]

brown 茶色の [chairo no]
- he has brown hair 茶色の髪をしています [chairo no kami o shite imasu]
- I'm looking for a brown leather belt 茶色の革のベルトを探しています [chairo no kawa no beruto o sagashite imasu]

brush *(for hair, clothes, with short handle)* ブラシ [burashi]; *(broom)* ほうき [hôki] ◆ *(hair)* とかす [tokasu]
- where are the brush and dustpan? ほうきとちりとりはどこですか [hôki to chiritori wa doko desu ka]
- to brush one's teeth 歯を磨く [ha o migaku]

bulb *(light)* 電球 [denkyû]
- the bulb's out in the bathroom 風呂場の電球が切れています [furoba no denkyû ga kirete imasu]

bunk beds 二段ベッド [ni dan beddo]
- are there bunk beds for the children? 子供用の二段ベッドはありますか [kodomo yô no ni dan beddo wa arimasu ka]

burn *(something)* 焦げる [kogeru]; *(body)* やけどをする [yakedo o suru]
- the food's completely burnt 食べ物は完全に焦げています [tabemono wa kanzen ni kogete imasu]
- I've burned my hand 手にやけどをしました [te ni yakedo o shimashita]

buses

Long distance buses run between major cities, and are cheaper than flying or taking the bullet train (新幹線 [shinkansen]). Overnight buses are affordable and reasonably comfortable; from Tokyo to Kyoto takes about 6 hours. On local buses, you can buy tickets when you get on or off the bus, depending on the company. Press the button to request a stop. Many city buses use a system where you get on at the rear of the bus and take a ticket from a machine. This has a number on it that indicates the fare zone, and a display screen at the front of the bus shows the fares; put the ticket and the right amount of money into the cash box by the driver when you leave the bus. If you plan to travel a lot on buses within a city over a few days, it will be cheaper to buy a book of tickets (回数券 [kaisûken]) from the driver.

---

burst *(tire)* パンクする [panku suru]
- one of my tires burst タイヤが一本パンクしました [taiya ga ippon panku shimashita]

bus バス [basu]
- does this bus go downtown? このバスは町の中心に行きますか [kono basu wa machi no chûshin ni ikimasu ka]
- which bus do I have to take to go to...? ..へ行くのにはどのバスに乗ればいいですか [...e iku no ni wa dono basu ni noreba î desu ka]

bus driver バスの運転手 [basu no untenshu]
- does the bus driver speak English? バスの運転手は英語を話しますか [basu no untenshu wa êgo o hanashimasu ka]

business *(commerce)* 仕事 [shigoto]; *(company)* 会社 [kaisha]; *(concern)* 関係があること [kankê ga aru koto]; *(affair, matter)* 用事 [yôji]
- it's none of your business あなたには関係ないでしょ [anata ni wa kankê nai desho]

business card 名刺 [mêshi]
- here's my business card 私の名刺をどうぞ [watashi no mêshi o dôzo]; see box on p. 22

business class ビジネスクラス [bijinesu kurasu] ◆ ビジネスクラスの [bijinesu kurasu no]
- are there any seats in business class? ビジネスクラスの席はありますか [bijinesu kurasu no seki wa arimasu ka]
- I prefer to travel business class ビジネスクラスの方がいいです [bijinesu kurasu no hô ga î desu]

bus station バスターミナル [basu tâminaru]
- I'm looking for the bus station バスターミナルを探しています [basu tâminaru o sagashite imasu]

business cards

These are extremely important when you meet someone through business as they show the position of the person you are talking to as well as all their contact details. Meetings usually begin with an exchange of business cards. You should give yours to the person with the highest status first – hierarchy is very important in Japan. Cards are always exchanged with great respect, and you should hold them at the corners with two hands and bow slightly when giving or receiving a card. You should look at the card for a while to show your interest and respect for the person, especially if he or she holds a high position; then put it away carefully – don't put it in your back pocket! People who work in an international business environment will often have bilingual business cards (English on one side and Japanese on the other). Japanese names are written in romanized form on the English side. Foreigners living and working in Japan will have their names written in katakana script on the Japanese side.

bus stop バス停 [basu tê]
- where's the nearest bus stop? 一番近いバス停はどこですか [ichi ban chikai basu tê wa doko desu ka]

busy *(person, period)* 忙しい [isogashî]; *(town, beach, street)* にぎやかな [nigiyaka na]; *(phone line)* 話し中 [hanashi chû]
- I'm afraid I'm busy tomorrow 申し訳ありませんが、明日は忙しいです [môshiwake arimasen ga, ashita wa isogashî desu]
- the line's busy 話し中です [hanashi chû desu]

butter バター [batâ]
- could you pass the butter please? バターをまわしてください [batâ o mawashite kudasai]

buy 買う [kau]
- where can I buy tickets? チケットはどこで買ったらいいですか [chiketto wa doko de kattara î desu ka]
- can I buy you a drink? 飲み物をおごりましょうか [nomimono o ogorimashô ka]

bye じゃ [ja]
- bye, see you tomorrow! じゃ、また明日 [ja, mata ashita]

C

cab タクシー [takushî]
- can you order me a cab to the airport? 空港までタクシーを頼んでくれませんか [kûkô made takushî o tanonde kuremasen ka]

cab driver タクシーの運転手 [takushî no untenshu]
- does the cab driver speak English? タクシーの運転手は英語を話しますか [takushî no untenshu wa êgo o hanashimasu ka]

cabin *(on boat)* 船室 [senshitsu]; *(on plane)* キャビン [kyabin]
- can I have breakfast in my cabin? 自分の船室で朝食が食べられますか [jibun no senshitsu de chôshoku ga taberaremasu ka]

cable ケーブルテレビ [kêburu terebi]
- does the hotel have cable? ホテルにはケーブルテレビがついていますか [hoteru ni wa kêburu terebi ga tsuite imasu ka]

café 喫茶店 [kissaten]
- is there a café near here? 近くに喫茶店はありますか [chikaku ni kissaten wa arimasu ka]

cake ケーキ [kêki]
- a piece of that cake, please そのケーキを一つください [sono kêki o hitotsu kudasai]

call *(on phone)* 電話 [denwa] ◆ *(name)* 呼ぶ [yobu]; *(on phone)* 電話する [denwa suru], 電話をかける [denwa o kakeru]
- I have to make a call 電話をしなければなりません [denwa o shinakereba narimasen]
- what is this called? これはなんと呼びますか [kore wa nan to yobimasu ka]
- who's calling? どちら様でしょうか [dochira sama deshô ka]

---

in the café

- is this table/seat free? この席は空いていますか [kono seki wa aite imasu ka]
- excuse me! すみません [sumimasen]
- can I have another coffee, please? コーヒーをもう一杯もらえますか [kôhî o mô ippai moraemasu ka]

cameras

The Japanese have long had a passion for photography. Discount stores such as Bic Camera, Yodobashi Camera and Sakuraya all offer a huge choice, whether you're looking for a cheap disposable camera or the most cutting-edge telephoto lens, a digital camera or an underwater camera. Having photos developed is fairly cheap in Japan, in specialist shops, supermarkets or convenience stores. The standard format is 3.5 inches by 5 inches.

call back 電話をかけなおす [denwa o kakenaosu]
- could you ask her to call me back? 電話をかけなおしてくれるよう、伝言してください [denwa o kakenaoshite kureru yô, dengon shite kudasai]
- I'll call back (later) (後で)またかけなおします [(ato de) mata kakenaoshimasu]

calm 落ち着いた [ochitsuita]
- keep calm! 落ち着いて！ [ochitsuite]

camera (for taking photos) カメラ [kamera]; (for filming) ビデオ（カメラ） [bideo (kamera)]
- can I use the camera here? ここでカメラを使ってもいいですか [koko de kamera o tsukatte mo î desu ka]

camper キャンピングカー [kyampingu kâ]
- do you have a space left for a camper? キャンピングカー一台分の場所は空いていますか [kyampingu kâ ichi dai bun no basho wa aite imasu ka]
- I'd like to book space for a camper for the night of August 15th 8月15日にキャンピングカー一台分、予約したいんですが [hachigatsu jûgonichi ni kyampingu kâ ichi dai bun, yoyaku shitai n desu ga]

campground キャンプ場 [kyampu jô]
- I'm looking for a campground キャンプ場を探しています [kyampu jô o sagashite imasu]

camping キャンプ [kyampu]
- I love going camping キャンプが大好きです [kyampu ga dai suki desu]

can 缶 [kan]
- a can of oil, please オイルを一缶ください [oiru o hito kan kudasai]

can (be able to) ...ことができる [...koto ga dekiru]; (know how to) できる [dekiru]
- can I help you? お手伝いしましょうか [otetsudai shimashô ka]
- can you speak French? フランス語を話すことができますか [furansugo o hanasu koto ga dekimasu ka]

Canada カナダ [kanada]
- I'm from Canada カナダから来ました [kanada kara kimashita]

▸ I live in Canada カナダに住んでいます [kanada ni sunde imasu]

▸ have you ever been to Canada? カナダに行ったことがありますか [kanada ni itta koto ga arimasu ka]

Canadian カナダの [kanada no] ◆ カナダ人 [kanadajin]

▸ I'm/we're Canadian(s) カナダ人です [kanadajin desu]

cancel 取り消す [torikesu]

▸ is it possible to cancel a reservation? 予約を取り消すことはできますか [yoyaku o torikesu koto wa dekimasu ka]

canoeing カヌー [kanû]

▸ I was told we could go canoeing カヌーができると言われました [kanû ga dekiru to iwaremashita]

car *(automobile)* 車 [kuruma], 自動車 [jidôsha]; *(on train)* 車両 [sharyô]

▸ I'd like to rent a car for a week 車を一週間借りたいんですが [kuruma o isshûkan karitai n desu ga]

▸ I've just crashed my car 衝突事故を起こしました [shôtotsu jiko o okoshimashita]

▸ can you help us push the car? 車を押してもらえませんか [kuruma o oshite moraemasen ka]

▸ my car's been towed away 車をレッカー車に持って行かれてしまいました [kuruma o rekkâsha ni motte ikarete shimaimashita]

▸ my car's broken down 車が故障しました [kuruma ga koshô shimashita]

car crash 自動車事故 [jidôsha jiko]

▸ he's been killed in a car crash 自動車事故で亡くなりました [jidôsha jiko de naku narimashita]

card *(finance)* クレジットカード [kurejitto kâdo]; *(greeting card)* カード [kâdo]; *(business card)* 名刺 [mêshi]

▸ the waiter hasn't brought my card back ウエイターが私のクレジットカードを持って行ったままです [wêtâ ga watashi no kurejitto kâdo o motte itta mama desu]

▸ I need to get a card for my parents for their anniversary 両親の結婚記念日

---

renting a car

▸ with comprehensive insurance 総合自動車保険付き [sôgô jidôsha hoken tsuki]

▸ can I leave the car at the airport? 車を空港に置いていってもいいですか [kuruma o kûkô ni oite itte mo î desu ka]

▸ can I see your driver's license, please? 免許証を見せていただけますか [menkyoshô o misete itadakemasu ka]

cash

Japan is still largely a cash-based society, even for quite large purchases. Only big stores and restaurants in the major cities accept credit cards, and traveler's checks are not usually accepted.

にカードを買わなければなりません [ryôshin no kekkon kinembi ni kâdo o kawanakereba narimasen]

▸ can I give you my card? 名刺を差し上げましょうか [mêshi o sashiagemashô ka]

cardigan カーディガン [kâdigan]

▸ should I take a cardigan for the evening? 夜はカーディガンを持ったほうがいいでしょうか [yoru wa kâdigan o motta hô ga î deshô ka]

carpet カーペット [kâpetto]

▸ the carpet hasn't been vacuumed カーペットに掃除機がかけてありません [kâpetto ni sôjiki ga kakete arimasen]

car rental レンタカー [rentakâ]

▸ is car rental expensive? レンタカーは高いですか [rentakâ wa takai desu ka]

car rental agency レンタカー会社 [rentakâ gaisha]

▸ do you know of any car rental agencies? レンタカー会社を知っていますか [rentakâ gaisha o shitte imasu ka]

carry (baggage) 運ぶ [hakobu] ◆ (sound) 伝わる [tsutawaru]

▸ could you help me carry something? 何か運んでもらえませんか [nani ka hakonde moraemasen ka]

carry-on bag 機内持ち込み（手荷物）[kinai mochikomi (tenimotsu)]

▸ am I only allowed one carry-on bag? 機内持ち込みは一つだけですか [kinai mochikomi wa hitotsu dake desu ka]

cart (for luggage, in supermarket) カート [kâto]

▸ where can I get a cart? カートはどこにありますか [kâto wa doko ni arimasu ka]

carton (of cigarettes) カートン [kâton]

▸ I'd like a carton of cigarettes タバコを１カートンください [tabako o ichi kâton kudasai]

cash (notes and coins) 現金 [genkin] ◆ (check) 現金化する [genkinka suru]

▸ I'll pay cash 現金で払います [genkin de haraimasu]

▸ I want to cash this traveler's check このトラベラーズチェックを現金化したいんですが [kono toraberâzu chekku o genkinka shitai n desu ga]

cellphones

Although some new foreign cellphones work in Japan, most don't, so check with your phone company. It is possible to rent Japanese cellphones from companies in the US, or at the major international airports after arriving in Japan.

castle 城 [shiro]
- what time does the castle open? 城は何時に開きますか [shiro wa nan ji ni akimasu ka]

catalog カタログ [katarogu]
- do you have a catalog? カタログはありますか [katarogu wa arimasu ka]

catch *(with hands)* つかまえる [tsukamaeru]; *(cold)* 引く [hiku]; *(hear clearly)* 聞き取る [kikitoru]
- I've caught a cold 風邪を引きました [kaze o hikimashita]
- I'm sorry, I didn't quite catch your name すみません、お名前を聞き取ることができませんでした [sumimasen, onamae o kikitoru koto ga dekimasen deshita]

Catholic カトリックの [katorikku no], カソリックの [kasorikku no] ◆ カトリック [katorikku], カソリック [kasorikku]
- where is there a Catholic church? カトリックの教会はどこにありますか [katorikku no kyôkai wa doko ni arimasu ka]

CD CD [shîdî]
- how much does this CD cost? このCDはいくらですか [kono shîdî wa ikura desu ka]

cellphone 携帯（電話）[kêtai (denwa)]
- is there an outlet so I can recharge my cellphone? 携帯を充電したいんですが、コンセントはありますか [kêtai o jûden shitai n desu ga, konsento wa arimasu ka]
- what's your cellphone number? 携帯の番号は何番ですか [kêtai no bangô wa nam ban desu ka]

center 中心 [chûshin]
- we want to be based near the center of the region その地方の中心に近いところに拠点を置きたいんですが [sono chihô no chûshin ni chikai tokoro ni kyoten o okitai n desu ga]

chair 椅子 [isu]
- could we have another chair in our room? 部屋にもう一つ椅子がほしいんですが [heya ni mô hitotsu isu ga hoshî n desu ga]

change *(alteration)* 変化 [henka]; *(money)* 小銭 [kozeni] ◆ かえる [kaeru]; *(baby)* おしめを換える [oshime o kaeru]; *(money)* 両替する [ryôgae suru] ◆ *(clothes)* 着替える [kigaeru]

- do you have any change? 小銭を持っていますか [kozeni o motte imasu ka]
- keep the change 小銭は取っておいてください [kozeni wa totte oite kudasai]
- I don't have exact change ぴったりの小銭がありません [pittari no kozeni ga arimasen]
- give me change for 1000 yen, please 1000円分の小銭をください [sen em bun no kozeni o kudasai]
- is it possible to change a reservation? 予約を変えることはできますか [yoyaku o kaeru koto wa dekimasu ka]
- I'd like to change 200 dollars into yen 200ドルを円に両替したいんですが [nihyaku doru o en ni ryôgae shitai n desu ga]
- I'd like to change these traveler's checks トラベラーズチェックを換えたいんですが [toraberâzu chekku o kaetai n desu ga]
- can you help me change the tire? タイヤを換えるのを手伝ってもらえませんか [taiya o kaeru no o tetsudatte moraemasen ka]
- the oil needs to be changed オイルを換えなければなりません [oiru o kaenakereba narimasen]

changing table *(for baby)* おしめ替えの台 [oshimekae no dai]

- is there a changing table? おしめ換えの台はありますか [oshimekae no dai wa arimasu ka]

charge *(cost)* 料金 [ryôkin]

- is there a charge for the parking lot? 駐車場は料金がかかりますか [chûshajô wa ryôkin ga kakarimasu ka]
- is there a charge for using the facilities? この施設を使うのに料金がかかりますか [kono shisetsu o tsukau no ni ryôkin ga kakarimasu ka]
- is there a charge for cancellations? キャンセルに料金がかかりますか [kyanseru ni ryôkin ga kakarimasu ka]
- in charge 責任を持っている [sekinin o motte iru]
- I'd like to speak to the person in charge 責任者と話したいんですが [sekininsha to hanashitai n desu ga]

charter flight チャーター機 [châtâ ki]

- where do we board the charter flight to Okinawa? 沖縄行きのチャーター機はどこで乗りますか [okinawa yuki no châtâ ki wa doko de norimasu ka]

cheap 安い [yasui]

- I'm trying to find a cheap flight home 帰りの安い飛行機を探しています [kaeri no yasui hikôki o sagashite imasu]

check *(in restaurant)* 勘定 [kanjô]; *(for paying)* 小切手 [kogitte] ◆ *(test, verify)* チェックする [chekku suru]

- the check, please! お勘定、お願いします [okanjô, onegai shimasu]
- can you check the oil? オイルをチェックしてもらえますか [oiru o chekku shite moraemasu ka]

check in *(baggage)* 預ける [azukeru] ◆ *(at airport)* 搭乗手続きをする [tôjô tetsuzuki o suru]; *(at hotel)* チェックインする [chekku-in suru]
- I'd like to check in both these bags, please 荷物を二つとも預けたいんですが [nimotsu o futatsu to mo azuketai n desu ga]
- what time do you have to be at the airport to check in? 搭乗手続きのためには、何時に空港にいなければなりませんか [tôjô tetsuzuki no tame ni wa, nan ji ni kûkô ni inakereba narimasen ka]

check-in desk *(at airport)* チェックインカウンター [chekku-in kauntâ]
- where is the United Airlines check-in desk? ユナイテッドエアラインのチェックインカウンターはどこですか [yunaiteddo earain no chekku-in kauntâ wa doko desu ka]

check out *(from hotel)* チェックアウトする [chekku-auto suru]
- what time do you have to check out by? チェックアウトは何時までですか [chekku-auto wa nan ji made desu ka]

cheers 乾杯！ [kampai]
- cheers and all the best! 前途を祝して、乾杯！ [zento o shukushite, kampai]

cheese チーズ [chîzu]
- where is the cheese shelf? チーズはどこにありますか [chîzu wa doko ni arimasu ka]

cherry blossom 桜 [sakura]
- will the cherry blossom be out soon? 桜はもうすぐ咲きますか [sakura wa môsugu sakimasu ka]; see box on p. 30

---

checking

- is it right and then left? 右に行ってそれから左ですね [migi ni itte sore kara hidari desu ne]
- is this the train for Kyoto? この列車は京都行きですか [kono ressha wa kyôto yuki desu ka]
- could you tell me where to get off, please? 降りるところを教えてくれませんか [oriru tokoro o oshiete kuremasen ka]
- is this the right stop for...? ...はここで降りればいいですか [...wa koko de orireba î desu ka]
- are you sure that he'll be able to come? 本当に彼は来られるんですか [hontô ni kare wa korareru n desu ka]

cherry blossom

Cherry blossom (桜 [sakura]) is one of the most famous symbols of Japan, loved for its delicate beauty and for reminding people of the transience of life. Television and newspapers report the progress of the blossom (桜前線 [sakura zensen]) from south to north from mid-March through April, so people can plan when to go and view the cherry blossom (花見 [hanami]). Families, friends and office colleagues have hanami parties under the trees in the parks, drinking, singing and dancing and generally having a good time. Foreigners admiring the blossom will usually be called over to join a group of revelers, so be prepared to join in the karaoke.

chicken チキン [chikin], 鶏肉 [toriniku]
- 200g of spicy fried chicken, please とりの唐揚げを２００グラムください [tori no kara-age o nihyaku guramu kudasai]
- a chicken sandwich and fries チキンサンドとフライドポテト [chikin sando to furaido poteto]

child 子供 [kodomo]
- do you have children? 子供さんはいらっしゃいますか [kodomo-san wa irasshaimasu ka]
- two adults and two children, please 大人二人と子供二人、お願いします [otona futari to kodomo futari, onegai shimasu]
- do you have discounts for children? 子供の割引はありますか [kodomo no waribiki wa arimasu ka]

chilled (wine) 冷やした [hiyashita]
- this wine isn't chilled enough このワインはよく冷えていません [kono wain wa yoku hiete imasen]

chocolate チョコレート [chokorêto]
- I'd like a bar of chocolate チョコレートを一枚ほしいです [chokorêto o ichi mai hoshî desu]

choose 選ぶ [erabu]
- I don't know which one to choose どちらを選んだらいいかわかりません [dochira o erandara î ka wakarimasen]

chopsticks はし [hashi]
- I can't use chopsticks; could I have a knife and a fork, please はしは使えません。ナイフとフォークをもらえますか [hashi wa tsukaemasen. naifu to fôku o moraemasu ka]

Christmas (day) クリスマス [kurisumasu]
- merry Christmas! メリークリスマス [merî kurisumasu]
- Christmas Day クリスマス [kurisumasu]

chopsticks

Most Japanese and Chinese restaurants use disposable chopsticks. These come in a paper packet and are joined together at the top, so you need to split them before use. If you want to take food from a communal dish with your chopsticks, it is polite to turn them around to do so. Never leave chopsticks sticking up in food, or use them to pass food to someone else, as these actions are associated with funerals.

church (Protestant, Catholic) 教会 [kyôkai]
▸ how old is the church? この教会はどれぐらい古いですか [kono kyôkai wa dore gurai furui desu ka]
▸ where can we find a Protestant church? プロテスタントの教会はどこにありますか [purotesutanto no kyôkai wa doko ni arimasu ka]
▸ where is there a Catholic church? カトリックの教会はどこですか [katorikku no kyôkai wa doko desu ka]

cigarette タバコ [tabako]
▸ can I ask you for a cigarette? タバコを一本いただけませんか [tabako o ippon itadakemasen ka]
▸ where can I buy cigarettes? どこでタバコは買えますか [doko de tabako wa kaemasu ka]

cigarette lighter ライター [raitâ]
▸ do you have a cigarette lighter? ライターをお持ちですか [raitâ o omochi desu ka]

city 都市 [toshi]
▸ what's the nearest big city? 一番近い大きな都市は何ですか [ichi ban chikai ôki na toshi wa nan desu ka]

clean きれいな [kirê na] ◆ 掃除する [sôji suru]
▸ the sheets aren't clean シーツがきれいじゃありません [shîtsu ga kirê ja arimasen]
▸ do we have to clean the apartment before leaving? アパートを出る前に掃除をしなければなりませんか [apâto o deru mae ni sôji o shinakereba narimasen ka]
▸ could you clean the windshield? フロントガラスを掃除してくれませんか [furonto garasu o sôji shite kuremasen ka]

cleaning 掃除 [sôji]
▸ who does the cleaning? 掃除は誰がしますか [sôji wa dare ga shimasu ka]

clear (easily understood) よくわかる [yoku wakaru]; (way) 空いている [aite iru] ◆ (road, path) 片付ける [katazukeru]

▸ is that clear? よくわかりましたか [yoku wakarimashita ka]

▸ is the road ahead clear? この先の道は空いていますか [kono saki no michi wa aite imasu ka]

▸ when will the road be cleared? 道はいつ片付きますか [michi wa itsu katazukimasu ka]

climb *(mountaineer)* 登る [noboru]; *(plane)* 上がる [agaru]; *(road)* 上り坂になる [noborizaka ni naru]

▸ the road climbs steadily after you leave the village 村を出ると道は上り坂になります [mura o deru to michi wa noborizaka ni narimasu]

climbing 登山 [tozan]

▸ can you go climbing here? ここは登山できますか [koko wa tozan dekimasu ka]

cloakroom *(in a museum, a theater)* 手荷物預かり所 [tenimotsu azukarijo]

▸ I'd like to leave my things in the cloakroom 手荷物預かり所に荷物を置いていきたいんですが [tenimotsu azukarijo ni nimotsu o oite ikitai n desu ga]

close *(door, window)* 閉める [shimeru] ✦ 閉まる [shimaru]

▸ what time do the stores close? 何時に店は閉まりますか [nan ji ni mise wa shimarimasu ka]

▸ what time do you close? 何時に閉めますか [nan ji ni shimemasu ka]

▸ the door won't close ドアが閉まりません [doa ga shimarimasen]

closed 閉まった [shimatta]

▸ are the stores closed on Sundays? 店は日曜日に閉まりますか [mise wa nichiyôbi ni shimarimasu ka]

clothes 服 [fuku]

▸ where can we wash our clothes? 服はどこで洗えますか [fuku wa doko de araemasu ka]

cloud 雲 [kumo]

▸ there are some rain clouds 雨雲が出ています [amagumo ga dete imasu]

cloudy 曇った [kumotta]

▸ it's cloudy today 今日は曇っています [kyô wa kumotte imasu]

club *(nightclub)* クラブ [kurabu]

▸ we could go to a club afterwards 後でクラブに行ってもいいですね [ato de kurabu ni itte mo î desu ne]

coach 長距離バス [chô kyori basu]

▸ what time does the coach leave? 長距離バスは何時に出ますか [chô kyori basu wa nan ji ni demasu ka]

coast 海岸 [kaigan]

▸ an island off the coast of Kamakura 鎌倉の海岸の向こうにある島 [kamakura no kaigan no mukô ni aru shima]

coffee *(drink, beans)* コーヒー [kôhî]
- black coffee ブラックコーヒー [burakku kôhî]
- I'd like a coffee コーヒーがほしいんですが [kôhî ga hoshî n desu ga]
- would you like some coffee? コーヒーはいかがですか [kôhî wa ikaga desu ka]

coin 硬貨 [kôka]
- the machine only takes coins この機械は硬貨しか使えません [kono kikai wa kôka shika tsukaemasen]

cold *(weather)* 寒い [samui]; *(temperature, object)* 冷たい [tsumetai] ◆ *(illness)* 風邪 [kaze]; *(low temperature)* 寒さ [samusa]
- it's cold today 今日は寒いです [kyô wa samui desu]
- I'm very cold とても寒いです [totemo samui desu]
- to have a cold 風邪を引く [kaze o hiku]
- I've caught a cold 風邪を引きました [kaze o hikimashita]

collect call コレクトコール [korekuto kôru]
- can I make a collect call? コレクトコールをかけられますか [korekuto kôru o kakeraremasu ka]

color 色 [iro]
- do you have it in another color? 違う色はありますか [chigau iro wa arimasu ka]

color film カラーフィルム [karâ firumu]
- I'd like a roll of color film カラーフィルムを一つほしいんですが [karâ firumu o hitotsu hoshî n desu ga]

come *(move toward speaker)* 来る [kuru]; *(move away from speaker)* 行く [iku]
- come here! 来なさい [kinasai]
- coming! 今、行きます [ima ikimasu]
- when does the bus come? バスはいつ来ますか [basu wa itsu kimasu ka]

come from ..から来る [...kara kuru]
- where do you come from? どこから来ましたか [doko kara kimashita ka]

come in *(enter)* 入る [hairu]; *(train)* 到着する [tôchaku suru]; *(tide)* 満ちてくる [michite kuru]
- may I come in? 入ってもいいですか [haitte mo î desu ka]
- come in! お入りください [ohairi kudasai]
- what time does the train for Osaka come in? 大阪行きの列車は何時に到着しますか [ôsaka yuki no ressha wa nan ji ni tôchaku shimasu ka]
- the tide's coming in 潮が満ちてきます [shio ga michite kimasu]

come on *(light, heating)* つく [tsuku]
- the heating hasn't come on ヒーターがつきません [hîtâ ga tsukimasen]
- come on! いい加減にしなさい [î kagen ni shinasai]

come with *(go with)* 一緒に行く [issho ni iku]; *(be served with)* 付いてくる [tsuite kuru]

- could you come with me to...? 一緒に...へ行ってくれませんか [issho ni ... e itte kuremasen ka]
- what does it come with? 何が一緒に付いてきますか [nani ga issho ni tsuite kimasu ka]

comfortable *(person)* くつろいで [kutsuroide]

- we're very comfortable here とてもくつろいでいます [totemo kutsuroide imasu]

commission 手数料 [tesûryô]

- what commission do you charge? 手数料はいくらかかりますか [tesûryô wa ikura kakarimasu ka]

company *(firm)* 会社 [kaisha]

- is it a big company? 大きな会社ですか [ôki na kaisha desu ka]

complete *(form)* 完成する [kansê suru]

- here's the completed form これが記入した申込書です [kore ga kinyû shita môshikomisho desu]

comprehensive insurance 総合自動車保険 [sôgô jidôsha hoken]

- how much extra is the comprehensive insurance coverage? 総合自動車保険に入ると、いくら余分にかかりますか [sôgô jidôsha hoken ni hairu to, ikura yobun ni kakarimasu ka]

computer コンピュータ [kompyûta]

- is there a computer I could use? 使ってもいいコンピュータはありますか [tsukatte mo î kompyûta wa arimasu ka]

concert コンサート [konsâto]

- did you like the concert? コンサートはよかったですか [konsâto wa yokatta desu ka]

condom コンドーム [kondômu]

- do you have any condoms? コンドームはありますか [kondômu wa arimasu ka]

confirm 確認する [kakunin suru]

- I confirmed my reservation by phone 電話で予約を確認しました [denwa de yoyaku o kakunin shimashita]
- I'd like to confirm my return flight 帰りの便の確認をしたいんですが [kaeri no bin no kakunin o shitai n desu ga]

congratulations おめでとう [omedetô]

- congratulations! おめでとう！ [omedetô]

connecting flight 乗り継ぎ便 [noritsugi bin]

- does the connecting flight leave from the same terminal? 乗り継ぎ便は同じターミナルから出ますか [noritsugi bin wa onaji tâminaru kara demasu ka]

connection *(on phone)* つながり [tsunagari]; *(transportation)* 乗り換え [norikae]
- the connection is very bad: I can't hear very well つながりが悪いです。よく聞こえません [tsunagari ga warui desu. yoku kikoemasen]
- I've missed my connection 乗り換え損ねました [norikae sokonemashita]

consulate 領事館 [ryôjikan]
- where is the American consulate? アメリカ領事館はどこですか [amerika ryôjikan wa doko desu ka]

contact *(communication)* 連絡 [renraku] ◆ *(communication)* 連絡する [renraku suru]
- I need to contact my family in the States アメリカの家族に連絡しなければなりません [amerika no kazoku ni renraku shinakereba narimasen]
- do you know how to get in contact with him? どうしたら彼に連絡がつくか分かりますか [dô shitara kare ni renraku ga tsuku ka wakarimasu ka]

contact lens コンタクト（レンズ）[kontakuto (renzu)]
- I've lost a contact (lens) コンタクトを失くしました [konkakuto o nakushimashita]

convenience store コンビニ [kombini]
- where is the nearest convenience store? 一番近いコンビにはどこですか [ichiban chikai kombini wa doko desu ka]

cookie *(food)* クッキー [kukkî]
- a box of cookies, please クッキーを一箱ください [kukkî o hito hako kudasai]

cooking 料理 [ryôri]
- we prefer to do our own cooking 自分達で料理する方がいいです [jibuntachi de ryôri suru hô ga î desu]
- do you like Chinese cooking? 中華料理は好きですか [chûka ryôri wa suki desu ka]; see box on p. 36

cork *(for a bottle)* コルク [koruku]
- where's the cork for the bottle? ビンのコルクはどこですか [bin no koruku wa doko desu ka]

corked コルク臭くなっている [koruku kusaku natte iru]
- this wine is corked このワインはコルク臭くなっています [kono wain wa koruku kusaku natte imasu]

corner *(of street, table)* 角 [kado]; *(spot)* 隅 [sumi]
- stop at the corner その角で止まってください [sono kado de tomatte kudasai]

coronary 心臓発作 [shinzô hossa]
- he's had a coronary 心臓発作を起こしました [shinzô hossa o okoshimashita]

correct *(check)* 正しい [tadashî]
- that's correct 正しいです [tadashî desu]

cuisine

Unlike European cooking, where the emphasis is on mixing ingredients together, Japanese food is all about juxtaposing different elements. It is very refined, and the delicious flavors are matched by careful presentation. 懐石料理 [kaiseki ryôri] is high-class formal seasonal Japanese cuisine which originated in Kyoto. Originally, it was a light meal of two or three vegetarian dishes accompanying the tea ceremony, but over the centuries, it has developed into a meal of many different courses of small dishes, such as raw fish (刺身 [sashimi]), てんぷら [tempura], grilled fish, vegetables, soup and rice. People go to kaiseki ryôri restaurants for special occasions, since it is time-consuming to prepare and therefore expensive. Some of the most expensive and sought-after dishes are ふぐ [fugu] (globe-fish), 鯨 [kujira] (whale), カニ [kani] (crab), ウナギ [unagi] (eel) and ウニ [uni] (sea urchin). The internal organs of the fugu contain a deadly poison, and the fish can only be served at restaurants with specially licensed chefs. It is eaten raw as 刺身 [sashimi] or in a 鍋 [nabe] (stew). Eels are eaten particularly in summer, when they are thought to combat lethargy from the humid heat (夏バテ [natsu bate]). They are served sliced and cooked and covered with a sweet sauce in specialized restaurants (ウナギ屋 [unagiya]).

cost かかる [kakaru]

▸ how much will it cost to go to the airport? 空港に行くのにいくらかかりますか [kûkô ni iku no ni ikura kakarimasu ka]

▸ it cost us 10,000 yen 1万円かかりました [ichiman en kakarimashita]

cot *(single bed)* 簡易ベッド [kan'i beddo]

▸ can you put a cot in the room for us? 部屋に簡易ベッドを入れてもらえませんか [heya ni kan'i beddo o irete moraemasen ka]

cough せき [seki] ◆ せきをする [seki o suru]

▸ I've got a cough せきが出ます [seki ga demasu]

▸ I need something for a cough せき止めがいります [sekidome ga irimasu]

could *(past tense of ''can'')* ことができた [...koto ga dekita]; *(in polite requests and suggestions)* てくれませんか [...te kuremasen ka]

▸ could you help me? 手伝ってくれませんか [tetsudatte kuremasen ka]

counter *(in store, bank)* カウンター [kauntâ]

▸ which counter do I have to go to? どのカウンターに行けばいいですか [dono kauntâ ni ikeba î desu ka]

country 国 [kuni]

▸ what country do you come from? お国はどちらですか [okuni wa dochira desu ka]

crosswalks

Japanese tend not to cross until the light is green. Many crosswalks play a traditional tune when it's OK to cross.

couple 夫婦 [fûfu]
- we need a room for a couple and two children 夫婦と子供二人用の部屋がいります [fûfu to kodomo futari yô no heya ga irimasu]

course *(of a meal, for a race, in yoga, sailing)* コース [kôsu]; *(of a ship, a plane)* 進路 [shinro] ◆ **of course** もちろん [mochiron]
- is the set meal three courses? セットメニューは三品コースですか [setto menyû wa sampin kôsu desu ka]
- how much does the sailing course cost? ヨットのコースはいくらですか [yotto no kôsu wa ikura desu ka]
- of course he'll come もちろん彼は来ます [mochiron kare wa kimasu]

cream *(for the skin)* クリーム [kurîmu]
- I need some cream for my sunburn 日焼けに塗るクリームがいります [hiyake ni nuru kurîmu ga irimasu]

credit card クレジットカード [kurejitto kâdo]
- do you take credit cards? クレジットカードで払えますか [kurejitto kâdo de haraemasu ka]

cross *(street, river)* 渡る [wataru]; *(border)* 越える [koeru]
- how do we cross this street? この道をどうやって渡りますか [kono michi o dô yatte watarimasu ka]

cross-country skiing クロスカントリースキー [kurosu kantorî sukî]
- where can I go cross-country skiing around here? この辺でクロスカントリースキーができるのはどこですか [kono hen de kurosu kantorî sukî ga dekiru no wa doko desu ka]

crosswalk 横断歩道 [ôdan hodô]
- always cross at the crosswalk いつも横断歩道を渡りなさい [itsumo ôdan hodô o watarinasai]

cry 泣く [naku]
- don't cry 泣かないで [nakanaide]

cup カップ [kappu]
- I'd like a cup of tea お茶を一杯、お願いします [ocha o ippai onegai shimasu]
- a coffee cup コーヒーカップ [kôhî kappu]
- could we have an extra cup? カップをもう一つもらえませんか [kappu o mô hitotsu moraemasen ka]

currency *(money)* 通貨 [tsûka]
- how much local currency do you have? この国の通貨をどれだけ持って いますか [kono kuni no tsûka o dore dake motte imasu ka]

cut 切る [kiru]
- I cut my finger 指を切りました [yubi o kirimashita]

d

daily 毎日の [mai nichi no] ◆ 日刊紙 [nikkanshi]
- what's the name of the local daily newspaper? 地元の日刊紙の名前は何 ですか [jimoto no nikkanshi no namae wa nan desu ka]

damage 傷をつける [kizu o tsukeru]
- my suitcase was damaged in transit 輸送の間にスーツケースに傷がつき ました [yusô no aida ni sûtsukêsu ni kizu ga tsukimashita]

damp じめじめした [jimejime shita]
- it's damp today 今日はじめじめしています [kyô wa jimejime shite imasu]

dance 踊る [odoru]
- shall we dance? 踊りましょうか [odorimashô ka]
- I can't dance 踊れません [odoremasen]

dancing ダンス [dansu]
- will there be dancing? ダンスはやっていますか [dansu wa yatte imasu ka]
- where can we go dancing? どこでダンスできますか [doko de dansu dekimasu ka]

dandruff ふけ [fuke]
- I have bad dandruff ひどくふけが出ます [hidoku fuke ga demasu]

danger 危険 [kiken]
- hurry! she's in danger! 急いで！すごく危険な状態です [isoide! sugoku kiken na jôtai desu]

dangerous 危ない [abunai]
- this stretch of the river is quite dangerous 川のこの辺りはかなり危ない です [kawa no kono atari wa kanari abunai desu]

dark *(room, night)* 暗い [kurai]; *(hair)* 黒っぽい [kuroppoi]
- it's very dark outside 外は暗いです [soto wa kurai desu]
- she has dark hair 黒っぽい髪をしています [kuroppoi kami o shite imasu]

dark chocolate ダークチョコ [dâku choko]
- I prefer dark chocolate ダークチョコのほうがいいです [dâku choko no hô ga î desu]

dates

The date can be written in two different ways, depending on whether it relates to the Western or Japanese calendar; the latter is based on imperial reigns. It is always written year (年 [nen]), month (月 [gatsu]), day (日 [nichi]). For example, 2007年３月15日 (15 March 2007) would be equivalent to 平成19年 (19th year of the Heisei era). The character 日 (day) is pronounced differently depending on whether it refers to a day of the week (Monday, Tuesday etc.), a day of the month (1st May, 2nd May etc.) or a period of time relating to a particular day (today, yesterday, the day before yesterday etc.). The same applies to the character 月 (month). The system for counting days and months combines Japanese numbers (1 to 10, with a few exceptions) and Chinese numbers.

date *(in time)* 日にち [hinichi]; *(appointment)* デート [dêto]
▸ I've got a date tonight 今晩デートをします [kom ban dêto o shimasu]

daughter *(one's own)* 娘 [musume]; *(someone else's)* 娘さん [musume-san]
▸ this is my daughter 娘です [musume desu]

day 日 [hi/nichi]; *(expressing duration)* 日間 [nichi kan]
▸ what day is it? 今日は何日ですか [kyô wa nan nichi desu ka]
▸ I arrived three days ago 三日前に着きました [mikka mae ni tsukimashita]
▸ I'd like to do a round trip in a day 一日で往復したいんですが [ichi nichi de ôfuku shitai n desu ga]
▸ how much is it per day? 一日いくらですか [ichi nichi ikura desu ka]

dead *(person)* 死亡した [shibô shita]; *(animal)* 死んだ [shinda]; *(battery)* 切れた [kireta]
▸ he was pronounced dead at the scene その場で死亡が確認されました [sono ba de shibô ga kakunin saremashita]
▸ the battery's dead 電池が切れました [denchi ga kiremashita]

lucky and unlucky days

Before Japan adopted the Gregorian calendar in the late 19th century, it used a lunar calendar with six days (六曜日 [rokuyô]), each of which had a name and meaning and was considered lucky or unlucky. This calendar is still used when choosing dates for important occasions, such as weddings, funerals, and opening new businesses.

dead end 行き止まり [ikidomari]
> it's a dead end 行き止まりです [ikidomari desu]

deal *(business agreement)* 取引き [torihiki]
> I got a good deal on the room 部屋の値段を割安にしてもらいました [heya no nedan o wariyasu ni shite moraimashita]

death *(state)* 死 [shi]; *(person)* 死亡 [shibô]
> there were two deaths 二人死亡しました [futari shibô shimashita]

decaf, decaffeinated カフェイン抜きのコーヒー [kafein nuki no kôhî] ◆ カフェイン抜きの [kafein nuki no]
> a decaf/decaffeinated coffee, please カフェイン抜きのコーヒーをお願いします [kafein nuki no kôhî o onegai shimasu]

December 十二月 [jûnigatsu]
> December 10th 十二月十日 [jûnigatsu tôka]

decide 決まる [kimaru]
> we haven't decided yet まだ決まっていません [mada kimatte imasen]

deck *(of ship)* デッキ [dekki]; *(of cards)* 一組 [hito kumi]
> how do I get to the upper deck? 上のデッキにはどうやって行ったらいいですか [ue no dekki ni wa dô yatte ittara î desu ka]

deckchair デッキチェア [dekkichea]
> I'd like to rent a deckchair デッキチェアを借りたいんですが [dekkichea o karitai n desu ga]

declare 申告する [shinkoku suru]
> I have nothing to declare 何も申告するものはありません [nani mo shinkoku suru mono wa arimasen]
> I have a bottle of spirits to declare お酒を一本申告します [osake o ippon shinkoku shimasu]

definitely 必ず [kanarazu]
> we'll definitely come back here ここに必ず戻ってきます [koko ni kanarazu modotte kimasu]

degree 度 [do]
> 5 degrees below freezing 氷点下５度 [hyôten ka go do]

delay 遅れ [okure]
> is there a delay for this flight? この便は遅れていますか [kono bin wa okurete imasu ka]

delayed 遅れた [okureta]
> how long will the flight be delayed? その便はどれぐらい遅れていますか [sono bin wa dore gurai okurete imasu ka]

delicious おいしい [oishî]
> this is delicious! おいしいです [oishî desu]

department stores

Department stores such as Isetan, Mitsukoshi, Takashimaya, Seibu and Odakyû sell high-quality goods, including kimono and traditional Japanese crafts, and Japanese and western food on the basement level. They also offer a wide range of services, such as ticket sales for local concerts and other events, luggage storage, and crêche facilities, and often have art or craft exhibitions on the top floor. The Tokyu Hands stores specialize in products relating to the home and hobbies. Department stores are usually open from 10 a.m. to 7 or 8 p.m, including Sunday, but are closed on one weekday.

delighted 喜んで [yorokonde]
- we're delighted you could make it お越しを喜んでいます [okoshi o yorokonde imasu]

dentist 歯医者 [haisha]
- I need to see a dentist urgently 緊急に歯医者に見てもらわなければなりません [kinkyû ni haisha ni mite morawanakereba narimasen]

department *(in store)* 売り場 [uriba]
- I'm looking for the menswear department 紳士服売り場を探しています [shinshi fuku uriba o sagashite imasu]

department store デパート [depâto]
- where are the department stores? デパートはどこにありますか [depâto wa doko ni arimasu ka]

departure 出発 [shuppatsu]
- 'departures' *(in airport)* 出発 [shuppatsu]

departure lounge 出発ロビー [shuppatsu robî]
- where's the departure lounge? 出発ロビーはどこですか [shuppatsu robî wa doko desu ka]

deposit *(against loss or damage)* 保証金 [hoshôkin]; *(down payment)* 頭金 [atamakin]
- is there a deposit to pay for using the equipment? 用具を使うのに保証金はいりますか [yôgu o tsukau no ni hoshôkin wa irimasu ka]
- how much is the deposit? 頭金はいくらですか [atamakin wa ikura desu ka]

desk *(in office, home)* 机 [tsukue]; *(at hotel)* フロント [furonto]; *(for cashier or airport)* カウンター [kauntâ]
- where can I find the American Airlines desk? アメリカンエアラインのカウンターはどこですか [amerikan earain no kauntâ wa doko desu ka]

desserts and cakes

Although Japan does not really have a tradition of desserts, there are traditional cakes and sweets called 和菓子 [wagashi] (Japanese cakes). Elegant small cakes made from rice (餅 [mochi]) and sweetened red bean paste (あんこ [anko]) are served at the tea ceremony. There are also many varieties of savory rice crackers (せんべい [sembê]) eaten as snacks.

dessert デザート [dezâto]
▸ what desserts do you have? デザートは何がありますか [dezâto wa nani ga arimasu ka]

dessert wine デザート用ワイン [dezâto yô wain]
▸ can you recommend a good dessert wine? デザート用ワインを何か推薦してくれますか [dezâto yô wain o nani ka suisen shite kuremasu ka]

detour 迂回路 [ukairo]
▸ is there a detour ahead? この先に迂回路はありますか [kono saki ni ukairo wa arimasu ka]

develop (film) 現像する [genzô suru]; (progress) 発達する [hattatsu suru]
▸ how much does it cost to develop a roll of 36 photos? ３６枚撮りを現像するのにいくらかかりますか [sanjûroku mai dori o genzô suru no ni ikura kakarimasu ka]

diabetic 糖尿病の [tônyôbyô no] ◆ 糖尿病 [tônyôbyô]
▸ I'm diabetic and I need a prescription for insulin 糖尿病なので、インシュリンの処方箋がいります [tônyôbyô na node, inshurin no shohôsen ga irimasu]

diarrhea 下痢 [geri]
▸ I'd like something for diarrhea 下痢に効くものがほしいんですが [geri ni kiku mono ga hoshî n desu ga]

difference (in price, cost) 差額 [sagaku]
▸ will you pay the difference? 差額を払ってもらえますか [sagaku o haratte moraemasu ka]

difficult 難しい [muzukashî]
▸ I find some sounds difficult to pronounce 発音するのに難しい音がいくつかあります [hatsuon suru no ni muzukashî oto ga ikutsu ka arimasu]

difficulty 難しさ [muzukashisa]
▸ I'm having difficulty finding the place 場所を探すのが難しいです [basho o sagasu no ga muzukashî desu]

digital camera デジ（タル）カメ（ラ）[deji(taru) kame(ra)]
▸ my digital camera's been stolen デジカメを盗まれました [deji kame o nusumaremashita]

disabled access

Since the introduction of the Law for Barrier-free Transport in 2000, escalators, elevators and ramps have been introduced in many stations, airports, bus terminals and ports, making travel much easier than it used to be for people with large luggage as well as those with disabilities. Other laws are making large buildings and tourist facilities more accessible for the disabled.

dining room 食堂 [shokudô]
▸ do you have to have breakfast in the dining room? 朝食は食堂で食べなければなりませんか [chôshoku wa shokudô de tabenakereba narimasen ka]

dinner 夕食 [yûshoku], 晩ごはん [bangohan]
▸ up to what time do they serve dinner? 夕食は何時までできますか [yûshoku wa nan ji made dekimasu ka]

direct 直通の [chokutsû no]
▸ is that train direct? その列車は直通ですか [sono ressha wa chokutsû desu ka]

direction 方角 [hôgaku]
▸ am I going in the right direction for the train station? 駅の方角に向かっていますか [eki no hôgaku ni mukatte imasu ka]

directory assistance 番号案内 [bangô annai]
▸ what's the number for directory assistance? 番号案内は何番ですか [bangô annai wa nam ban desu ka]

dirty *(room, tablecloth)* 汚い [kitanai]
▸ the sheets are dirty シーツが汚いです [shîtsu ga kitanai desu]

disability 障害 [shôgai]
▸ do you have facilities for people with disabilities? 障害者用の設備はありますか [shôgaisha yô no setsubi wa arimasu ka]

disabled 身体障害の [shintai shôgai no]
▸ where's the nearest disabled parking spot? 一番近い身体障害者用の駐車場はどこですか [ichi ban chikai shintai shôgaisha yô no chûshajô wa doko desu ka]

disco *(club)* ディスコ [disuko]
▸ are there any discos around here? この辺にディスコはありますか [kono hen ni disuko wa arimasu ka]

discount 割引 [waribiki]
▸ is there any chance of a discount? 割引してもらうことはできませんか [waribiki shite morau koto wa dekimasen ka]

dish *(plate)* 皿 [sara]; *(food)* 料理 [ryôri] ✦ **dishes** 皿洗い [sara arai]
- what's the dish of the day? 今日のお勧め料理は何ですか [kyô no osusume ryôri wa nan desu ka]
- can I help you with the dishes? 皿洗いを手伝いましょうか [sara arai o tetsudaimashô ka]

disposable 使い捨て [tsukaisute]
- I need some disposable razors 使い捨てかみそりがいります [tsukaisute kamisori ga irimasu]
- do you sell disposable cameras? 使い捨てカメラを売っていますか [tsukaisute kamera o utte imasu ka]

distance 距離 [kyori]
- the hotel is only a short distance from here ホテルはここからたいした距離ではありません [hoteru wa koko kara taishita kyori dewa arimasen]

district *(of town)* 地区 [chiku]
- which district do you live in? どの地区に住んでいますか [dono chiku ni sunde imasu ka]

dive ダイビングをする [daibingu o suru] ✦ ダイビング [daibingu]
- can we do a night dive? *(scuba diving)* 夜のスキューバダイビングはできますか [yoru no sukyûba daibingu wa dekimasu ka]

diving *(scuba diving)* ダイビング [daibingu]
- I'd like to take diving lessons ダイビングレッスンを受けたいんですが [daibingu ressun o uketai n desu ga]
- do you rent out diving equipment? ダイビングの道具を貸し出しますか [daibingu no dôgu o kashidashimasu ka]

diving board 飛込み台 [tobikomidai]
- is there a diving board? 飛込み台はありますか [tobikomidai wa arimasu ka]

dizzy spell めまい [memai]
- I've been having dizzy spells めまいがしています [memai ga shite imasu]

do *(perform action)* する [suru]; *(cover distance)* 進む [susumu]
- what do you do for a living? 仕事は何をしていますか [shigoto wa nani o shite imasu ka]
- is there anything I can do (to help)? 何か私にできることはありますか [nani ka watashi ni dekiru koto wa arimasu ka]
- what are you doing tonight? 今夜は何をしますか [kon ya wa nani o shimasu ka]
- what is there to do here during the festival? 祭りの間、ここで何がありますか [matsuri no aida, koko de nani ga arimasu ka]

doctor 医者 [isha]
- I have to see a doctor 医者に見てもらわなければなりません [isha ni mite morawanakereba narimasen]

dollar ドル [doru]

▸ I'd like to change some dollars into yen ドルを円に換えたいんですが [doru o en ni kaetai n desu ga]

door ドア [doa]

▸ do you want me to answer the door? 私が応対しましょうか [watashi ga ôtai shimashô ka]

dormitory *(in youth hostel)* 相部屋 [aibeya]; *(for students)* 寮 [ryô]

▸ are you staying in the dormitory? 寮にいますか [ryô ni imasu ka]

double 二倍の [ni bai no] ✦ 二倍になる [ni bai ni naru]

▸ it's spelled with a double 'l' つづりはエルが二つです [tuzuri wa eru ga futatsu desu]

▸ prices have doubled since last year 値段は去年の二倍になりました [nedan wa kyonen no ni bai ni narimashita]

double bed ダブルベッド [daburu beddo]

▸ does the room have a double bed? 部屋にあるのはダブルベッドですか [heya ni aru no wa daburu beddo desu ka]

double room ダブルベッドの部屋 [daburu beddo no heya]

▸ I'd like a double room for five nights, please ダブルベッドの部屋を五泊お願いします [daburu beddo no heya o go haku onegai shimasu]

downtown 町の中心の [machi no chûshin no] ✦ 町の中心で [machi no chûshin de] ✦ 町の中心 [machi no chûshin]

▸ we're looking for a good downtown hotel 町の中心にあるいいホテルを探しています [machi no chûshin ni aru î hoteru o sagashite imasu]

▸ does this bus go downtown? このバスは町の中心に行きますか [kono basu wa machi no chûshin ni ikimasu ka]

draft beer 生ビール [nama bîru]

▸ a draft beer, please 生ビールをください [nama bîru o kudasai]

dream 夢 [yume] ✦ 夢を見る [yume o miru]

▸ to have a dream 夢を見る [yume o miru]

▸ I dreamt (that)... ...という夢を見ました [...to yû yume o mimashita]

drink 飲み物 [nomimono] ✦ 飲む [nomu]

▸ I'll have a cold drink 冷たいものを飲みます [tsumetai mono o nomimasu]

▸ I could do with a drink 飲み物がほしいです [nomimono ga hoshî desu]

▸ what kind of hot drinks do you have? 温かい飲み物は何がありますか [atatakai nomimono wa nani ga arimasu ka]

▸ shall we go for a drink? 飲みに行きましょうか [nomi ni ikimashô ka]

▸ can I buy you a drink? 飲み物をおごりましょうか [nomimono o ogorimashô ka]

driving

In Japan, you drive on the left. There are right of way signs at every junction. If you see 止まれ [tomare], either written on the road or on a roadsign, it means STOP. Speed limits are 100 km/h on freeways and 60 km/h on other types of road, and built-up areas often have a 20 km/h limit. Freeway tolls are very expensive and there is almost always a charge for street parking.

drinking water 飲み水 [nomi mizu]
- this is not drinking water 飲めません [nomemasen]

drive *(in vehicle)* ドライブ [doraibu] ◆ *(vehicle)* 運転する [unten suru]
- is it a long drive? 長くドライブしますか [nagaku doraibu shimasu ka]
- could you drive me home? 家まで乗せてくれませんか [ie made nosete kuremasen ka]
- she was driving too close to the car in front 前の車と車間距離を取らずに運転していました [mae no kuruma to shakan kyori o torazu ni unten shite imashita]

driver 運転手 [untenshu]
- the other driver wasn't looking where he was going 向こうの運転手はよそ見をしていました [mukô no untenshu wa yosomi o shite imashita]

driver's license （運転）免許証 [(unten) menkyoshô]
- can I see your driver's license? 免許証を見せてください [menkyoshô o misete kudasai]

drop *(of liquid)* しずく [shizuku]; *(small amount)* 少量 [shôryô] ◆ *(let fall)* 落とす [otosu]; *(let out of vehicle)* おろす [orosu]
- could I just have a drop of milk? ミルクをほんの少しだけ入れてください [miruku o hon no sukoshi dake irete kudasai]
- I dropped my scarf スカーフを落としました [sukâfu o otoshimashita]
- could you drop me off at the corner? あの角でおろしてくれませんか [ano kado de oroshite kuremasen ka]

drop off *(let out of vehicle)* おろす [orosu]
- could you drop me off here? ここでおろしてくれませんか [koko de oroshite kuremasen ka]

driver's license

You need an International Driving Permit to drive in Japan.

drown 溺れる [oboreru]
- he's drowning: somebody call for help 人が溺れています。助けを呼んでください [hito ga oborete imasu; tasuke o yonde kudasai]

drugstore 薬屋 [kusuriya]
- where is the nearest drugstore? 一番近い薬屋はどこですか [ichi ban chikai kusuriya wa doko desu ka]

drunk 酔った [yotta]
- he's very drunk ひどく酔っています [hidoku yotte imasu]

dry *(clothing)* 乾いた [kawaita]; *(wine)* 辛口の [karakuchi no]; *(skin, day, climate)* 乾燥した [kansô shita] ◆ 乾かす [kawakasu]; *(with a cloth, a towel)* ふく [fuku] ◆ 乾く [kawaku]
- a small glass of dry white wine 辛口の白ワインを小さなグラスに一杯 [karakuchi no shiro wain o chîsa na gurasu ni ippai]
- where can I put my towel to dry? どこでタオルを乾かしたらいいですか [doko de taoru o kawakashitara î desu ka]

dry cleaner's クリーニング屋 [kurîningu ya]
- is there a dry cleaner's nearby? 近くにクリーニング屋がありますか [chikaku ni kurîningu ya ga arimasu ka]

dryer *(for laundry)* 乾燥機 [kansôki]
- is there a dryer? 乾燥機はありますか [kansôki wa arimasu ka]

dub *(movie)* 吹き替えをする [fukikae o suru]
- do they always dub English-language movies? 英語の映画は必ず吹き替えされていますか [êgo no êga wa kanarazu fukikae sarete imasu ka]

during の間 [...no aida]
- is there restricted parking during the festival? 祭りの間、駐車は規制されていますか [matsuri no aida, chûsha wa kisê sarete imasu ka]

duty *(tax)* 関税 [kanzê]
- do I have to pay duty on this? これに関税はかかりますか [kore ni kanzê wa kakarimasu ka]

---

at the drugstore

- I'd like something for a headache/a sore throat/diarrhea 頭痛/のどの痛み止め/下痢止めの薬がほしいんですが [zutsû/nodo no itamidome/geridome no kusuri ga hoshî n desu ga]
- I'd like some aspirin/some Band-Aids® アスピリン/バンドエイド®がほしいんですが [asupirin/bando-êdo ga hoshî n desu ga]
- could you recommend a doctor? お医者さんを紹介してくれませんか [oisha-san o shôkai shite kuremasen ka]

duty-free shop 免税店 [menzê ten]
- ▸ where are the duty-free shops? 免税店はどこですか [menzê ten wa doko desu ka]

DVD DVD [dîbuidî]
- ▸ can I play this DVD in the States? このDVDはアメリカで見られますか [kono dîbuidî wa amerika de miraremasu ka]

e

ear 耳 [mimi]
- ▸ I have a ringing in my ears 耳鳴りがします [mimi nari ga shimasu]

earache 耳の痛み [mimi no itami]
- ▸ he has an earache 耳が痛いようです [mimi ga itai yô desu]

ear infection 耳の炎症 [mimi no enshô]
- ▸ I think I have an ear infection 耳が炎症を起こしたようです [mimi ga enshô o okoshita yô desu]

early *(before the expected time)* 早い [hayai]; *(in the day)* 早く [hayaku]; *(at the beginning)* 始めの [hajime no]
- ▸ is there an earlier flight? もっと早い便はありますか [motto hayai bin wa arimasu ka]
- ▸ we arrived early 早く着きました [hayaku tsukimashita]
- ▸ I'll be leaving early in the morning 朝、早く出ます [asa hayaku demasu]

earthquake 地震 [jishin]
- ▸ when was the last earthquake? この前の地震はいつありましたか [kono mae no jishin wa itsu arimashita ka]

easy 簡単な [kantan na]
- ▸ is it easy to use? 使い方は簡単ですか [tsukaikata wa kantan desu ka]
- ▸ I'd like something easy to carry 持ち運びの簡単なものが何かほしいんですが [mochihakobi no kantan na mono ga nani ka hoshî n desu ga]

eat 食べる [taberu]
- ▸ I'm afraid I don't eat fish 残念ながら魚は食べません [zannen nagara sakana wa tabemasen]
- ▸ where can we get something to eat? どこで食事ができますか [doko de shokuji ga dekimasu ka]

economy (class) エコノミークラス [ekonomî kurasu] ◆ エコノミークラスの [ekonomî kurasu no]

earthquakes

Earthquakes are common in Japan, with minor tremors occurring almost daily in the Tokyo area, but very few are big enough to cause serious damage. If you are involved in such an earthquake, try not to panic; even severe tremors usually only last for a minute or two. If you are inside, try to protect yourself from falling objects, for example, by hiding under a table. Don't run outside and don't use elevators or escalators. If you are in the street, get inside a building. If you are in an apartment, switch off any gas appliances and the main gas valve. If you are in a train, hang on to a strap or seat, and don't leave the train until told to do so. Be aware of the danger of a tsunami if you are on or near the beach, and of landslides in the mountains.

- are there any seats in economy class? エコノミークラスの席はあります か [ekonomî kurasu no seki wa arimasu ka]
- I'd prefer to go economy エコノミークラスの方がいいです [ekonomî kurasu no hô ga î desu]

egg 卵 [tamago]
- I'd like my eggs sunny side up, please 目玉焼きにしてください [medamayaki ni shite kudasai]

eight 八 [hachi]
- there are eight of us 全部で八人です [zembu de hachi nin desu]

electric heater 電気ヒーター [denki hîtâ]
- do you have an electric heater? 電気ヒーターはありますか [denki hîtâ wa arimasu ka]

electricity 電気 [denki]
- there's no electricity in the room 部屋に電気が来ていません [heya ni denki ga kite imasen]

eating – manners

It's polite to say いただきます [itadakimasu] before a meal, and ごちそうさ までした [gochisôsama deshita] afterwards as thanks, particularly if someone else is treating you. It is not considered rude to make a noise when eating noodles – in fact, slurping shows enjoyment! Lifting up one's rice bowl or soup bowl to eat is considered good manners. You should try not to leave any grains of rice in the bowl when you finish.

electronics

There are whole areas of big cities that sell nothing but electronics, such as Akihabara in Tokyo and Nihombashi in Osaka. They have a truly enormous range of products, far more advanced than available in the US. Most shops will deduct sales tax for tourists, and you will need your passport for this. If you do buy any electronic appliances in Japan, make sure they will be compatible when you take them home.

electric razor, electric shaver 電気かみそり [denki kamisori]
▸ where can I plug in my electric razor? 電気かみそりのコンセントはどこ ですか [denki kamisori no konsento wa doko desu ka]

electronics 電気製品 [denki sêhin]
▸ where is the electronics department? 電気製品売り場はどこですか [denki sêhin uriba wa doko desu ka]

elevator エレベーター [erebêtâ]
▸ is there an elevator? エレベーターはありますか [erebêtâ wa arimasu ka]
▸ the elevator is out of order エレベーターは故障中です [erebêtâ wa koshô chû desu]

eleven 十一 [jûichi]
▸ there are eleven of us 全部で十一人です [zembu de jûichi nin desu]

e-mail （電子）メール [(denshi) mêru]
▸ I'd like to send an e-mail メールを送りたいんですが [mêru o okuritai n desu ga]
▸ where can I check my e-mail? どこでメールをチェックできますか [doko de mêru o chekku dekimasu ka]

e-mail address メールアドレス [mêru adoresu]
▸ do you have an e-mail address? メールアドレスはありますか [mêru adoresu wa arimasu ka]

emergency 緊急 [kinkyû]
▸ it's an emergency! 緊急です [kinkyû desu]
▸ what number do you call in an emergency? 緊急時の電話番号は何番です か [kinkyû ji no denwa bangô wa nam ban desu ka]

emergency brake サイドブレーキ [saido burêki]
▸ I'm sure I put the emergency brake on 確かにサイドブレーキをかけまし た [tashika ni saido burêki o kakemashita]

emergency cord 緊急停止装置 [kinkyû têshi sôchi]
▸ someone's pulled the emergency cord 誰かが緊急停止装置を引きました [dare ka ga kinkyû têshi sôchi o hikimashita]

emergencies

In an emergency dial 110 for police and 119 for the fire brigade or an ambulance. If you dial 119 you will need to specify which service you require: shôbôsha o onegai shimasu for the fire brigade, or kyûkyûsha o onegai shimasu for an ambulance. Japan has a system of local police boxes/offices (交番 [kôban]) open 24 hours a day, where the neighborhood police officers (おまわりさん [omawari san]) are based. If you need to ask directions or have lost something, or there is some kind of emergency, this is a good place to go.

emergency exit 非常口 [hijôguchi]
▸ where is the nearest emergency exit? 一番近い非常口はどこですか [ichi ban chikai hijôguchi wa doko desu ka]

emergency room 救急病院 [kyûkyû byôin]
▸ I need to go to the emergency room right away すぐに救急病院に行かなければなりません [sugu ni kyûkyû byôin ni ikanakereba narimasen]

emergency services 救急隊 [kyûkyû tai]
▸ please call the emergency services 救急隊を呼んでください [kyûkyû tai o yonde kudasai]

end *(conclusion, finish)* 終わり [owari]
▸ at the end of July 七月の終わり [shichigatsu no owari]

engine エンジン [enjin]
▸ the engine is making a funny noise エンジンが変な音を立てています [enjin ga hen na oto o tatete imasu]

English *(nation)* イングランドの [ingurando no]; *(language)* 英語の [êgo no] ◆ *(language)* 英語 [êgo]
▸ I'm English イングランド人です [ingurandojin desu]
▸ how do you say that in English? 英語で何と言いますか [êgo de nan to îmasu ka]
▸ do you understand English? 英語はわかりますか [êgo wa wakarimasu ka]
▸ the English イングランド人 [ingurandojin]

English

English on signs is becoming more widespread in the big cities and tourist areas. You will also hear English announcements on the bullet trains (新幹線 [shinkansen]) and on some buses in the major tourist areas, such as Kyoto.

enjoy 楽しむ [tanoshimu]
- to enjoy oneself 楽しく過ごす [tanoshiku sugosu]
- did you enjoy your meal? お食事はいかがでしたか [oshokuji wa ikaga deshita ka]

enough 充分に [jûbun ni] ◆ 充分な量 [jûbun na ryô]
- I don't have enough money お金が足りません [okane ga tarimasen]
- that's enough! もう充分です [mô jûbun desu]
- no thanks, I've had quite enough もう結構です [mô kekkô desu]

enter *(type in)* 入れる [ireru] ◆ 入る [hairu]
- do I enter my PIN number now? ここで暗証番号を入れるんですか [koko de anshô bangô o ireru n desu ka]

entrance 入口 [iriguchi]
- where's the entrance to the subway? 地下鉄の入口はどこですか [chikatetsu no iriguchi wa doko desu ka]

entry *(to place)* 入場 [nyûjô]
- entry to the exhibit is free 展覧会の入場は無料です [tenrankai no nyûjô wa muryô desu]

envelope 封筒 [fûtô]
- I'd like a pack of envelopes 封筒を一パックください [fûtô o hito pakku kudasai]

equipment 道具 [dôgu]
- do you provide the equipment? 道具は含まれていますか [dôgu wa fukumarete imasu ka]

escalator エスカレーター [esukarêtâ]
- is there an escalator? エスカレーターはありますか [esukarêtâ wa arimasu ka]

evening 晩 [ban]
- why don't we meet up this evening? 今晩、会いませんか [kom ban aimasen ka]
- in the evening *(of every day)* 毎晩 [mai ban]

event *(cultural)* イベント [ibento]
- what's the program of events? 何がイベントの予定に入っていますか [nani ga ibento no yotê ni haitte imasu ka]

ever *(at any time)* いつも [itsumo]; *(before now)* これまでに [kore made ni]
- have you ever been to Boston? ボストンに行ったことがありますか [bosuton ni itta koto ga arimasu ka]

everything 全部 [zembu]
- that's everything, thanks それで全部です、ありがとう [sore de zembu desu, arigatô]

exchange ⓘ

You are strongly advised to change money before you go to Japan. Outside airports, only the larger branches of the major banks have foreign currency exchange facilities, and these are only open on weekdays from 9 a.m. to 3 p.m.

▸ we didn't have time to see everything 全部見る時間はありませんでした [zembu miru jikan wa arimasen deshita]

excess baggage 重量オーバーの荷物 [jûryô ôbâ no nimotsu]
▸ what's your policy on excess baggage? 重量オーバーの荷物に対するきまりはどうなっていますか [jûryô ôbâ no nimotsu ni taisuru kimari wa dô natte imasu ka]

exchange 交換する [kôkan suru]
▸ I'd like to exchange this T-shirt このTシャツを交換したいんですが [kono tîshatsu o kôkan shitai n desu ga]

exchange rate 両替率 [ryôgae ritsu]
▸ what is today's exchange rate? 今日の両替率はいくらですか [kyô no ryôgae ritsu wa ikura desu ka]

excursion オプショナルツアー [opushonaru tsuâ]
▸ I'd like to sign up for the excursion on Saturday 土曜日のオプショナルツアーに加わりたいんです [doyôbi no opushonaru tsuâ ni kuwawaritai n desu ga]

excuse *(behavior, person)* 許す [yurusu]
▸ excuse me? *(asking for repetition)* もう一度お願いします [mô ichi do onegai shimasu]
▸ excuse me! *(to get attention; to get by; interrupting, apologizing, expressing disagreement)* すみません [sumimasen]
▸ you'll have to excuse my (poor) Japanese 下手な日本語は大目に見てください [heta na nihongo wa ôme ni mite kudasai]

exhaust 排気管 [haikikan]
▸ the exhaust is making a strange noise 排気管が変な音を立てています [haikikan ga hen na oto o tatete imasu]

exhausted *(tired)* へとへとの [hetoheto no]
▸ I'm exhausted へとへとです [hetoheto desu]

exhibit 展覧会 [tenrankai]
▸ I'd like a ticket for the temporary exhibit 特別展のチケットをください [tokubetsu ten no chiketto o kudasai]
▸ is this ticket valid for the exhibit too? このチケットで展覧会も入れますか [kono chiketto de tenrankai mo hairemasu ka]

exit 出口 [deguchi]
- where's the exit? 出口はどこですか [deguchi wa doko desu ka]
- is it far to the next exit? 次の出口は遠いですか [tsugi no deguchi wa tôi desu ka]

expect *(letter)* 来るのを待つ [kuru no o matsu]; *(baby)* 産む予定で [umu yotê de]
- I'll be expecting you at eight o'clock at... 8時に...で待っています [hachi ji ni...de matte imasu]
- when do you expect it to be ready? いつできると思いますか [itsu dekiru to omoimasu ka]

expensive 高い [takai]
- do you have anything less expensive? それより高くないものは何かありませんか [sore yori takakunai mono wa nani ka arimasen ka]

expire *(visa)* 期限が切れる [kigen ga kireru]
- my passport has expired パスポートの期限が切れてしまいました [pasupôto no kigen ga kirete shimaimashita]

explain 説明する [setsumê suru]
- please explain how to get to the airport どうやって空港に行ったらいいか説明してください [dô yatte kûkô ni ittara î ka setsumê shite kudasai]
- can you explain what this means? どういうことか説明してもらえますか [dô yû koto ka setsumê shite moraemasu ka]

express (train) 急行（列車） [kyûkô (ressha)]
- how long does it take by express train? 急行でどれぐらいかかりますか [kyûkô de dore gurai kakarimasu ka]

extension *(phone line)* 内線 [naisen]
- could I have extension 358, please? 内線番号358をお願いできますか [naisen bangô san go hachi o onegai dekimasu ka]

extra 追加の [tsuika no]
- is it possible to add an extra bed? 追加のベッドを入れてもらえますか [tsuika no beddo o irete moraemasu ka]
- would it be possible to stay an extra night? もう一泊できますか [mô ippaku dekimasu ka]

extra charge 追加料金 [tsuika ryôkin]
- what would the extra charge be for this service? 追加料金はいくらですか [tsuika ryôkin wa ikura desu ka]
- at no extra charge 追加料金なしで [tsuika ryôkin nashi de]

eye 目 [me]
- she has blue eyes 青い目をしています [aoi me o shite imasu]
- can you keep an eye on my bag for a few minutes? かばんをちょっと見ていてくれませんか [kaban o chotto mite ite kuremasen ka]

eye drops 目薬 [megusuri]
▸ do you have any eye drops? 目薬はありますか [megusuri wa arimasu ka]

eye shadow アイシャドウ [ai shadô]
▸ is this the only eye shadow you've got? アイシャドウはこれしかありませんか [ai shadô wa kore shika arimasen ka]

eyesight 視力 [shiryoku]
▸ I don't have very good eyesight 視力があまりよくありません [shiryoku ga amari yoku arimasen]

face (of person) 顔 [kao]
▸ the attacker had a broad face 襲ってきた人は幅の広い顔をしていました [osotte kita hito wa haba no hiroi kao o shite imashita]

facilities 設備 [setsubi]
▸ what kind of exercise facilities do you have here? ここにはどんな運動の設備がありますか [koko ni wa donna undô no setsubi ga arimasu ka]
▸ do you have facilities for people with disabilities? 身障者のための設備はありますか [shinshôsha no tame no setsubi wa arimasu ka]
▸ are there facilities for children? 子供用の設備はありますか [kodomo yô no setsubi wa arimasu ka]

faint 失神する [shisshin suru]
▸ I fainted twice last week 先週、2度失神しました [senshû ni do shisshin shimashita]

fair (person, situation) 公平な [kôhê na]; (price) 適正な [tekisê na]; (hair) 金髪の [kimpatsu no]; (skin, complexion) 色白な [irojiro na]
▸ this isn't a fair price これは適正な値段じゃありません [kore wa tekisê na nedan ja arimasen]
▸ it's not fair! 公平じゃない [kôhê ja nai]

fall 倒れる [taoreru] ◆ (season) 秋 [aki]
▸ I fell on my back 後ろに倒れました [ushiro ni taoremashita]
▸ in (the) fall 秋に [aki ni]; see box on p. 56

family 家族 [kazoku]
▸ do you have any family in the area? その地域にご家族がいますか [sono chi-iki ni go-kazoku ga imasu ka]

fan (electric) 扇風機 [sempûki]; (Japanese) 扇子 [sensu]; (enthusiast) ファン [fan]

fall leaf-viewing

In the fall equivalent of cherry blossom viewing, people go to see the spectacular foliage of maple, gingko and other trees in October and November (紅葉狩り [momijigari]). The Kyoto temples and hills are particularly famous, but each place has its own local spot to view the bright red, gold and orange leaves against clear blue fall skies.

» how does the fan work? 扇風機はどうやって使いますか [sempûki wa dô yatte tsukaimasu ka]

far *(in distance, time)* 遠い [tôi]

» am I far from the village? 村からはまだ遠いですか [mura kara wa mada tôi desu ka]
» is it far to walk? 歩くのには遠いですか [aruku no ni wa tôi desu ka]
» is it far by car? 車で行くのには遠いですか [kuruma de iku no ni wa tôi desu ka]
» how far is the market from here? 市場はここからどのぐらい離れていますか [ichiba wa koko kara dono gurai hanarete imasu ka]
» far away/off *(in distance, time)* 遠い [tôi]
» so far 今までのところは [ima made no tokoro wa]

fast 速い [hayai] ♦ 速く [hayaku]

» please don't drive so fast そんなにスピードを出さないでください [sonna ni supîdo o dasanaide kudasai]
» to be fast *(watch, clock)* 進んでいる [susunde iru]
» my watch is five minutes fast 私の時計は5分進んでいます [watashi no tokê wa go fun susunde imasu]

fat *(in diet)* 脂肪 [shibô]

» it's low in fat 脂肪が少ないです [shibô ga sukunai desu]

father *(one's own)* 父 [chichi]; *(someone else's)* お父さん [otô-san]

» this is my father 父です [chichi desu]

fault *(responsibility)* 責任 [sekinin]

» it was my fault 私の責任です [watashi no sekinin desu]

favor *(kind act)* 好意 [kôi]

» can I ask you a favor? お願いがあるんです [onegai ga aru n desu]

favorite お気に入りの [oki ni iri no] ♦ お気に入り [oki ni iri]

» it's my favorite book 私のお気に入りの本です [watashi no oki ni iri no hon desu]

feather 羽 [hane]

» are these feather pillows? これは羽毛の枕ですか [kore wa umô no makura desu ka]

February 二月 [nigatsu]
- February 8th ２月８日 [nigatsu yôka]

feed 食べ物を与える [tabemono o ataeru]
- where can I feed the baby? どこで赤ん坊にミルクをやったらいいですか [doko de akambô ni miruku o yattara î desu ka]

feel *(touch)* 触る [sawaru]; *(sense)* 感じる [kanjiru] ◆ *(physically)* 感じる [kanjiru]
- I can't feel my feet 足の感覚がありません [ashi no kankaku ga arimasen]
- I don't feel well 気分が悪いです [kibun ga warui desu]

ferry フェリー [ferî]
- when does the next ferry leave? 次のフェリーは何時に出ますか [tsugi no ferî wa nan ji ni demasu ka]

ferry terminal フェリー乗り場 [ferî noriba]
- which way is the ferry terminal? フェリー乗り場はどちらですか [ferî noriba wa dochira desu ka]

fever 熱 [netsu]
- the baby's got a fever 赤ん坊が熱を出しました [akambô ga netsu o dashimashita]

festival 祭り [matsuri]
- will it be crowded at the festival? 祭りの時は混みますか [matsuri no toki wa komimasu ka]

few 少しも [sukoshi mo] ◆ **a few** 少しだけ [sukoshi dake]
- there are few sights worth seeing around here この辺に見る価値のあるところは少しもありません [kono hen ni miru kachi no aru tokoro wa sukoshi mo arimasen]
- we're thinking of staying a few more days もう数日いようと思います [mô sû nichi iyô to omoimasu]
- I spent a month in France a few years ago 数年前にフランスで一ヶ月過ごしました [sû nen mae ni furansu de ikka getsu sugoshimashita]

fifth 五番目の [go bam me no] ◆ *(gear)* トップギア [toppu gia]
- I can't get it into fifth トップギアが入りません [toppu gia ga hairimasen]

filling *(in a tooth)* 詰め物 [tsumemono]
- one of my fillings has come out 詰め物が取れてしまいました [tsumemono ga torete shimaimashita]

fill up いっぱいにする [ippai ni suru] ◆ いっぱいになる [ippai ni naru]
- fill it up, please いっぱいにしてください [ippai ni shite kudasai]

film *(for camera)* フィルム [firumu] ◆ 撮影する [satsuê suru]
- I'd like to have this film developed このフィルムを現像してほしいんですが [kono firumu o genzô shite hoshî n desu ga]

‣ do you have black-and-white film? 白黒のフィルムはありますか [shiro kuro no firumu wa arimasu ka]

‣ is filming allowed in the museum? 博物館の中で撮影してもいいですか [hakubutsukan no naka de satsuê shite mo î desu ka]

find 見つける [mitsukeru]; *(lost object)* 拾う [hirou]

‣ has anyone found a watch? 誰か時計を拾いましたか [dare ka tokê o hiroimashita ka]

‣ where can I find a doctor on a Sunday? 日曜の当番医はどこですか [nichiyôbi no tôban i wa doko desu ka]

find out 調べる [shiraberu]

‣ I need to find out the times of trains to Osaka 大阪行きの列車の時間を調べなければなりません [ôsaka yuki no ressha no jikan o shirabenakereba narimasen]

fine *(in health etc.)* 大丈夫 [daijôbu] ◆ 罰金 [bakkin]

‣ fine thanks, and you? 大丈夫です、あなたは？ [daijôbu desu. anata wa]

‣ how much is the fine? 罰金はいくらですか [bakkin wa ikura desu ka]

finger 指 [yubi]

‣ I've cut my finger 指を切りました [yubi o kirimashita]

finish 終わる [owaru]

‣ can we leave as soon as we've finished our meal? 食事が終わったらすぐに出られますか [shokuji ga owattara sugu ni deraremasu ka]

fire 火 [hi]; *(out of control)* 火事 [kaji]

‣ to make a fire 火を起こす [hi o okosu]

‣ on fire *(forest, house)* 燃えている [moete iru]

fire department 消防署 [shôbôsho]

‣ call the fire department! 消防署に電話してください！ [shôbôsho ni denwa shite kudasai]

fireworks 花火 [hanabi]

‣ what time do the fireworks start? 花火は何時に始まりますか [hanabi wa nan ji ni hajimarimasu ka]

first 最初の [saisho no] ◆ *(before all others)* 初め [hajime]; *(gear)* ファーストギア [fâsuto gia]; *(class – train)* グリーン車 [gurîn sha]

‣ it's the first time I've been here ここに来たのは初めてです [koko ni kita no wa hajimete desu]

‣ you have to take the first left after the lights 信号を過ぎて最初を左です [shingô o sugite saisho o hidari desu]

‣ put it into first ファーストに入れる [fâsuto ni ireru]

first-aid kit 救急箱 [kyûkyû bako]

‣ do you have a first-aid kit? 救急箱はどこですか [kyûkyû bako wa doko desu ka]

fish and seafood　(i)

There is a huge variety of fish and seafood available in Japan, some of which is not found in the West. It is often eaten raw (刺身 [sashimi]). Freshness is strictly controlled both in restaurants and supermarkets. In specialized 寿司 [sushi] restaurants (すし屋 [sushiya]), the price varies considerably. If ordered from a menu, the sushi can be extremely high quality – but at prices to match. A 盛り合わせ [moriawase], or typical selection, usually includes 18 pieces. In a conveyor belt sushi bar (回転寿司 [kaitenzushi]), you pick up dishes as they pass you, then pile the empty plates up next to you. The bill is calculated based on the number and color of plates you end up with.

first class carriage グリーン車 [gurîn sha] ♦ グリーン車の [gurîn sha no]
 ▸ are there any seats in first class? グリーン車の席はありますか [gurîn sha no seki wa arimasu ka]
 ▸ I prefer to travel first class グリーン車の方がいいです [gurîn sha no hô ga î desu]

fish 魚 [sakana]
 ▸ I don't eat fish 魚は食べません [sakana wa tabemasen]

fishing permit つり許可証 [tsuri kyokashô]
 ▸ do you need a fishing permit to fish here? ここで釣りをするのに許可証が要りますか [koko de tsuri o suru no ni kyokashô ga irimasu ka]

fit (seizure) 発作 [hossa] ♦ (be correct size) 合う [au]
 ▸ I think she's having some kind of fit 何か発作を起こしたようです [nani ka hossa o okoshita yô desu]
 ▸ those pants you are wearing fit you better そのズボンのほうが合います [sono zubon no hô ga aimasu]
 ▸ the key doesn't fit in the lock 鍵が合いません [kagi ga aimasen]
 ▸ we won't all fit around one table 一つのテーブルに全員座れません [hitotsu no têburu ni zen in suwaremasen]

fit in (go in) 中に入る [naka ni hairu] ♦ (put in) 中に入れる [naka ni ireru]
 ▸ I can't get everything to fit in my suitcase スーツケースに全部は入りません [sûtsukêsu ni zembu wa hairimasen]
 ▸ how many people can you fit in this car? この車に何人乗れますか [kono kuruma ni nan nin noremasu ka]

fitting room 試着室 [shichaku shitsu]
 ▸ where are the fitting rooms? 試着室はどこですか [shichaku shitsu wa doko desu ka]

five 五 [go]
 ▸ there are five of us 全部で五人です [zembu de go nin desu]

fix 直す [naosu]

▸ where can I find someone to fix my bike? バイクを直せる人はどこにいますか [baiku o naoseru hito wa doko ni imasu ka]

fixed price 定額 [têgaku]

▸ are there any taxis that go to the airport that charge a fixed price? 定額で空港へ行くタクシーはありますか [têgaku de kûkô e iku takushî wa arimasu ka]

flash フラッシュ [furasshu]

▸ I'd like some batteries for my flash フラッシュの電池がほしいんですが [furasshu no denchi ga hoshî n desu ga]

flash photography フラッシュをたいて撮った写真 [furasshu o taite totta shashin]

▸ is flash photography allowed here? ここでフラッシュをたいて写真を撮ってもいいですか [koko de furasshu o taite shashin o totte mo î desu ka]

flat *(tire)* パンクした [panku shita]

▸ the tire's flat タイヤがパンクしました [taiya ga panku shimashita]

flavor 味 [aji]

▸ I'd like to try a different flavor of ice cream 別の味のアイスクリームを食べてみたいんですが [betsu no aji o aisukurîmu o tabete mitai n desu ga]

flight 便 [bin]

▸ how many flights a day are there? 一日に何便ありますか [ichi nichi ni nam bin arimasu ka]

▸ what time is the flight? その便は何時ですか [sono bin wa nan ji desu ka]

flight of stairs 階段 [kaidan]

▸ your room's up that flight of stairs 部屋は階段の上です [heya wa kaidan no ue desu]

floor *(story)* 階 [kai]

▸ which floor is it on? 何階ですか [nan kai desu ka]

▸ it's on the top floor 最上階です [saijô kai desu]

flower 花 [hana]

▸ do you sell flowers? 花は売っていますか [hana wa utte imasu ka]

flu インフルエンザ [infuruenza]

▸ I'd like something for flu インフルエンザに効くものが何かほしいんですが [infuruenza ni kiku mono ga nani ka hoshî n desu ga]

flush 排水 [haisui] ◆ *(toilet)* 水を流す [mizu o nagasu] ◆ *(person)* 顔が赤くなる [kao ga akaku naru]; *(toilet)* 水が流れる [mizu ga nagareru]

▸ the toilet won't flush トイレの水が流れません [toire no mizu ga nagaremasen]

deep-fried food

てんぷら [tempura], battered and deep-fried fish and vegetables are one of the rare traditional dishes that originates in the West: cooking in oil was introduced by the Portuguese in the 16th century. てんぷら定食 [tempura têshoku] (tempura set meal) consists of an assortment of several pieces of fish, prawns and vegetables served on a paper napkin; these are dipped in a sauce made of soya sauce mixed with grated white radish. Miso soup, rice and pickles are served with the tempura.

---

fog 霧 [kiri]
  ▸ is there a lot of fog today? 今日は霧が深いですか [kyô wa kiri ga fukai desu ka]

food 食べ物 [tabemono]
  ▸ is there someplace to buy food nearby? 近くに食べ物が買えるところはありますか [chikaku ni tabemono ga kaeru tokoro wa arimasu ka]
  ▸ the food here is excellent ここの食べ物はすばらしいです [koko no tabemono wa subarashî desu]

food cart *(on train)* 車内販売 [shanai hambai]
  ▸ is there food cart service on this train? この列車には車内販売がありますか [kono ressha ni wa shanai hambai ga arimasu ka]

food section *(in store)* 食品売り場 [shokuhin uriba]
  ▸ where's the food section? 食品売り場はどこですか [shokuhin uriba wa doko desu ka]

foot 足 [ashi]
  ▸ on foot 歩いて [aruite]

for *(expressing purpose, function)* ために [tame ni]; *(indicating direction, destination)* 行き [yuki]; *(indicating duration)* 間 [kan]; *(since)* から [kara]
  ▸ what's that for? それは何のためですか [sore wa nan no tame desu ka]
  ▸ the flight for Okinawa 沖縄行きの便 [okinawa yuki no bin]
  ▸ is this the right train for Sendai? この列車は仙台行きですか [kono ressha wa sendai yuki desu ka]
  ▸ I'm staying for two months ２ヶ月間います [ni ka getsu kan imasu]
  ▸ I've been here for a week ここに一週間います [koko ni isshû kan imasu]
  ▸ I need something for a cough セキに利くものが何かいります [seki ni kiku mono ga nani ka irimasu]

foreign *(country, language)* 外国の [gaikoku no]
  ▸ I don't speak any foreign languages 外国語は話しません [gaikokugo wa hanashimasen]

foreign currency 外国のお金 [gaikoku no okane]
- do you change foreign currency? 外国のお金を両替してくれますか [gaikoku no okane o ryôgae shite kuremasu ka]

foreigner 外国人 [gaikokujin]
- as a foreigner, this custom seems a bit strange to me 外国人にとってこの習慣はちょっと不思議です [gaikokujin ni totte kono shûkan wa chotto fushigi desu]

forever いつまでも [itsu made mo]
- our money won't last forever お金がいつまでも続くわけではありません [okane ga itsu made mo tsuzuku wake de wa arimasen]

fork フォーク [fôku]
- could I have a fork? フォークをもらえませんか [fôku o moraemasen ka]

forward 転送する [tensô suru]
- can you forward my mail? 郵便を転送してもらえますか [yûbin o tensô shite moraemasu ka]

four 四 [yon/shi]
- there are four of us 全部で四人です [zembu de yo nin desu]

fourth 四番目の [yom bam me no] ◆ *(gear)* 四速 [yon soku]
- it's hard to get it into fourth 四速のギアが入りにくいです [yon soku no gia ga hairinikui desu]

four-wheel drive 四輪駆動 [yon rin kudô]
- I'd like a four-wheel drive 四輪駆動がいいんですが [yon rin kudô ga î n desu ga]

fracture 骨折 [kossetsu]
- is it a hairline fracture? 細かいひびですか [komakai hibi desu ka]

free *(offered at no charge)* 無料の [muryô no]; *(not occupied)* 空いている [aite iru]; *(available)* 暇な [hima na]
- is it free? 無料ですか [muryô desu ka]
- is this seat free? この席は空いていますか [kono seki wa aite imasu ka]
- are you free on Thursday evening? 木曜日の夜は暇ですか [mokuyôbi no yoru wa hima desu ka]

freeway 高速道路 [kôsoku dôro]
- what is the speed limit on freeways? 高速道路の制限速度は何キロですか [kôsoku dôro no sêgen sokudo wa nan kiro desu ka]
- how do I get onto the freeway? どうやって高速道路に入ったらいいですか [dô yatte kôsoku dôro ni haittara î desu ka]

freezing (cold) *(room, day)* すごく寒い [sugoku samui]
- I'm freezing (cold) すごく寒いです [sugoku samui desu]

frequent 頻繁に [himpan ni]
- how frequent are the trains to the city? どれくらい頻繁に町への列車がありますか [dore kurai himpan ni machi e no ressha ga arimasu ka]

fresh *(food)* 新鮮な [shinsen na]
- I'd like some fresh orange juice 新鮮なオレンジジュースがほしいんですが [shinsen na orenji jûsu ga hoshî n desu ga]

freshly *(ironed)* …したての [...shitate no]
- freshly ironed shirt アイロンしたてのシャツ [airon shitate no shatsu]

Friday 金曜日 [kin'yôbi]
- we're arriving/leaving on Friday 金曜日に着きます/出ます [kin'yôbi ni tsukimasu/demasu]

fried egg 目玉焼き [medama yaki]
- I'd like a fried egg 目玉焼きがほしいんですが [medama yaki ga hoshî n desu ga]

friend 友達 [tomodachi]
- are you with friends? 友達と一緒ですか [tomodachi to issho desu ka]
- I've come with a friend 友達と一緒に来ました [tomodachi to issho ni kimashita]
- I'm meeting some friends 友達に会います [tomodachi ni aimasu]

from から [kara]
- I'm from the United States アメリカからです [amerika kara desu]
- how many flights a day are there from Tokyo to Sapporo? 東京から札幌までは一日何便ありますか [tôkyô kara sapporo made wa ichi nichi nam bin arimasu ka]

front *(of train)* 前 [mae] ✦ **in front** 前の [mae no] ✦ **in front of** …の前で […no mae de]
- I'd like a seat toward the front of the train 列車の前のほうの席がいいです [ressha no mae no hô no seki ga î desu]
- the car in front braked suddenly 前の車が急ブレーキをかけました [mae no kuruma ga kyû burêki o kakemashita]
- I'll meet you in front of the museum 博物館の前で会いましょう [hakubutsukan no mae de aimashô]

front door 玄関 [genkan]
- which is the key to the front door? どれが玄関の鍵ですか [dore ga genkan no kagi desu ka]
- the front door is closed 玄関は閉まっています [genkan wa shimatte imasu]

frozen *(person)* 凍えて [kogoete]; *(pipes)* 凍って [kôtte]
- I'm absolutely frozen 完全に凍えてしまいました [kanzen ni kogoete shimaimashita]
- the lock is frozen 鍵が凍っています [kagi ka kôtte imasu]

fruit

Fruit is cultivated, selected and presented with great care, often grown to very large sizes and selling for exorbitant prices. It is usually peeled when served, including grapes (which can have quite tough skins), and larger fruit is cut into pieces and eaten with small forks.

frozen food 冷凍食品 [rêtô shokuhin]
- ▸ is that all the frozen food you have? この冷凍食品で全てですか [kono rêtô shokuhin de subete desu ka]

fruit フルーツ [furûtsu], くだもの [kudamono]
- ▸ where can I buy some fruit? フルーツはどこで買えますか [furûtsu wa doko de kaemasu ka]

fruit juice フルーツジュース [furûtsu jûsu]
- ▸ what types of fruit juice do you have? どんなフルーツジュースがありますか [donna furûtsu jûsu ga arimasu ka]

full *(hotel, restaurant, train)* いっぱいの [ippai no]; *(with food)* お腹がいっぱいの [onaka ga ippai no]
- ▸ is it full? いっぱいですか [ippai desu ka]
- ▸ I'm quite full, thank you お腹がいっぱいです [onaka ga ippai desu]

fun *(pleasure, amusement)* 面白み [omoshiromi]
- ▸ we had a lot of fun とても面白かったです [totemo omoshirokatta desu]

g

gallery *(for art)* 美術館 [bijutsukan]
- ▸ what time does the gallery open? 美術館は何時に開きますか [bijutsukan wa nan ji ni akimasu ka]

game *(fun activity)* ゲーム [gêmu]; *(of sport)* 試合 [shiai]
- ▸ do you want to play a game of tennis tomorrow? 明日テニスの試合をしませんか [ashita tenisu no shiai o shimasen ka]

garage *(for car repair)* 修理工場 [shûri kôjô]
- ▸ is there a garage near here? この近くに車の修理工場はありますか [kono chikaku ni kuruma no shûri kôjô wa arimasu ka]
- ▸ could you tow me to a garage? 修理工場まで引っ張ってもらえませんか [shûri kôjô made hippatte moraemasen ka]

garbage can ゴミ箱 [gomi bako]
- where is the garbage can? ゴミ箱はどこですか [gomi bako wa doko desu ka]

garden 庭 [niwa]
- what a beautiful garden なんてきれいな庭なんでしょう [nante kirê na niwa na n deshô]
- I'd like to see a Japanese garden 日本庭園が見たいですんですが [nihon tê-en ga mitai n desu ga]

gas *(for vehicle)* ガソリン [gasorin]; *(for domestic, medical use)* ガス [gasu]
- where can I get gas? ガソリンはどこで入れられますか [gasorin wa doko de ireraremasu ka]
- I've run out of gas ガス欠になりました [gasu ketsu ni narimashita]

gas station ガソリンスタンド [gasorin sutando]
- where can I find a gas station? ガソリンスタンドはどこにありますか [gasorin sutando wa doko ni arimasu ka]

gas stove ガスこんろ [gasu konro]
- do you have a gas stove we could borrow? ガスこんろを借りられませんか [gasu konro o kariraremasen ka]

gas tank ガソリンのタンク [gasorin no tanku]
- the gas tank is leaking ガソリンのタンクが漏れています [gasorin no tanku ga morete imasu]

gate *(of a house, a temple)* 門 [mon]; *(at an airport)* ゲート [gêto]
- where is Gate 2? 2番ゲートはどこですか [ni ban gêto wa doko desu ka]

gear *(of a car, a bike)* ギア [gia]
- how many gears does the bike have? そのバイクにはギアがいくつついていますか [sono baiku ni wa gia ga ikutsu tsuite imasu ka]

get *(obtain)* 手に入れる [te ni ireru]; *(understand)* 分かる [wakaru] ◆ *(make one's way)* 行く [iku]
- where can we get something to eat this time of night? こんな夜遅く、どこで食事ができますか [konna yoru osoku, doko de shokuji ga dekimasu ka]
- I can't get it into reverse バックに入りません [bakku ni hairimasen]
- now I get it やっと分かりました [yatto wakarimashita]
- I got here a month ago 一ヶ月前に着きました [ikka getsu mae ni tsukimashita]
- can you get there by car? 車でそこまで行けますか [kuruma de soko made ikemasu ka]
- how can I get to... ...にどうしたら行けますか [...ni dô shitara ikemasu ka]
- could you tell me the best way to get to Akihabara? 秋葉原に行く一番いい方法を教えてくれませんか [akihabara ni iku ichi ban î hôhô o oshiete kuremasen ka]

▸ how do we get to Terminal 2? 第２ターミナルにはどうやって行ったら
いいですか [dai ni tâminaru ni wa dô yatte ittara î desu ka]

get back *(money)* 払い戻してもらう [haraimodoshite morau]

▸ I just want to get my money back お金を払い戻してもらいたいだけで
す [okane o haraimodoshite moraitai dake desu]

get back onto *(road)* 戻る [modoru]

▸ how can I get back onto the freeway? どうしたら高速道路に戻れますか
[dô shitara kôsoku dôro ni modoremasu ka]

get in *(arrive)* 着く [tsuku]; *(gain entry)* 入る [hairu] ◆ *(car)* 乗り込む
[norikomu]

▸ what time does the train get in to Kyoto? 列車は何時に京都に着きます
か [ressha wa nan ji ni kyôto ni tsukimasu ka]

▸ what time does the flight get in? 飛行機は何時に着きますか [hikôki wa
nan ji ni tsukimasu ka]

▸ do you have to pay to get in? 入るのにお金を払わなければなりません
か [hairu no ni okane o harawanakereba narimasen ka]

get off *(bus, train, bike)* 降りる [oriru]; *(road)* 出る [deru]

▸ where do we get off the bus? どこでバスを降りたらいいですか [doko de
basu o oritara î desu ka]

▸ where do I get off the freeway? 高速道路をどこで出たらいいですか
[kôsoku dôro o doko de detara î desu ka]

get on *(train, bus, plane)* 乗る [noru]

▸ which bus should we get on to go downtown? 町の中心に行くのにはど
のバスに乗ったらいいですか [machi no chûshin ni iku no ni wa dono basu ni
nottara î desu ka]

get past 通る [tôru]

▸ sorry, can I get past, please? すみません、通してください [sumimasen,
tôshite kudasai]

get up *(in morning)* 起きる [okiru]

▸ I got up very early とても早く起きました [totemo hayaku okimashita]

gift-wrap プレゼント用に包む [purezento yô ni tsutsumu]

▸ could you gift-wrap it for me? プレゼント用に包んでくれませんか
[purezento yô ni tsutsunde kuremasen ka]

girl *(young female)* 女の子 [onna no ko]; *(daughter)* 娘 [musume]

▸ who is that girl? あの女の子は誰ですか [ano onna no ko wa dare desu ka]

▸ I've got two girls 娘が二人います [musume ga futari imasu]

girlfriend ガールフレンド [gârufurendo]

▸ is she your girlfriend? ガールフレンドですか [gârufurendo desu ka]

gifts

Gift-giving plays a vital role in Japanese culture, used as a means of maintaining good relationships with friends and business associates. As in other countries, it is usual to take a gift if visiting someone (for example, food, flowers or drink), and something from your own country will be particularly appreciated. In addition, gifts are exchanged in early July (中元 [chûgen]) and at the end of the year (歳暮 [sêbo]) by businesses as well as individuals, to thank people for their custom or kindness. It is important to reciprocate by giving an appropriate gift in return at the appropriate time. It is customary to refuse a gift several times before eventually accepting it, and to put it aside to open later, usually not in front of the giver. However, this is changing, particularly among younger people and those familiar with western customs. Wrapping a gift appropriately is as important as the gift itself. Store staff are adept at beautifully wrapping purchases intended as gifts.

---

give *(to me)* くれる [kureru]; *(to someone else)* あげる [ageru]
- I can give you my e-mail address 私のメールアドレスをあげましょう [watashi no mêru adoresu o agemashô]
- can you give me a hand? 手伝ってくれますか [tetsudatte kuremasu ka]

glass *(material)* ガラス [garasu]; *(for drinking)* コップ [koppu] ◆ **glasses** メガネ [megane]
- can I have a clean glass? きれいなコップをください [kirê na koppu o kudasai]
- would you like a glass of champagne? シャンペンはいかがですか [champen wa ikaga desu ka]
- I've lost my glasses メガネを失くしました [megane o nakushimashita]

glove 手袋 [tebukuro]
- I've lost a brown glove 茶色い手袋を失くしました [chairoi tebukuro o nakushimashita]

go *(move, vehicle, travel)* 行く [iku]; *(depart)* 出る [deru]; *(lead)* 続く [tsuzuku]
- let's go to the beach 海岸に行きましょう [kaigan ni ikimashô]
- where can we go for breakfast? どこへ朝ごはんを食べに行きましょうか [doko e asagohan o tabe ni ikimashô ka]
- where does this path go? この道はどこに続いていますか [kono michi wa doko ni tsuzuite imasu ka]
- I must be going もうそろそろ行かなければならなりません [mô sorosoro ikanakereba narimasen]
- we're going home tomorrow 明日帰ります [ashita kaerimasu]

go away *(person)* 向こうへ行く [mukô e iku]; *(pain)* なくなる [naku naru]
▸ go away and leave me alone! 向こうへ行ってくれ！放っておいてくれ！ [mukô e itte kure! hôtte oite kure]

go back *(return)* 戻る [modoru]
▸ we're going back home tomorrow 明日帰ります [ashita kaerimasu]

go down *(stairs)* 下りる [oriru]; *(street)* 下る [kudaru]
▸ go down that street and turn left at the bottom その道を下って、行き止まりを左に曲がりなさい [sono michi o kudatte, ikidomari o hidari ni magarinasai]

gold *(metal)* 金 [kin]
▸ is it made of gold? 金でできていますか [kin de dekite imasu ka]

golf ゴルフ [gorufu]
▸ I play golf ゴルフをします [gorufu o shimasu]

golf club ゴルフクラブ [gorufu kurabu]
▸ where can I rent golf clubs? ゴルフクラブはどこで借りられますか [gorufu kurabu wa doko de kariraremasu ka]

golf course ゴルフコース [gorufu kôsu]
▸ is there a golf course nearby? 近くにゴルフコースはありますか [chikaku ni gorufu kôsu wa arimasu ka]

good いい [î]
▸ this isn't a very good restaurant あまりいいレストランじゃありません [amari î resutoran ja arimasen]
▸ you're really good at cooking! 料理が上手ですね！ [ryôri ga jôzu desu ne]
▸ we had a good time 楽しかったです [tanoshikatta desu]

good afternoon こんにちは [konnichiwa]
▸ good afternoon! isn't it a beautiful day? こんにちは、いい天気ですね [konnichiwa, î tenki desu ne]

goodbye さようなら [sayônara]
▸ I'd better say goodbye now そろそろ失礼します [sorosoro shitsurê shimasu]

good evening こんばんは [kombanwa]

good morning おはよう（ございます） [ohayô (gozaimasu)]

good night *(when leaving)* じゃ、また [ja mata]; *(when going to bed)* おやすみ（なさい） [oyasumi (nasai)]
▸ I'll say good night, then では、失礼します [de wa, shitsurê shimasu]

go out *(leave house)* 出かける [dekakeru]; *(socially)* 出歩く [dearuku]; *(on date)* つきあう [tsukiau]; *(tide)* 引く [hiku]
▸ what's a good place to go out for a drink? 飲みに出かけるのにいい場所はどこですか [nomi ni dekakeru no ni î basho wa doko desu ka]
▸ the tide's going out 潮が引いてきました [shio ga hîte kimashita]

grapefruit グレープフルーツ [gurêpufurûtsu]
- I'll just have the grapefruit グレープフルーツにします [gurêpufurûtsu ni shimasu]

great (very good) すばらしい [subarashî]
- that's great! すばらしい！ [subarashî]
- it was really great! すばらしかった！ [subarashikatta]

green 緑の [midori no]
- the green one 緑の [midori no]

grocery store 雑貨屋 [zakkaya]
- is there a grocery store around here? この辺に雑貨屋はありますか [kono hen ni zakkaya wa arimasu ka]

group グループ [gurûpu], 団体 [dantai]
- there's a group of twelve of us　１２人のグループです [jûni nin no gurûpu desu]
- are there reductions for groups? 団体割引はありますか [dantai waribiki wa arimasu ka]

group rate 団体料金 [dantai ryôkin]
- are there special group rates? 団体の特別料金はありますか [dantai no tokubetsu ryôkin wa arimasu ka]

guarantee (for purchased product) 保証 [hoshô]
- it's still under guarantee まだ保証期間内です [mada hoshô kikan nai desu]

guide (person) ガイド [gaido]; (book) ガイドブック [gaidobukku]
- does the guide speak English? ガイドは英語ができますか [gaido wa êgo ga dekimasu ka]

guidebook ガイドブック [gaidobukku]
- do you have a guidebook in English? 英語のガイドブックはありますか [êgo no gaidobukku wa arimasu ka]

guided tour ガイド付き見学コース [gaido tsuki kengaku kôsu]
- what time does the guided tour begin? 何時にガイド付き見学コースは出ますか [nan ji ni gaido tsuki kengaku kôsu wa demasu ka]
- is there a guided tour in English? 英語のガイド付き見学コースはありますか [êgo no gaido tsuki kengaku kôsu wa arimasu ka]
- are there guided tours of the museum? 博物館のガイド付き見学コースはありますか [hakubutsukan no gaido tsuki kengaku kôsu wa arimasu ka]

h

hair 髪の毛 [kami no ke]
- she has short hair 髪の毛が短いです [kami no ke ga mijikai desu]
- he has red hair 赤毛です [akage desu]

hairbrush ヘアブラシ [heaburashi]
- do you sell hairbrushes? ヘアブラシは売っていますか [heaburashi wa utte imasu ka]

hairdryer ドライヤー [doraiyâ]
- do the rooms have hairdryers? 部屋にドライヤーはついていますか [heya ni doraiyâ wa tsuite imasu ka]

hair salon 美容院 [biyôin]
- does the hotel have a hair salon? ホテルに美容院はありますか [hoteru ni biyôin wa ariimasu ka]

half 半分の [hambun no] ◆ 半分 [hambun]
- shall we meet in half an hour? ３０分後に会いましょうか [sanjippun go ni aimashô ka]
- it's half past eight 八時半です [hachi ji han desu]

ham ハム [hamu]
- I'd like a packet of ham ハムを一パックほしいんですが [hamu o hito pakku hoshî n desu ga]

hand 手 [te]
- where can I wash my hands? どこで手を洗ったらいいですか [doko de te o arattara î desu ka]

handbag ハンドバッグ [handobaggu]
- someone's stolen my handbag ハンドバッグを盗まれました [handobaggu o nusumaremashita]

hand baggage 手荷物 [tenimotsu]
- I have one suitcase and one piece of hand baggage スーツケースが一つと手荷物が一つです [sûtsuksêsu ga hitotsu to tenimotsu ga hitotsu desu]

---

hair salons

Japanese hair salons and barbers usually give complementary brief head and neck massages after a haircut.

---

handkerchief ハンカチ [hankachi]
- do you have a spare handkerchief? 予備のハンカチを持っていますか [yobi no hankachi o motte imasu ka]

handle 取っ手 [totte]
- the handle's broken 取っ手が壊れています [totte ga kowarete imasu]

handmade 手作りの [tezukuri no]
- is this handmade? これは手作りですか [kore wa tezukuri desu ka]

happen 起きる [okiru]
- what happened? 何が起きたんですか [nani ga okita n desu ka]
- these things happen こんなこともありますよ [konna koto mo arimasu yo]

happy (not sad) うれしい [ureshī]; (satisfied) 満足して [manzoku shite]
- I'd be happy to help 喜んでお手伝いします [yorokonde otetsudai shimasu]
- Happy Birthday! 誕生日おめでとう！ [tanjôbi omedetô]
- Happy New Year! 新年おめでとう！ [shin nen omedetô]

hat 帽子 [bôshi]
- I think I left my hat here ここに帽子を忘れたと思うんですが [koko ni bôshi o wasureta to omou n desu ga]

hate 嫌いだ [kirai da]
- I hate golf ゴルフが嫌いです [gorufu ga kirai desu]

have (possess) ある [aru]; (meal) 食べる [taberu]; (drink) 飲む [nomu]; (as characteristic) している [shite iru] ◆ (be obliged) なければならない [...nakereba naranai]
- do you have any bread? パンはありますか [pan wa arimasu ka]
- do you have them in red? 赤いのはありますか [akai no wa arimasu ka]
- he has brown hair 茶色い髪をしています [chairoi kami o shite imasu]
- where should we go to have a drink? どこに飲みに行きましょうか [doko ni nomi ni ikimashô ka]
- I have to be at the airport by six (o'clock) 6時までに空港に行かなければなりません [roku ji made ni kûkô ni ikanakereba narimasen]
- we have to go もう行かなければなりません [mô ikanakereba narimasen]

head (of a person) 頭 [atama]; (of a shower) ヘッド [heddo]
- I hit my head when I fell 倒れた時に頭を打ちました [taoreta toki ni atama o uchimashita]
- The shower head is broken シャワーヘッドが壊れています [shawâ heddo ga kowarete imasu]

headache 頭痛 [zutsû]
- I've got a headache 頭が痛いです [atama ga itai desu]
- do you have anything for a headache? 頭痛に効くものは何かありますか [zutsû ni kiku mono wa nani ka arimasu ka]

headlight ヘッドライト [heddoraito]
▸ one of my headlights got smashed ヘッドライトが割れました [heddoraito ga waremashita]

headphones ヘッドホーン [heddohôn]
▸ did you find my headphones? 私のヘッドホーンは見つかりましたか [watashi no heddohôn wa mitsukarimashita ka]

health 健康 [kenkô]
▸ in good/poor health 体の調子がいい/悪い [karada no chôshi ga î/warui]

hear 聞く [kiku]; (learn of) 聞いて知っている [kîte shitte iru]
▸ I've heard a lot about you あなたのことは何度も聞いて知っています [anata no koto wa nan do mo kîte shitte imasu]

heart 心臓 [shinzô]
▸ he's got a weak heart 心臓が弱いです [shinzô ga yowai desu]

heart attack 心臓発作 [shinzô hossa]
▸ he had a heart attack 心臓発作を起こしました [shinzô hossa o okoshimashita]
▸ I nearly had a heart attack! 心臓が止まりそうになりました！ [shinzô ga tomarisô ni narimashita]

heart condition 心臓の問題 [shinzô no mondai]
▸ to have a heart condition 心臓に問題がある [shinzô ni mondai ga aru]

heat (hot quality) 熱 [netsu]; (weather) 暑さ [atsusa]; (for cooking) 温度 [ondo]
▸ there's no heat from the heater in my room 部屋のヒーターがききません [heya no hîtâ ga kikimasen]

heating 暖房器具 [dambô kigu]
▸ how does the heating work? 暖房器具はどうやって使ったらいいですか [dambô kigu wa dô yatte tsukattara î desu ka]

heavy 重い [omoi]
▸ my bags are very heavy かばんがとても重いです [kaban ga totemo omoi desu]

heel (of a foot) かかと [kakato]; (of a shoe) ヒール [hîru]
▸ is it possible to put new heels on these shoes? 新しいヒールに換えられますか [atarashî hîru ni kaeraremasu ka]

hello (as a greeting) こんにちは [konnichiwa]; (on the phone) もしもし [moshi moshi]
▸ hello, is this...? もしもし、...さんですか [moshi moshi, ... san desu ka]

helmet ヘルメット [herumetto]
▸ do you have a helmet you could lend me? ヘルメットを借りられますか [herumetto o kariraremasu ka]

help *(assistance)* 手伝い [tetsudai]; *(emergency aid)* 助け [tasuke] ◆ 手伝う [tetsudau]

- help! 助けて！ [tasukete]
- go and get help quickly! 早く助けを呼んで！ [hayaku tasuke o yonde]
- thank you for your help 手伝ってくれてありがとう [tetsudatte kurete arigatô]
- could you help me? 手伝ってくれませんか [tetsudatte kuremasen ka]
- could you help us push the car? 車を押すのを手伝ってくれませんか [kuruma o osu no o tetsudatte kuremasen ka]
- let me help you with that 手伝いましょうか [tetsudaimashô ka]
- could you help me carry my bags? かばんを運ぶのを手伝ってくれませんか [kaban o hakobu no o tetsudatte kuremasen ka]

here *(in this place)* ここで [koko de]; *(to this place)* ここに [koko ni] ◆ *(giving)* はい [hai]

- I've been here two days ここに二日間います [koko ni futsuka kan imasu]
- I came here three years ago 三年前にここに来ました [san nen mae ni koko ni kimashita]
- are you from around here? この辺からですか [kono hen kara desu ka]
- I'm afraid I'm a stranger here myself すみません、私もよそ者なので [sumimasen, watashi mo yosomono na node]
- it's five minutes from here ここから５分です [koko kara go fun desu]
- here is/are... はい、...です [hai, ... desu]
- here are my passport and ticket はい、私のパスポートとチケットです [hai, watashi no pasupôto to chiketto desu]

high chair 子供用の椅子 [kodomo yô no isu]

- could we have a high chair for the baby? 赤ん坊に子供用の椅子を貸してもらえますか [akambô ni kodomo yô no isu o kashite moraemasu ka]

high season 観光シーズン [kankô shîzun]

- is it very expensive in the high season? 観光シーズンは高いですか [kankô shîzun wa takai desu ka]

high tide 満潮 [manchô]

- what time is high tide? 満潮は何時ですか [manchô wa nan ji desu ka]

hike ハイキング [haikingu]

- are there any good hikes around here? この辺にハイキングにいいところはありますか [kono hen ni haikingu ni î tokoro wa arimasu ka]

hiking ハイキング [haikingu]

- to go hiking ハイキングに行く [haikingu ni iku]
- are there any hiking trails? ハイキングコースはありますか [haikingu kôsu wa arimasu ka]

hiking boot ハイキングシューズ [haikingu shûzu]

holidays

The main holiday seasons are at New Year (正月 [shôgatsu]) and お盆 [obon] (festival of the dead) in mid-August. People tend to return to their family homes at these times. In addition, several public holidays fall close together in 'Golden Week' from the end of April through the beginning of May, and this is the most popular holiday period. If you plan to travel at this time, be warned that it will be incredibly crowded everywhere, and you should book overnight accommodations months in advance and be prepared for steep price increases.

‣ do you need to wear hiking boots? ハイキングシューズをはかなければなりませんか [haikingu shûzu o hakanakereba narimasen ka]

hitchhike ヒッチハイクをする [hitchihaiku o suru]

‣ we hitchhiked here ここまでヒッチハイクをして来ました [koko made hitchihaiku o shite kimashita]

holiday 休日 [kyûjitsu]

‣ is tomorrow a holiday? 明日は休日ですか [ashita wa kyûjitsu desu ka]

home *(house)* 家 [uchi] ◆ 家に [uchi ni]

‣ to stay at home 家にいる [uchi ni iru]

‣ we're going home tomorrow 明日、家に帰ります [ashita uchi ni kaerimasu]

homemade 自家製 [jikasê]

‣ is it homemade? 自家製ですか [jikasê desu ka]

hood *(of car)* ボンネット [bonnetto]

‣ I've dented the hood ボンネットがへこんでしまいました [bonnetto ga hekonde shimaimashita]

horrible ひどい [hidoi]

‣ what horrible weather! なんてひどい天気なんでしょう！ [nante hidoi tenki na n deshô]

horseback riding 乗馬 [jôba]

‣ can we go horseback riding? 乗馬はできますか [jôba wa dekimasu ka]

hospital 病院 [byôin]

‣ where is the nearest hospital? 一番近い病院はどこですか [ichiban chikai byôin wa doko desu ka]

hot *(in temperature)* あつい [atsui]; *(spicy)* 辛い [karai]

‣ I'm too hot 暑すぎます [atsusugimasu]

‣ this dish is really hot この料理は本当に辛いです [kono ryôri wa hontô ni karai desu]

‣ there's no hot water お湯が出ません [oyu ga demasen]

hospitals

Healthcare in Japan is provided by large hospitals and small clinics, and medical facilities have a high international reputation. English-speaking doctors are available in some hospitals.

hot spring 温泉 [onsen]
▸ I'd like to go to a hot spring 温泉に行きたいんですが [onsen ni ikitai n desu ga]

hotel ホテル [hoteru]
▸ do you have a list of hotels in this area? この地域のホテルのリストはありますか [kono chi-iki no hoteru no risuto wa arimasu ka]
▸ are there any reasonably priced hotels near here? 近くにまあまあの値段のホテルはありますか [chikaku ni mâmâ no nedan no hoteru wa arimasu ka]
▸ is the hotel downtown? ホテルは町の中心にありますか [hoteru wa machi no chûshin ni arimasu ka]
▸ could you recommend another hotel? 他のホテルを紹介してくれませんか [hoka no hoteru o shôkai shite kuremasen ka]

hour 時間 [jikan]
▸ I'll be back in an hour 一時間で戻ります [ichi jikan de modorimasu]
▸ the flight takes three hours 飛行機は３時間かかります [hikôki wa san jikan kakarimasu]

house 家 [ie]
▸ is this your house? これはあなたの家ですか [kore wa anata no ie desu ka]

house wine ハウスワイン [hausu wain]
▸ a bottle of house wine, please ハウスワインを一本、お願いします [hausu wain o ippon onegai shimasu]

at the hotel

▸ we'd like a double room/two single rooms ダブルルームを一つ/シングルルームを二つお願いします [daburu rûmu o hitotsu/shinguru rûmu o futatsu onegai shimasu]
▸ I have a reservation in the name of Jones ジョーンズの名前で予約してあります [jônzu no namae de yoyaku shite arimasu]
▸ what time is breakfast/dinner served? 朝食/夕食は何時ですか [chôshoku/yûshoku wa nan ji desu ka]
▸ could I have a wake-up call at seven a.m.? 朝７時にモーニングコールをお願いできますか [asa shichi ji ni môningu kôru o onegai dekimasu ka]

hotels, guesthouses and hostels

There is a great range of accommodations available in Japan. Western-style hotels range from good-value business hotels to more luxurious ones. Japanese-style inns (旅館 [ryokan]) are a wonderful way to experience a traditional Japanese way of life. A cheaper alternative is the 民宿 [minshuku] (guesthouse). The ultimate response to lack of space in the major cities is the capsule hotel (カプセルホテル [kapuseru hoteru]), which offers just enough space to lie down and sleep; they are popular with businessmen who have missed their last train home after a drinking session with colleagues. Youth hostels run by the Japan Youth Hostel Organization and independent hostels are popular among students.

how どう [dô]
▸ how are you? お元気ですか [ogenki desu ka]
▸ how do you spell it? どうつづりますか [dô tsuzurimasu ka]
▸ how about a drink? 飲み物はどうですか [nomimono wa dô desu ka]

humid 蒸し暑い [mushiatsui]
▸ it's very humid today 今日はとても蒸し暑いです [kyô wa totemo mushiatsui desu]

hungry
▸ to be hungry おなかが減っている [onaka ga hette iru]
▸ I'm starting to get hungry おなかが減り始めました [onaka ga herihajimemashita]

hurry
▸ to be in a hurry 急いでいる [isoide iru]

hurry up 急ぐ [isogu]
▸ hurry up! 急いで！ [isoide]

hurt *(to cause physical pain)* 傷つける [kizu tsukeru] ◆ 痛む [itamu]
▸ you're hurting me! 痛いです！ [itai desu]
▸ to hurt oneself 怪我をする [kega o suru]
▸ I hurt myself 怪我をしました [kega o shimashita]
▸ I hurt my hand 手に怪我をしました [te ni kega o shimashita]
▸ it hurts 痛いです [itai desu]

i

ice *(frozen water)* 氷 [kôri]; *(cubes)* 角氷 [kakugôri]
- the car skidded on the ice 車が氷で滑りました [kuruma ga kôri de suberimashita]
- a Diet Coke® without ice, please ダイエットコーク®を氷なしでお願いします [daietto kôku o kôri nashi de onegai shimasu]

ice cream アイスクリーム [aisukurîmu]
- I'd like some ice cream アイスクリームがほしいんですが [aisukurîmu ga hoshî n desu ga]

ice cube 角氷 [kakugôri]
- do you sell ice cubes? 角氷を売っていますか [kakugôri o utte imasu ka]

iced coffee アイスコーヒー [aisu kôhî]
- I'd like an iced coffee アイスコーヒーがほしいんですが [aisu kôhî ga hoshî n desu ga]

ice rink アイススケート場 [aisu sukêto jô]
- is there an ice rink nearby? 近くにアイススケート場はありますか [chikaku ni aisu sukêto jô wa arimasu ka]

ice skate スケート靴 [sukêto gutsu]
- I'd like to rent some ice skates スケート靴を借りたいんですが [sukêto gutsu o karitai n desu ga]

ice-skating アイススケート [aisu sukêto]
- would you like to go ice-skating tomorrow? 明日アイススケートに行きませんか [ashita aisu sukêto ni ikimasen ka]

ID card 身分証明書 [mibunshômêsho]
- I don't have an ID card: will a passport work? 身分証明書は持っていません：パスポートでもいいですか [mibunshômêsho wa motte imasen. pasupôto de mo î masu ka]

if もし [moshi]
- we'll go if you want もしお望みなら行きます [moshi onozomi nara ikimasu]

ill 病気の [byôki no]
- my son is ill 息子が病気です [musuko ga byôki desu]

immediately すぐに [sugu ni]
- can you do it immediately? すぐにできますか [sugu ni dekimasu ka]

improve うまくなる [umaku naru]

▸ I'm hoping to improve my Japanese while I'm here ここにいる間に日本語がうまくなりたいです [koko ni iru aida ni nihongo ga umaku naritai desu]

in に [ni]
▸ our bags are still in the room かばんはまだ部屋にあります [kaban wa mada heya ni arimasu]
▸ do you live in Tokyo? 東京に住んでいますか [tôkyô ni sunde imasu ka]

in case の場合 [...no bâi]
▸ just in case 万一に備えて [man'ichi ni sonaete]

included 含まれている [fukumarete iru]
▸ is breakfast included? 朝食は含まれていますか [chôshoku wa fukumarete imasu ka]
▸ is sales tax included? 消費税は含まれていますか [shôhizê wa fukumarete imasu ka]

indoor 屋内 [shitsunai]
▸ is there an indoor pool? 屋内プールはありますか [shitsunai pûru wa arimasu ka]

infection 炎症 [enshô]
▸ I have an eye infection 目が炎症を起こしています [me ga enshô o okoshite imasu]

information *(facts)* 情報 [jôhô]; *(service, department)* 案内 [annai]
▸ may I ask you for some information? ちょっと教えてほしいんですが [chotto oshiete hoshî n desu ga]
▸ where can I find information on...? ...についての情報はどこで手に入りますか [...ni tsuite no jôhô wa doko de te ni hairimasu ka]

injection *(medicine)* 注射 [chûsha]
▸ am I going to need an injection? 注射が必要ですか [chûsha ga hitsuyô desu ka]

injure 怪我をする [kega o suru]
▸ to injure oneself 怪我をする [kega o suru]
▸ I injured myself 怪我をしました [kega o shimashita]

inside の中に [...no naka ni] ◆ 中の [naka no]
▸ are you allowed inside the castle? 城の中に入れますか [shiro no naka ni hairemasu ka]
▸ we'd prefer a table inside 中のテーブルのほうがいいです [naka no têburu no hô ga î desu]

insurance 保険 [hoken]
▸ what does the insurance cover? その保険には何が含まれていますか [sono hoken ni wa nani ga fukumarete imasu ka]

Internet

There are plenty of Internet cafés in cities, particularly in the trendy areas. You may need to become a member to use the computers, but this is a simple procedure. The Japanese use an adapted English keyboard, on which the keys have both roman and Japanese characters (using the hiragana writing system) – so for example, you would find A and あ on the same key. You can select English or Japanese entry on-screen. The icon for this can vary, so it's best to ask for help. Exchanging e-mail addresses is common in Japan, and young people often e-mail each other via their cellphones, which have their own e-mail addresses.

---

insure *(house, car)* 保険をかける [hoken o kakeru]
 ▸ yes, I'm insured はい、保険をかけてあります [hai, hoken o kakete arimasu]

interesting おもしろい [omoshiroi]
 ▸ it's not a very interesting place あまりおもしろい所じゃありません
 [amari omoshiroi tokoro ja arimasen]

international call 国際電話 [kokusai denwa]
 ▸ I'd like to make an international call 国際電話をかけたいんですが
 [kokusai denwa o kaketai n desu ga]

Internet インターネット [intânetto]
 ▸ where can I connect to the Internet? インターネットはどこで接続でき
 ますか [intânetto wa doko de setsuzoku dekimasu ka]

introduce *(present)* 紹介する [shôkai suru]
 ▸ to introduce oneself 自己紹介する [jiko shôkai suru]
 ▸ allow me to introduce myself: I'm Michael 自己紹介させてください：マ
 イケルです [jiko shôkai sasete kudasai. maikeru desu]

invite 招待する [shôtai suru]
 ▸ I'd like to invite you to dinner next weekend 来週の週末、夕食に招待し
 たいんですが [rai shû no shûmatsu, yûshoku ni shôtai shitai n desu ga]

iron *(for ironing)* アイロン [airon] ◆ アイロンをかける [airon o kakeru]
 ▸ I need an iron アイロンがいります [airon ga irimasu]

itch かゆみ [kayumi]
 ▸ I've got an itch on my left leg 左足がかゆいです [hidari ashi ga kayui desu]

itinerary 旅程 [ryotê]
 ▸ is it possible to modify the planned itinerary? 旅程を少し変更することは
 できますか [ryotê o sukoshi henkô suru koto wa dekimasu ka]

j

January 一月 [ichigatsu]
▸ January 4th 1月4日 [ichigatsu yokka]

Jet Ski® ジェットスキー® [jettosukī]
▸ I'd like to rent a Jet Ski® ジェットスキー®を借りたいんですが [jettosukī o karitai n desu ga]

job *(employment)* 仕事 [shigoto]
▸ I'm looking for a summer job in the area この辺で夏の仕事を探しています [kono hen de natsu no shigoto o sagashite imasu]

joke 冗談 [jōdan] ◆ 冗談を言う [jōdan o yū]
▸ it's beyond a joke! 冗談じゃない！ [jōdan ja nai]
▸ I was just joking ちょっとふざけてみただけです [chotto fuzakete mita dake desu]

journey 旅 [tabi]
▸ how long does the journey take? 旅はどのぐらい時間がかかりますか [tabi wa dono gurai jikan ga kakarimasu ka]

juice *(from fruit)* ジュース [jūsu]
▸ what types of juice do you have? どんなジュースがありますか [donna jūsu ga arimasu ka]

July 七月 [shichigatsu]
▸ July 4th 7月4日 [shichigatsu yokka]

June 六月 [rokugatsu]
▸ June 2nd 6月2日 [rokugatsu futsuka]

just *(recently)* ばかり [bakari]; *(at that moment)* ちょうど [chōdo]; *(only, simply)* だけ [dake]
▸ he just left 今、出たばかりです [ima deta bakari desu]
▸ I'll just have one 一つだけにします [hitotsu dake ni shimasu]

k

karaoke カラオケ [karaoke]
- where is the nearest karaoke box? 一番近いカラオケボックスはどこですか [ichiban chikai karaoke bokkusu wa doko desu ka]

kayak カヤック [kayakku]
- can we rent kayaks? カヤックを借りられますか [kayakku o kariraremasu ka]

keep *(retain)* 取っておく [totte oku]; *(promise, appointment)* 守る [mamoru]
- I'm sorry, I won't be able to keep the appointment すみません、約束を守れそうにありません [sumimasen, yakusoku o mamoresô ni arimasen]
- keep the change お釣りは取っておいてください [otsuri wa totte oite kudasai]

key *(for a door, a container)* かぎ [kagi]; *(on a keyboard)* 鍵盤 [kemban]; *(of a phone)* 番号ボタン [bangô botan]
- which is the key to the front door? どちらが玄関の鍵ですか [dochira ga genkan no kagi desu ka]

kilometer キロ（メーター） [kiro(mêtâ)]
- how much is it per kilometer? 一キロにつき、いくらですか [ichi kiro ni tsuki ikura desu ka]

kind *(nice)* 親切な [shinsetsu na] ◆ *(sort, type)* 種類 [shurui]
- that's very kind of you どうもご親切に [dômo goshinsetsu ni]
- what's your favorite kind of music? どんな種類の音楽が好きですか [donna shurui no ongaku ga suki desu ka]

kitchen 台所 [daidokoro]
- is the kitchen shared? 台所は共用ですか [daidokoro wa kyôyô desu ka]

Kleenex® ティッシュペーパー [tisshu pêpâ]
- do you have any Kleenex®? ティッシュペーパーはありますか [tisshu pêpâ wa arimasu ka]

knife ナイフ [naifu]
- could I have a knife? ナイフをもらえますか [naifu o moraemasu ka]

know 知っている [shitte iru]
- I don't know this town very well この町のことはあまり知りません [kono machi no koto wa amari shirimasen]
- I know the basics but no more than that 基本的なことは知っていますが、それだけです [kihonteki na koto wa shitte imasu ga, sore dake desu]
- do you know each other? お互いに知っていますか [otagai ni shitte imasu ka]

knowledge 知っていること [shitte iru koto]

- she has a good knowledge of French フランス語をよく知っています
  [furansugo o yoku shitte imasu]
- without my knowledge 知らぬ間に [shiranu ma ni]

ladies' room 女性用お手洗い [josê yô otearai], 女性用トイレ [josê yô toire]

- where's the ladies' room? 女性用お手洗いはどこですか [josê yô otearai wa doko desu ka]

lake 湖 [mizu-umi]

- can you go swimming in the lake? 湖で泳げますか [mizu-umi de oyogemasu ka]

lamp 電気スタンド [denki sutando]

- the lamp doesn't work 電気スタンドが壊れています [denki sutando ga kowarete imasu]

land *(plane)* 着陸する [chakuriku suru]

- what time is the plane scheduled to land? 飛行機は何時に着陸する予定ですか [hikôki wa nan ji ni chakuriku suru yotê desu ka]

landmark 目印になるもの [mejirushi ni naru mono]

- do you recognize any landmarks? 目印になるものに見覚えがありますか [mejirushi ni naru mono ni mioboe ga arimasu ka]

lane 車線 [shasen]

- a four-lane highway 四車線の高速道路 [yon shasen no kôsoku dôro]

laptop ラップトップ [rapputoppu]

- my laptop's been stolen ラップトップを盗まれました [rapputoppu o nusumaremashita]

last 最後の [saigo no] ◆ 続く [tsuzuku]

- when does the last bus go? 最後のバスはいつ出ますか [saigo no basu wa itsu demasu ka]
- when is the last subway train? 最後の地下鉄はいつですか [saigo no chikatetsu wa itsu desu ka]

last name 苗字 [myôji]

- could I have your last name? 苗字を教えていただけませんか [myôji o oshiete itadakemasen ka]

late 遅い [osoi] ◆ 遅れて [okurete]; *(in the day)* 遅く [osoku]

- the plane was two hours late 飛行機は二時間遅れました [hikôki wa ni jikan okuremashita]

smiling and laughing

In Japan, smiling or laughing do not necessarily mean that all is well. A smile or laugh can hide shame, embarrassment or suppressed anger. In general, you should always avoid getting annoyed, and try to keep your cool. In social situations it is second nature to the Japanese to 'save face,' which relates to one's reputation and image. You must try to compromise and not get into direct confrontation.

▸ could you tell me if the train to Yokohama is running late? 横浜行きの列車が遅れているかどうか教えてくれませんか [yokohama yuki no ressha ga okurete iru ka dô ka oshiete kuremasen ka]

later もっと後の [motto ato de] ◆ 後で [ato de]
▸ is there a later train? もっと後の列車はありますか [motto ato no ressha wa arimasu ka]
▸ see you later! じゃ、また後で！ [ja, mata ato de]

latest *(most recent)* 最新の [saishin no]; *(very last)* 一番遅い [ichiban osoi]
▸ what's the latest time we can check out? 一番遅いチェックアウトの時間は何時ですか [ichiban osoi chekku-auto no jikan wa nan ji desu ka]

laugh 笑い [warai] ◆ 笑う [warau]
▸ I just did it for a laugh 冗談でやったんです [jôdan de yatta n desu]

Laundromat® コインランドリー [koin randorî]
▸ is there a Laundromat® nearby? 近くにコインランドリーはありますか [chikaku ni koin randorî wa arimasu ka]

laundry *(washed clothes)* 洗濯 [sentaku]; *(unwashed clothes)* 洗濯物 [sentakumono]; *(business)* クリーニング屋 [kurîningu ya]; *(room)* 洗濯室 [sentaku shitsu]
▸ where can we do our laundry? 洗濯はどこでできますか [sentaku wa doko de dekimasu ka]
▸ where's the nearest laundry? 一番近いクリーニング屋はどこですか [ichiban chikai kurîningu ya wa doko desu ka]

lawyer 弁護士 [bengoshi]
▸ I'm a lawyer 弁護士です [bengoshi desu]
▸ I need a lawyer 弁護士がいります [bengoshi ga irimasu]

leaflet リーフレット [rîfuretto]
▸ do you have any leaflets in English? 英語のリーフレットはありますか [êgo no rîfuretto wa arimasu ka]

learn 勉強する [benkyô suru]
▸ I've just learned a few words from a book 本で単語をいくつか勉強しました [hon de tango o ikutsuka benkyô shimashita]

least 一番少ない [ichiban sukunai] ◆ 最少 [saishô] ◆ 一番少なく [ichiban sukunaku] ◆ **at least** 少なくとも [sukunaku tomo]
- it's the least I can do どういたしまして [dô itashimashite]
- not in the least とんでもない [tondemonai]
- to say the least 控えめに言っても [hikaeme ni itte mo]
- it's at least a three-hour drive 少なくとも３時間の運転です [sukunaku tomo san jikan no unten desu]

leave *(go away from)* 去る [saru]; *(let stay)* 置いて行く [oite iku]; *(forget to take)* 置き忘れる [okiwasureru] ◆ *(go away)* 出る [deru]
- can I leave my backpack at the reception desk? バックパックを受付に置いて行ってもいいですか [bakkupakku o uketsuke ni oite itte mo î desu ka]
- can I leave the car at the airport? 車は空港に置いていってもいいですか [kuruma wa kûkô ni oite itt emo î desu ka]
- leave us alone! 放っておいてくれ！ [hôtte oite kure]
- I've left something on the plane 飛行機に置き忘れたものがあります [hikôki ni okiwasureta mono ga arimasu]
- I'll be leaving at nine o'clock tomorrow morning 明日の朝、９時に出ます [ashita no asa ku ji ni demasu]
- what platform does the train for Kobe leave from? 神戸行きの列車は何番ホームから出ますか [kôbe yuki no ressha wa nam ban hômu kara demasu ka]

left *(not right)* 左の [hidari no] ◆ 左 [hidari]
- to be left 残っている [nokotte iru]
- are there any tickets left for...? ...のチケットは残っていますか [...no chiketto wa nokotte imasu ka]
- to the left (of) の左側 [...no hidari gawa]

left-hand 左側の [hidari gawa no]
- on your left-hand side 左側に [hidari gawa ni]

leg 足 [ashi]
- I have a pain in my left leg 左足が痛いです [hidari ashi ga itai desu]
- I can't move my leg 足が動かせません [ashi ga ugokasemasen]

lemon レモン [remon]
- can I have two lemons? レモンを二つください [remon o futatsu kudasai]

lend 貸す [kasu]
- could you lend us your car? 車を貸してくれませんか [kuruma o kashite kuremasen ka]

lens *(of camera)* レンズ [renzu]; *(contact lens)* （コンタクト）レンズ [(kontakuto) renzu]
- there's something on the lens レンズに何か付いています [renzu ni nani ka tsuite imasu]

letters

When addresses are written in roman letters, they follow the same pattern that we use. However when they are written in Japanese, the order is reversed as follows: prefecture, city or town, area, street, house or apartment and room number, and finally the addressee's name with the title 様 [sama]. The Japanese zip code is preceded by the symbol 〒 and is written side-on in the bottom right-hand corner of the envelope if the address is written horizontally.

- I have hard lenses ハードレンズを使っています [hâdo renzu o tsukatte imasu]
- I have soft lenses ソフトレンズを使っています [sofuto renzu o tsukatte imasu]

less より少ない [yori sukunai] ◆ より少ない数 [yori sukunai kazu] ◆ より少なく [yori sukunaku]

- less and less ますます少なく [masumasu sukunaku]
- a little less ちょっと少ない [chotto sukunai]

lesson レッスン [ressun]

- how much do lessons cost? レッスンはいくらですか [ressun wa ikura desu ka]
- can we take lessons? レッスンが受けられますか [ressun ga ukeraremasu ka]

let off *(allow to disembark)* 降ろす [orosu]

- could you let me off here, please? ここで降ろしてくれませんか [koko de oroshite kuremasen ka]

letter 手紙 [tegami]

- I would like to send this letter to the States この手紙をアメリカに送りたいんですが [kono tegami o amerika ni okuritai n desu ga]
- I confirmed my reservation by letter 予約を手紙で確認しました [yoyaku o tegami de kakunin shimashita]

level *(amount)* レベル [reberu]; *(of a building, a ship)* 階 [kai]

- do you know if cabin 27 is on this level? ２７号室はこの階ですか [nijûnana gô shitsu wa kono kai desu ka]

license 許可証 [kyokashô]; *(for driving)* （運転）免許証 [(unten) menkyoshô]

- do you need a license to hunt here? ここで狩りをするのには許可証が要りますか [koko de kari o suru no ni wa kyokashô ga irimasu ka]
- I left my driver's license in my hotel room 免許証をホテルの部屋に置いてきました [menkyoshô o hoteru no heya ni oite kimashita]

license number 登録番号 [tôroku bangô]
- I got the license number 登録番号は分かっています [tôroku bangô wa wakatte imasu]

lie down 横になる [yoko ni naru]
- I'm tired, so I need to lie down 疲れたので、横になりたいんですが [tsukareta node, yoko ni naritai n desu ga]

lifebelt 救命ベルト [kyûmê beruto]
- throw me a lifebelt! 救命ベルトを投げてくれ！ [kyûmê beruto o nagete kure]

lifeboat 救命ボート [kyûmê bôto]
- how many lifeboats are there? 救命ボートは何艘ありますか [kyûmê bôto wa nan so arimasu ka]

lifejacket 救命胴着 [kyûmê dôgi]
- are there any lifejackets? 救命胴着はありますか [kyûmê dôgi wa arimasu ka]

light *(brightness)* 光 [hikari]; *(on a car)* ライト [raito]; *(regulating traffic)* 信号 [shingô]; *(for a cigarette)* マッチかライター [matchi ka raitâ]; *(in a lamp)* 明かり [akari]
- the light doesn't work 明かりがつきません [akari ga tsukimasen]
- could you check the lights? ライトをチェックしてくれませんか [raito o chekku shite kuremasen ka]
- stop at the next light 次の信号で止まってください [tsugi no shingô de tomatte kudasai]
- do you have a light? マッチかライターを持っていますか [matchi ka raitâ o motte imasu ka]

lighter ライター [raitâ]
- can I borrow your lighter? ライターを貸してもらえますか [raitâ o kashite moraemasu ka]

lighthouse 灯台 [tôdai]
- shall we have our picnic near the lighthouse? 灯台の近くでお弁当にしましょうか [tôdai no chikaku de obentô ni shimashô ka]

like *(similar to)* 似ている [nite iru]; *(such as)* のような [...no yô na] ◆ 好きだ [suki da]
- it's quite like English 英語によく似ています [êgo ni yoku nite imasu]
- I like it 好きです [suki desu]
- I don't like it 好きじゃありません [suki ja arimasen]
- do you like it here? ここが気に入りましたか [koko ga ki ni irimashita ka]
- I like Japanese food very much 日本料理がとても好きです [nihon ryôri ga totemo suki desu]
- do you like the movies? 映画が好きですか [êga ga suki desu ka]

likes

- I really love that painting あの絵が大好きです [ano e ga dai suki desu]
- I like your younger brother 弟さんはいい人ですね [otôto-san wa î hito desu ne]
- I've got a soft spot for her 彼女には甘くなってしまうんです [kanojo ni wa amaku natte shimau n desu]
- I think she's very nice 素敵な人だと思います [suteki na hito da to omoimasu]

- would you like a drink? - yes, I'd love one 飲み物はいかがですか–はい、喜んで [nomimono wa ikaga desu ka – hai, yorokonde]
- I'd like to speak to the manager 責任者と話したいんですが [sekininsha to hanashitai n desu ga]

lime ライム [raimu]

- can I have three limes? ライムを三つください [raimu o mittsu kudasai]

limit 限度 [gendo] ◆ 制限する [sêgen suru]

- is that area off limits? そこは立ち入り禁止ですか [soko wa tachi-iri kinshi desu ka]

line *(phone connection)* 電話 [denwa]; *(of people waiting)* 列 [retsu]; *(of railroad, subway, bus)* 線 [sen]

- the line was busy 話し中でした [hanashi chû deshita]
- we had to stand in line for 15 minutes 15分、列で待たなければなりませんでした [jûgo fun retsu de matanakereba narimasen deshita]
- which line do I take to get to...? ...に行くのにはどの線に乗ればいいですか [... ni iku no ni wa dono sen ni noreba î desu ka]

dislikes

- I hate football フットボールは嫌いです [futtobôru wa kirai desu]
- I can't stand him あの人には耐えられません [ano hito ni wa taeraremasen]
- I don't really like him/her あの人はあまり好きじゃありません [ano hito wa amari suki ja arimasen]
- I'm not really into walking 散歩にそんなに関心があるというわけじゃありません [sampo ni sonna ni kanshin ga aru to yû wake ja arimasen]

lipstick 口紅 [kuchibeni]
- I need to buy some lipstick 口紅を買わなければなりません [kuchibeni o kawanakereba narimasen]

listen 聞く [kiku]
- listen, I really need to see a doctor 聞いてください、医者に見てもらわなければなりません [kîte kudasai, isha ni mite morawanakereba narimasen]
- listen to me carefully 注意して聞いてください [chûi shite kîte kudasai]

liter リットル [rittoru]
- a two-liter bottle of soda 2リットル入りの清涼飲料水 [ni rittoru iri no sêryô inryôsui]

little 小さい [chîsai] ◆ ほとんどない [hotondo nai] ◆ **a little** ほんのわずかなもの [hon no wazuka na mono] ◆ 少し [sukoshi]
- it's for a little girl ちいさな女の子用です [chîsa na onna no ko yô desu]
- as little as possible できるだけ少なく [dekiru dake sukunaku]
- I speak a little Japanese 日本語を少しだけ話します [nihongo o sukoshi dake hanashimasu]
- we've only got a little money left お金は少し残っているだけです [okane wa sukoshi nokotte iru dake desu]
- a little bit ちょっと [chotto]
- a little less ちょっと少なく [chotto sukunaku]
- a little more もうちょっと [mô chotto]

live 住んでいる [sunde iru]
- do you live around here? この近くに住んでいますか [kono chikaku ni sunde imasu ka]
- I live in Nara 奈良に住んでいます [nara ni sunde imasu]

live music ライブ [raibu]
- I'd like to go to a bar with live music ライブをやっているバーに行きたいんですが [raibu o yatte iru bâ ni ikitai n desu ga]

living room 居間 [ima]
- Mr Suzuki is in the living room 鈴木さんは居間にいます [suzuki-san wa ima ni imasu]

loaf (of bread) 食パン一つ [shokupan hitotsu]
- I'd like one of those large loaves あの大きな食パンを一つほしいんですが [ano ôki na shokupan o hitotsu hoshî n desu ga]

local 土地の [tochi no]
- what's the local specialty? 土地の名物は何ですか [tochi no mêbutsu wa nan desu ka]

lock 鍵 [kagi] ◆ 鍵をかける [kagi o kakeru]
- the lock's broken 鍵が壊れています [kagi ga kowarete imasu]
- I locked the door ドアに鍵をかけました [doa ni kagi o kakemashita]

lock out

▸ to lock oneself out 閉め出す [shimedasu]
▸ I've locked myself out 鍵を中に入れたまま閉めてしまいました [kagi o naka ni ireta mama shimete shimaimashita]

long 長い [nagai] ◆ 長く [nagaku]

▸ it's ten meter long 長さ１０メートルあります [nagasa jû mêtoru arimasu]
▸ I waited for a long time 長く待ちました [nagaku machimashita]
▸ how long? どれぐらい？ [dore gurai]
▸ how long will it take? どれぐらいかかりますか [dore gurai kakarimasu ka]
▸ we're not sure how long we're going to stay どれぐらいいるか分かりません [dore gurai iru ka wakarimasen]

look (with eyes) 見ること [miru koto]; (appearance) 外見 [gaiken] ◆ (with eyes) 見る [miru]; (seem) ようだ [yô da]

▸ could you have a look at my car? 車をちょっと見てもらえませんか [kuruma o chotto mite moraemasen ka]
▸ no, thanks, I'm just looking いいえ結構です、見ているだけです [îe kekkô desu, mite iru dake desu]
▸ what does she look like? どんな感じの人ですか [donna kanji no hito desu ka]
▸ you look like your elder brother お兄さんによく似ていますね [onî-san ni yoku nite imasu ne]
▸ it looks like it's going to rain 雨が降るようです [ame ga furu yô desu]

look after (child, ill person) 世話をする [sewa o suru]; (luggage) 見ている [mite iru]

▸ can someone look after the children for us? 誰か子供の世話をしてくれますか [dare ka kodomo no sewa o shite kuremasu ka]
▸ can you look after my things for a minute? ちょっと荷物を見ていてくれますか [chotto nimotsu o mite ite kuremasu ka]

look for 探す [sagasu]

▸ I'm looking for a good restaurant that serves regional cuisine 地元の料理を出すよいレストランを探しています [jimoto no ryôri o dasu yoi resutoran o sagashite imasu]

lose (be unable to find) 失くす [nakusu]

▸ I've lost the key to my room 部屋の鍵をなくしました [heya no kagi o nakushimashita]
▸ I've lost my way 道に迷いました [michi ni mayoimashita]

lost 失くなった [naku natta]

▸ who do you have to see about lost luggage? 失くなった荷物は誰に届け出ればいいですか [naku natta nimotsu wa dare ni todoke dereba î desu ka]
▸ could you help me? I seem to be lost 助けてくれませんか。道に迷ったようです [tasukete kuremasen ka. michi ni mayotta yô desu]

- to get lost 迷子になる [maigo ni naru]
- get lost! いい加減にしろ！ [î kagen ni shiro]

lost-and-found 遺失物取扱所 [ishitsubutsu toriatsukaijo]
- where's the lost-and-found? 遺失物取扱所はどこですか [ishitsubutsu toriatsukaijo wa doko desu ka]

lot ◆ a lot たくさん [takusan]
- a lot of ... たくさんの... [takusan no ...]
- are there a lot of things to see around here? ここには見るものがたくさんありますか [koko ni wa miru mono ga takusan arimasu ka]
- will there be a lot of other people there? そこには他の人がたくさんいますか [soko ni wa hoka no hito ga takusan imasu ka]
- thanks a lot どうもありがとう [dômo arigatô]

loud (noise) うるさい [urusai]; (voice) 大きい [ôkî]; (music) やかましい [yakamashî]
- the television is too loud テレビの音が大きすぎます [terebi no oto ga ôkisugimasu]

loudly (speak) 大きな声で [ôki na koe de]
- can you speak a little more loudly? もう少し大きな声で話してくれますか [mô sukoshi ôki na koe de hanashite kuremasu ka]

love 大好きだ [dai suki da]
- I love you 愛しています [ai shite imasu]
- I love the movies 映画が大好きです [êga ga dai suki desu]
- I love cooking 料理が大好きです [ryôri ga dai suki desu]

lovely 素敵な [suteki na]
- what a lovely room! なんて素敵な部屋なんでしょう [nante suteki na heya na n deshô]
- it's lovely today 今日はすばらしい日ですね [kyô wa subarashî hi desu ne]

low (temperature) 低い [hikui]; (speed) 遅い [osoi]
- temperatures are in the low twenties 気温は２０度ちょっとです [kion wa nijû do chotto desu]

lower 下げる [sageru] ◆ 下の [shita no]
- is it OK if I lower the blind a little? ブラインドをちょっと下げてもいいですか [buraindo o chotto sagete mo î desu ka]
- how do we get to the lower level? 下の階へはどうやって行きますか [shita no kai e wa dô yatte ikimasu ka]

low-fat (yogurt) 低脂肪の [tê shibô no]
- do you have any low-fat yogurt? 低脂肪のヨーグルトはありますか [tê shibô no yôguruto wa arimasu ka]

luggage

Stations don't have luggage carts, so take wheeled suitcases if you can. On long-distance trains there are luggage storage sections at the ends of carriages, but space in other trains is more limited. There are luggage lockers (コインロッカー [koin rokkâ]) at stations and other transportation facilities, and left luggage offices at major stations and other facilities.

---

low season シーズンオフ [shîzun ofu]
▸ what are prices like in the low season? シーズンオフの料金はどうですか [shîzun ofu no ryôkin wa dô desu ka]

low tide 干潮 [kanchô]
▸ what time is low tide today? 今日の干潮は何時ですか [kyô no kanchô wa nan ji desu ka]

luck 幸運 [kôun]
▸ good luck! がんばって！ [gambatte]

luggage 荷物 [nimotsu]
▸ my luggage hasn't arrived 荷物がまだ届いていません [nimotsu ga mada todoite imasen]
▸ I'd like to report the loss of my luggage 荷物の紛失を届け出たいんですが [nimotsu no funshitsu o todoke detai n desu ga]

luggage cart カート [kâto]
▸ I'm looking for a luggage cart カートを探しています [kâto o sagashite imasu]

lunch 昼食 [chûshoku], 昼ごはん [hirugohan]
▸ to have lunch 昼ごはんを食べる [hirugohan o taberu]
▸ what time is lunch served? 昼食は何時ですか [chûshoku wa nan ji desu ka]

machine-washable 洗濯機で洗える [sentakki de araeru]
▸ is it machine-washable? 洗濯機で洗えますか [sentakki de araemasu ka]

maid メイド [mêdo]
▸ what time does the maid come? メイドさんは何時に来ますか [mêdo-san wa nan ji ni kimasu ka]

mail

As well as airmail (航空便 [kôkûbin]) and surface mail/seamail (船便 [funabin]), there is economy airmail (SAL) which is between the two in cost and speed of delivery. Books etc. can be sent more cheaply as printed matter (印刷物 [insatsu butsu]). Size and weight restrictions for all mail are applied strictly.

---

mailbox *(for getting mail)* 郵便受け [yûbin uke]; *(for sending mail)* ポスト [posuto]
 ‣ where's the nearest mailbox? 一番近いポストはどこですか [ichiban chikai posuto wa doko desu ka]

main course メインコース [mên kôsu]
 ‣ what are you having for your main course? メインコースは何にしますか [mên kôsu wa nan ni shimasu ka]

make *(create, produce)* 作る [tsukuru]; *(cause to become)* させる [saseru]
 ‣ how is this dish made? この料理はどうやって作りますか [kono ryôri wa dô yatte tsukurimasu ka]
 ‣ I hope to make new friends here ここで新しい友達を作りたいと思います [koko de atarashî tomodachi o tsukuritai to omoimasu]

make up *(compensate for)* 埋め合わせる [umeawaseru]; *(invent)* 創り出す [tsukuridasu]
 ‣ will we be able to make up the time we've lost? 遅れた時間を埋め合わせられるでしょうか [okureta jikan o umeawaserareru deshô ka]

man 男の人 [otoko no hito]
 ‣ that man is bothering me あの男の人に困らされています [ano otoko no hito ni komarasarete imasu]

man-made 人工の [jinkô no]
 ‣ it's man-made 人工のものです [jinkô no mono desu]

---

delivery services

Domestic door-to-door delivery services (宅配便 [takuhaibin]) such as Kuroneko-Yamato Takkyûbin and Sagawa Kyûbin deliver parcels and packages within Japan very quickly, reliably and often more cheaply than the post office. You can even use them to send your luggage ahead of you to the airport if you allow a few days before your departure. Hotels and many convenience stores deal with these companies.

flea markets

Flea markets and antique markets are held regularly at weekends in the grounds of certain temples and shrines around Tokyo and Kyoto as well as in other areas. They sell a wide range of second-hand goods – kimonos and other clothing, pottery, furniture, dolls and many other items – and bargaining is acceptable.

many たくさん [takusan]
▸ there are many good restaurants here ここにはいいレストランがたくさんあります [koko ni wa î resutoran ga takusan arimasu]
▸ how many? いくつ？ [ikutsu]
▸ how many days will you be staying? 何日いますか [nan nichi imasu ka]

map *(of a country, town)* 地図 [chizu]; *(of a train, bus)* 路線図 [rosenzu]
▸ where can I buy a map of the area? この地域の地図はどこで買えますか [kono chi-iki no chizu wa doko de kaemasu ka]
▸ can you show me where we are on the map? 今、どこにいるかこの地図で教えてくれませんか [ima doko ni iru ka kono chizu de oshiete kuremasen ka]
▸ can I have a map of the subway? 地下鉄の路線図をもらえますか [chikatetsu no rosenzu o moraemasu ka]

March 三月 [sangatsu]
▸ March 1st 3月1日 [sangatsu tsuitachi]

market 市場 [ichiba]
▸ is there a market here every day? 市場は毎日、ここに立ちますか [ichiba wa mai nichi koko ni tachimasu ka]

married 結婚している [kekkon shite iru]
▸ are you married? 結婚していますか [kekkon shite imasu ka]

mass *(religion)* ミサ [misa]
▸ what time is mass? ミサは何時ですか [misa wa nan ji desu ka]

match *(for lighting)* マッチ [matchi]
▸ do you have any matches? マッチはありますか [matchi wa arimasu ka]

matter 重要だ [jûyô da]
▸ it doesn't matter 重要じゃありません [jûyô ja arimasen]

mattress マットレス [mattoresu]; *((Japanese) futon mattress)* 布団 [futon]
▸ the mattresses are saggy マットレスがへこんでいます [mattoresu ga hekonde imasu]

May 五月 [gogatsu]
▸ May 9th 5月9日 [gogatsu kokonoka]

---

meals

Meals often consist of several small dishes served at the same time; alternate eating from each dish. Breakfast may be eaten very early for people with a long commute. Lunch is usually between 12 and 1p.m., and the evening meal around 6–7 p.m. Presentation of food is important in Japan, even for the most basic of meals served at home. Rather than matching tableware, a variety of shapes and designs is considered more pleasing.

---

maybe たぶん [tabun]
  ▸ maybe the weather will be better tomorrow たぶん明日の天気はもっといいでしょう [tabun ashita no tenki wa motto î deshô]

meal 食事 [shokuji]
  ▸ are meals included? 食事は含まれていますか [shokuji wa fukumarete imasu ka]

mean *(signify)* 意味する [imi suru]; *(intend)* つもりだ [tsumori da]
  ▸ what does that word mean? その言葉はどういう意味ですか [sono kotoba wa dô yû imi desu ka]
  ▸ I mean it 本気です [honki desu]
  ▸ I didn't mean it そんなつもりはなかったんです [sonna tsumori wa nakatta n desu]

meat 肉 [niku]
  ▸ I don't eat meat 肉は食べません [niku wa tabemasen]

mechanic 整備士 [sêbishi]
  ▸ what did the mechanic say was wrong with the car? 整備士は車のどこに問題があると言っていましたか [sêbishi wa kuruma no doko ni mondai ga aru to itte imashita ka]

medication 薬 [kusuri]
  ▸ I'm not taking any other medication at the moment 今は他にどんな薬も飲んでいません [ima wa hoka ni donna kusuri mo nonde imasen]

---

meat

Meat is very popular in Japan, and is served in a variety of ways: in fondues (すき焼き [sukiyaki]), on skewers, breaded and deep-fried or even raw. Fondues are prepared at the table. First a kind of stock is made in a cast iron pot, and vegetables and then tofu are gradually added. Then small strips of pieces of raw meat are dipped into the pot to be cooked. Small pieces of meat are cooked on bamboo skewers and grilled over a wood fire, particularly chicken (焼き鳥 [yakitori]).

---

meeting people

Among friends and in casual situations, a slight nod of the head is enough, but more obvious bowing is needed in a more formal situation, for example, when meeting older people or new work acquaintances. The greater the formality, the lower the bow and the longer it lasts. You should bow from the waist, keeping your neck and back straight from head to hips. Women should place one hand over the other with their arms held down in front of their bodies, and men should keep their arms at their sides. Japanese people used to meeting foreigners may shake hands instead. Punctuality is highly valued in Japan, as is clear from the precision with which the trains run. It is better to arrive a little early than late, even for what may seem a fairly casual meeting.

medicine 薬 [kusuri]
- how many times a day do I have to take the medicine? 一日何回、薬を飲まなければいけませんか [ichi nichi nan kai kusuri o nomanakereba ikemasen ka]

medium *(size)* Mサイズの [emu saizu no]; *(steak)* ミディアムの [midiamu no]
◆ *(size)* Mサイズ [emu saizu]
- I'd like my steak medium, please ステーキはミディアムでお願いします [sutêki wa midiamu de onegai shimasu]
- do you have this shirt in a medium? このシャツのMサイズはありますか [kono shatsu no emu saizu wa arimasu ka]

meet *(by chance)* 出会う [deau]; *(by arrangement)* 会う [au]; *(make the acquaintance of)* 知り合いになる [shiriai ni naru]; *(go to collect someone)* 迎えに行く [mukae ni iku]
- meet you at 9 o'clock in front of the town hall 市役所の前で9時に会いましょう [shiyakusho no mae de ku ji ni aimashô]
- I have to meet my friend at nine o'clock 9時に友達と会わなければなりません [ku ji ni tomodachi to awanakereba narimasen]
- pleased to meet you/delighted to meet you/it was a pleasure meeting you どうぞよろしく [dôzo yoroshiku]
- goodbye! it was nice meeting you さようなら、お会いできてよかったです [sayônara, oai dekite yokatta desu]
- Charles, I'd like you to meet Mr. Tanaka チャールズさん、こちらは田中さんです [châruzu-san, kochira wa tanaka-san desu]
- where shall we meet? どこで会いましょうか [doko de aimashô ka]
- what time are we meeting tomorrow? 明日、何時に会いましょうか [ashita nan ji ni aimashô ka]
- could you meet me at the station? 駅に迎えに来てもらえませんか [eki ni mukae ni kite moraemasen ka]

menus

Menus may have English translations in popular restaurants in major tourist areas, but the vast majority are only in Japanese. However, many restaurants and coffee-shops have very realistic plastic models of the dishes available on display in the windows, so the easiest thing to do is take the waiter or waitress and point to what you want.

member *(of a club)* 会員 [kai-in]
- do you have to be a member? 会員にならなければなりませんか [kai-in ni naranakereba narimasen ka]

men's room 男性用お手洗い [dansê yô otearai], 男性用トイレ [dansê yô toire]
- where's the men's room? 男性用トイレはどこですか [dansê yô toire wa doko desu ka]

menu メニュー [menyû]
- can we see the menu? メニューを見せてくれますか [menyû o misete kuremasu ka]
- do you have a menu in English? 英語のメニューはありますか [êgo no menyû wa arimasu ka]
- do you have a children's menu? 子供用のメニューはありますか [kodomo yô no menyû wa arimasu ka]

message 伝言 [dengon]
- can you take a message? 伝言してもらえますか [dengon shite moraemasu ka]
- can I leave a message? 伝言を残せますか [dengon o nokosemasu ka]
- did you get my message? 伝言を聞いてもらえましたか [dengon o kîte moraemashita ka]

meter *(measurement)* メートル [mêtoru]; *(device)* メーター [mêtâ]
- it's about 5 meters long 約5メートルです [yaku go mêtoru desu]

midday 正午 [shôgo]
- we have to be there by midday 正午までに着かなければなりません [shôgo made ni tsukanakereba narimasen]

midnight 真夜中 [mayonaka]
- it's midnight 真夜中です [mayonaka desu]

milk ミルク [miruku], 牛乳 [gyûnyû]
- a liter of milk ミルクを1リットル [miruku o ichi rittoru]
- tea with milk ミルクティー [miruku tî]

milk chocolate ミルクチョコ [miruku choko]
- I prefer milk chocolate ミルクチョコのほうがいいです [miruku choko no hô ga î desu]

mind *(object)* かまう [kamau]
- I don't mind かまいません [kamaimasen]
- do you mind if I smoke? タバコを吸ってもかまいませんか [tabakao o sutte mo kamaimasen ka]
- do you mind if I open the window? 窓を開けてもかまいませんか [mado o akete mo kamaimasen ka]
- never mind 気にしないで [ki ni shinaide]

mineral water ミネラルウォーター [mineraru wôtâ]
- could I have a bottle of mineral water, please? ミネラルウォーターを一本くれませんか [mineraru wôtâ o ippon kuremasen ka]

minus マイナス [mainasu]
- it's minus 2 degrees outside! 外はマイナス2度です [soto wa mainasu ni do desu]

minute 分 [fun/pun]
- we'll go in a minute すぐに行きます [sugu ni ikimasu]

mirror 鏡 [kagami]
- the mirror's cracked 鏡が割れました [kagami ga waremashita]

miss *(be too late for)* 逃す [nogasu]; *(regret the absence of)* いなくて寂しい [inakute sabishī]
- I've missed my connection 乗り換え損ねました [norikae sokonemashita]
- we're going to miss the train 列車を逃してしまいますよ [ressha o nogashite shimaimasu yo]
- I missed you いなくて寂しかったです [inakute sabishikatta desu]

missing ない [nai]
- one of my suitcases is missing スーツケースが一つありません [sûtsukêsu ga hitotsu arimasen]

mistake 間違い [machigai]
- I think there's a mistake with the bill 勘定に間違いがあるんじゃないかと思いますが [kanjô ni machigai ga aru n ja nai ka to omoimasu ga]
- you've made a mistake with my change おつりが間違っています [otsuri ga machigatte imasu]

moment 瞬間 [shunkan]
- for the moment, we prefer staying in Tokyo しばらく東京にいるほうがいいです [shibaraku tôkyô ni iru hô ga î desu]

Monday 月曜日 [getsuyôbi]
- we're arriving/leaving on Monday 月曜日に着きます/出ます [getsuyôbi ni tsukimasu/demasu]

money お金 [okane]
- I don't have much money あまりお金がありません [amari okane ga arimasen]

▸ where can I change money? どこでお金の両替ができますか [doko de okane no ryôgae ga dekimasu ka]

▸ I want my money back 返金してほしいです [henkin shite hoshî desu]

money order 為替 [kawase]

▸ I'm waiting for a money order 為替を待っています [kawase o matte imasu]

month 月 [tsuki/getsu]

▸ I'm leaving in a month 一ヵ月後に出ます [ikka getsu go ni demasu]

monument 記念碑 [kinenhi]

▸ what does this monument commemorate? この記念碑は何を記念していますか [kono kinenhi wa nani o kinen shite imasu ka]

more もっと [motto] ◆ もう少し [mô sukoshi] ◆ それ以上 [sore ijô]

▸ can we have some more bread? パンをもう少しもらえますか [pan o mô sukoshi moraemasu ka]

▸ a little more もう少し [mô sukoshi]

▸ could I have a little more wine? ワインをもう少しもらえませんか [wain o mô sukoshi moraemasen ka]

▸ I don't want any more, thank you もう結構です [mô kekkô desu]

▸ I don't want to spend any more これ以上、お金を使いたくありません [kore ijô okane o tsukaitaku arimasen]

morning 朝 [asa]; (expressing duration) 午前中 [gozen chû]

▸ the museum is open in the morning 博物館は午前中、開いています [hakubutsukan wa gozen chû aite imasu]

mosque モスク [mosuku]

▸ where's the nearest mosque? 一番近いモスクはどこですか [ichiban chikai mosuku wa doko desu ka]

most (the majority of) ほとんどの [hotondo no]; (the largest amount of) 一番多い [ichiban ôi] ◆ (the majority) 大部分 [dai bubun]; (the largest amount) 一番多いもの [ichiban ôi mono] ◆ (to the greatest extent) 最も [mottomo]; (very) とても [totemo]

▸ are you here most days? ほとんど毎日、ここにいますか [hotondo mai nichi koko ni imasu ka]

▸ that's the most I can offer これができる最大限です [kore ga dekiru saidaigen desu]

mother (one's own) 母 [haha]; (someone else's) お母さん [okâ-san]

▸ this is my mother 母です [haha desu]

motorboat モーターボート [môtâ bôto]

▸ can we rent a motorboat? モーターボートは借りられますか [môtâ bôto wa kariraremasu ka]

motorcycle バイク [baiku], オートバイ [ôtobai]
- I'd like to rent a motorcycle バイクを借りたいんですが [baiku o karitai n desu ga]

mountain 山 [yama]
- in the mountains 山で [yama de]

mountain hut 山小屋 [yama goya]
- we slept in a mountain hut 山小屋で寝ました [yama goya de nemashita]

mouth 口 [kuchi]
- I've got a strange taste in my mouth 変な味が口の中でします [hen na aji ga kuchi no naka de shimasu]

move (*movement*) 動き [ugoki]; (*step, measure*) 処置 [shochi] ◆ 動く [ugoku] ◆ 動かす [ugokasu]
- I can't move my leg 足が動かせません [ashi ga ugokasemasen]
- don't move him 動かさないで！ [ugokasanaide]

movie 映画 [êga]
- have you seen ...'s latest movie? ...の最新の映画を見ましたか [...no saishin no êga o mimashita ka]
- it's a subtitled movie 字幕つきの映画です [jimaki tsuki no êga desu]

movie theater 映画館 [êgakan]
- where is there a movie theater? 映画館はどこにありますか [êgakan wa doko ni arimasu ka]
- what's on at the movie theater? 映画館では今、何をやっていますか [êgakan dewa ima nani o yatte imasu ka]

much たくさんの [takusan no] ◆ たくさん [takusan] ◆ (*considerably*) とても [totemo]; (*often*) しょっちゅう [shotchû]
- I don't have much money あまりお金を持っていません [amari okane o motte imasen]
- how much is it? いくらですか [ikura desu ka]
- how much is it for one night? 一晩いくらですか [hito ban ikura desu ka]
- how much is it per day and per person? 一人一日に付きいくらですか [hitori ichi nichi ni tsuki ikura desu ka]
- how much does it cost per hour? 一時間に付きいくらですか [ichi jikan ni tsuki ikura desu ka]
- how much is a ticket to Fukuoka? 福岡までの切符はいくらですか [fukuoka made no kippu wa ikura desu ka]

museum 博物館 [hakubutsukan]
- what time does the museum open? 博物館は何時に開きますか [hakubutsukan wa nan ji ni akimasu ka]

music 音楽 [ongaku]
- ▶ what kind of music do they play in that club? そのクラブではどんな音楽をやっていますか [sono kurabu de wa donna ongaku o yatte imasu ka]

must *(obligation, necessity)* ...なければならない [...nakereba naranai]; *(certainty)* ...に違いない [...ni chigai nai]
- ▶ I must be at the airport by 7a.m. 午前 7 時までに空港に行かなければなりません [gozen shichi ji made ni kûkô ni ikanakereba narimasen]
- ▶ that must cost a lot 高いに違いありません [takai ni chigai arimasen]

mustard 辛子 [karashi]
- ▶ is it strong mustard? 辛い辛子ですか [karai karashi desu ka]

n

nail *(on a finger, a toe)* 爪 [tsume]
- ▶ I need to cut my nails 爪を切らなければなりません [tsume o kiranakereba narimasen]

nail polish マニキュア [manikyua]
- ▶ I'd like to find nail polish in a dark shade of red 黒っぽい赤のマニキュアを探しているんですが [kuroppoi aka no manikyua o sagashite iru n desu ga]

name 名前 [namae]
- ▶ what is your name? 名前は何ですか [namae wa nan desu ka]
- ▶ my name is Patrick 名前はパトリックです [namae wa patorikku desu]
- ▶ hello, my name's John こんにちは、ジョンです [konnichiwa, jon desu]
- ▶ I have a reservation in the name of Jackson ジャクソンの名前で予約してあります [jakkuson no namae de yoyaku shite arimasu]

napkin ナプキン [napukin]
- ▶ could I have a napkin, please? ナプキンをもらえませんか [napukin o moraemasen ka]

national holiday 祝日 [shukujitsu]
- ▶ is tomorrow a national holiday? 明日は祝日ですか [ashita wa shukujitsu desu ka]

nationality 国籍 [kokuseki]
- ▶ what nationality are you? 国籍は何ですか [kokuseki wa nan desu ka]

nature *(plants and animals)* 自然 [shizen]; *(essential qualities)* 本質 [honshitsu]; *(character)* 性質 [sêshitsu]
- ▶ I like to take long walks outdoors and enjoy nature 外を歩いて自然を楽しむのが好きです [soto o aruite shizen o tanoshimu no ga suki desu]

names

Given names are only used among family members and close friends; colleagues and even good friends use family names. The title さん [san] (Mr/Mrs/Miss/Ms) is added after the family name or given name. Note that direct use of pronouns meaning 'you' is considered rude and aggressive, and names with titles are used instead. Within the family, affectionate terms of address are used: dad (お父さん [otô-san]), mom (お母さん [okâ-san]), big sister (お姉さん [onê-san]), and big brother (お兄さん [onî-san]). The title san is only used for older family members, while younger brothers and sisters are referred to by their given names or abbreviations of them, often with the familiar title ちゃん [chan] added – for example, Mika-chan. Note that chan can also be used for older family members (e.g. onê-chan) and close friends, who may also have nicknames. Boys and young men are also addressed with the familiar title 君 [kun] after their names.

nausea 吐き気 [hakike]
> I've had nausea all day 一日中、吐き気がしています [ichi nichi jû hakike ga shite imasu]

near 近い [chikai] ◆ 近く [chikaku]
> where's the nearest subway station? 一番近い地下鉄の駅はどこですか [ichiban chikai chikatetsu no eki wa doko desu ka]
> it's near the railway station 駅の近くです [eki no chikaku desu]
> very near ... ...のすぐ近く [...no sugu chikaku]

nearby 近くに [chikaku ni]
> is there a supermarket nearby? 近くにスーパーはありますか [chikaku ni sûpâ wa arimasu ka]

neck 首 [kubi]
> I have a sore neck 首が痛いです [kubi ga itai desu]

need 必要 [hitsuyô] ◆ いる [iru] ◆ なければならない [nakereba naranai]
> I need something for a cough セキに効くものが何かいります [seki ni kiku mono ga nani ka irimasu]
> I need to be at the airport by six (o'clock) 6時までに空港に着かなければなりません [roku ji made ni kûkô ni tsukanakereba narimasen]
> we need to go 行かなければなりません [ikanakereba narimasen]

neither どちらもない [dochira mo nai] ◆ どちらの...も...でない [dochira no ... mo ... de nai]
> neither of us 私たちのどちらでもない [watashi-tachi no dochira de mo nai]
> me neither 私も違います [watashi mo chigaimasu]

newspapers

There are several daily and weekly English-language newspapers: the Japan Times, the Mainichi Daily News and the Daily Yomiuri. The Nikkei Shimbun is Japan's daily financial newspaper and it has an English version, the Nikkei Weekly.

never 決してない [kesshite nai]
> I've never been to Japan before 日本に来たことは一度もありません [nihon ni kita koto wa ichi do mo arimasen]

new 新しい [atarashî]
> could we have a new towel, please? 新しいタオルをもらえませんか [atarashî taoru o moraemasen ka]

news *(information)* 知らせ [shirase]; *(on TV, radio)* ニュース [nyûsu]
> a piece of news 知らせ [shirase]
> that's great news! それはすごい知らせだ！ [sore wa sugoi shirase da]
> I heard it on the news ニュースで聞きました [nyûsu de kikimashita]

newspaper 新聞 [shimbun]
> do you have any English-language newspapers? 英字新聞はありますか [êji shimbun wa arimasu ka]

New Year 新年 [shin nen]
> Happy New Year! 新年おめでとう [shin nen omedetô]

New Year's Day 元日 [gan jitsu]
> are stores open on New Year's Day? 元日に店は開いていますか [gan jitsu ni mise wa aite imasu ka]

next 次の [tsugi no] ◆ **next to** ...の隣に [...no tonari ni]
> when is the next guided tour? 次のガイド付き見学コースはいつですか [tsugi no gaido tsuki kengaku kôsu wa itsu desu ka]
> when is the next train to Tokyo? 東京行きの次の列車はいつですか [tôkyô yuki no tsugi no ressha wa itsu desu ka]
> what time is the next flight to London? ロンドン行きの次の便は何時ですか [rondon yuki no tsugi no bin wa nan ji desu ka]
> can we park next to the tent? テントの隣に駐車してもいいですか [tento no tonari ni chûsha shite mo î desu ka]

nice *(wonderful)* 素敵な [suteki na]; *(kind)* 親切な [shinsetsu na]; *(likable)* よい [yoi]、いい [î]
> have a nice vacation! よい休暇を！ [yoi kyûka o]
> we found a really nice little hotel 小さくてとても素敵なホテルを見つけました [chîsakute totemo suteki na hoteru o mitsukemashita]

no (i)

It is considered rude to express open disagreement, unless you clearly have higher status than the other person, so the Japanese tend to use vaguer phrases whose meanings are nevertheless understood by both sides.

▸ goodbye! it was nice meeting you さようなら、会えてよかったです [sayônara, aete yokatta desu]

night 晩 [ban]
▸ how much is it per night? 一晩いくらですか [hito ban ikura desu ka]
▸ I'd like to stay an extra night 一晩余分に泊まりたいんですが [hito ban yobun ni tomoritai n desu ga]

nightclub ナイトクラブ [naitokurabu]
▸ are there any good nightclubs in this town? この町にいいナイトクラブは ありますか [kono machi ni î naitokurabu wa arimasu ka]

nine 九 [kyû/ku]
▸ there are nine of us 全部で九人です [zembu de kyû nin desu]
▸ we have a reservation for nine (o'clock) 9 時に予約してあります [ku ji ni yoyaku shite arimasu]

no *(opposite of yes)* いいえ [ie] ◆ なしの [nashi no]
▸ no thanks! 結構です [kekkô desu]
▸ a cup of tea with no milk or sugar, please 紅茶をミルクと砂糖なしでお願 いします [kôcha o miruku to satô nashi de onegai shimasu]

nobody 誰も…ない [dare mo … nai]
▸ there's nobody at the reception desk フロントには誰もいません [furonto ni wa dare mo imasen]

noise 音 [oto]
▸ to make a noise 音を立てる [oto o tateru]
▸ I heard a funny noise 変な音を聞きました [hen na oto o kikimashita]

noisy うるさい [urusai]
▸ I'd like another room: mine is too noisy 別の部屋にしてほしいんです が：うるさすぎます [betsu no heya ni shite hoshî n desu ga. urusasugimasu]

nonsmoker タバコを吸わない人 [tabako o suwanai hito]
▸ we're nonsmokers タバコは吸いません [tabako wa suimasen]

nonsmoking 禁煙 [kin'en]
▸ is this restaurant nonsmoking? このレストランは禁煙ですか [kono resutoran wa kin'en desu ka]

nonsmoking carriage 禁煙車 [kin'en sha]
▸ I'd like a seat in a nonsmoking carriage 禁煙車の席がいいです [kin'en sha no seki ga î desu]

noodles

Noodles made from buckwheat or wheat are very popular, eaten hot or cold according to type and season. ラーメン [râmen] come from China, whereas うどん [udon] and そば [soba] originate in Japan. Each city or region has its own râmen specialty.

nonsmoking section 禁煙コーナー [kin'en kônâ]
▸ do you have a nonsmoking section? 禁煙コーナーはありますか [kin'en kônâ wa arimasu ka]

nonstop 直行の [chokkô no] ◆ 直行で [chokkô de]
▸ I'd like a nonstop flight from Tokyo to New York 東京からニューヨークまでの直行便がいいんですが [tôkyô kara nyûyôku made no chokkô bin ga î n desu ga]

noodles 麺類 [menrui]
▸ I'd like some noodles, please 麺類にします [menrui ni shimasu]

noon 正午 [shôgo]
▸ we leave at noon 正午に出ます [shôgo ni demasu]

no one 誰も…ない [dare mo ... nai]
▸ there's no one there 誰もいません [dare mo imasen]

normal 普通の [futsû no]
▸ is it normal for it to rain as much as this? こんなに雨が降るのは普通ですか [konna ni ame ga furu no wa futsû desu ka]

nose 鼻 [hana]
▸ I have a blocked nose 鼻が詰まっています [hana ga tsumatte imasu]

not ない [nai]
▸ I don't like spinach ほうれん草は好きじゃありません [hôrensô wa suki ja arimasen]
▸ I don't think so そうは思いませんが [sô wa omoimasen ga]
▸ not at all 全然ない [zenzen nai]

nose-blowing

Nose-blowing is considered very rude in Japan. If you can't avoid doing it, be sure to turn your head away and use tissues. In contrast, you may be irritated by Japanese sniffing instead of blowing their noses! You may also see people wearing mouth masks in winter in an attempt to avoid catching or passing on colds.

numbers four and nine

The Japanese consider the numbers 4 and 9 unlucky. One of the Japanese pronunciations of 4 is the same as that of the character 死 [shi], meaning 'death.' Similarly, 9 can be pronounced the same as the character 苦 [ku], meaning 'pain.'

note メモ [memo]
- could I leave a note for him? メモを残してもいいですか [memo o nokoshite mo î desu ka]

nothing 何も…ない [nani mo ... nai]
- there's nothing to do here in the evening ここでは夜、何もすることがありません [koko de wa yoru nani mo suru koto ga arimasen]
- there's nothing I can do about it それに関しては何もできることはありません [sore ni kanshite wa nani mo dekiru koto wa arimasen]

November 十一月 [jûichigatsu]
- November 7th １１月７日 [jûichigatsu nanoka]

now 今 [ima]
- what should we do now? さあ、どうしましょうか [sâ, dô shimashô ka]

number *(of a phone, a car, a room, an apartment)* 番号 [bangô]; *(numeral)* 数字 [sûji]; *(quantity)* 数 [kazu]
- my name is... and my number is... 名前は…、番号は…です [namae wa ..., bangô wa ... desu]

numbers

The Japanese number system is quite complex – even native speakers sometimes get confused! It combines Japanese and Chinese-derived pronunciations. The Chinese-based ones are used to count numbers and do sums. Various 'counters' are added onto these to count objects; the counter depends on the type of objects being counted. For example, 個 [ko] is used when talking about medium-sized objects (three apples ringo san ko); 本 [hon] for long thin objects (two pencils enpitsu ni hon), and 枚 [mai] for flat objects (five stamps kitte go mai). There are also native Japanese numbers for 1 to 10, which can be used to count any type of object; after 10, you need to use the Chinese-based numbers with the appropriate counter. Don't panic though – people will still follow what you're talking about even if you get one of these counters wrong. It's useful to know that ko is by far the most commonly used one.

occupied *(bathroom)* 使用中 [shiyô chû]
- the restroom's occupied トイレは使用中です [toire wa shiyô chû desu]

ocean 海 [umi]
- we'd like to see the ocean while we're here ここにいる間に海が見たいんですが [koko ni iru aida ni umi ga mitai n desu ga]

o'clock 時 [ji]
- it's eight o'clock 8 時です [hachi ji desu]

October 十月 [jûgatsu]
- October 12th 10月12日 [jûgatsu jûninichi]

of の [no]
- one of us 私たちのうちの一人 [watashi-tachi no uchi no hitori]

off *(indicating movement)* 離れて [hanarete] ◆ *(at a distance from)* 向こうに [mukô ni]; *(deducted from)* 引いて [hîte]
- an island off the coast of Atami 熱海の海岸の向こうにある島 [atami no kaigan no mukô ni aru shima]
- this sweater is fifty percent off! このセーターは50パーセント引きです [kono sêtâ wa gojippâsento biki desu]

offer 提供する [têkyô suru]
- can I offer you a cigarette? タバコをさしあげましょうか [tabako o sashiagemashô ka]

office 事務所 [jimusho]
- where is the hotel office? ホテルの事務所はどこですか [hoteru no jimusho wa doko desu ka]

often よく [yoku]
- how often does the ferry sail? フェリーは何回出ますか [ferî wa nan kai demasu ka]

oil *(for car, machine)* オイル [oiru]; *(for cooking)* 油 [abura]
- could you check the oil, please? オイルをチェックしてくれませんか [oiru o chekku shite kuremasen ka]

OK 大丈夫な [daijôbu na] ◆ オッケー [okkê]
- that's OK 大丈夫です [daijôbu desu]
- do you think it's OK? 大丈夫だと思いますか [daijôbu da to omoimasu ka]

old *(in discussing age)* 歳 [sai]; *(not young)* 年を取った [toshi o totta]; *(not new)* 古い [furui]

▸ how old are you? 何歳ですか [nan sai desu ka]

▸ I'm 18 years old 18歳です [jûhassai desu]

▸ have you visited the old temple? あの古いお寺には行きましたか [ano furui otera ni wa ikimashita ka]

on *(working)* ついている [tsuite iru]; *(happening)* やっている [yatte iru] ◆ …に […ni]

▸ how long is it on for? いつまでやっていますか [itsu made yatte imasu ka]

▸ the heater is on 暖房がついています [dambô ga tsuite imasu]

once *(on one occasion)* 一度 [ichi do]; *(previously)* 前に [mae ni] ◆ **at once** すぐに [sugu ni]

▸ I've been here once before 以前一度ここに来たことがあります [izen ichi do koko ni kita koto ga arimasu]

▸ please do it at once すぐにやってください [sugu ni yatte kudasai]

one 一 [ichi]

▸ a table for one, please 一人分のテーブルをお願いします [hitori bun no têburu o onegai shimasu]

one-way (ticket) 片道 [katamichi]

▸ how much is a one-way ticket downtown? 町の中心までの片道切符はいくらですか [machi no chûshin made no katamichi kippu wa ikura desu ka]

▸ a one-way ticket to Kyoto, please 京都までの片道切符をください [kyôto made no katamichi kippu o kudasai]

only だけ [dake]

▸ that's the only one left 一つだけ残っています [hitotsu dake nokotte imasu]

open 開いている [aite iru] ◆ 開ける [akeru] ◆ 開く [aku]

▸ is the bank open at lunchtime? 銀行は昼食の時間も開いていますか [ginkô wa chûshoku no jikan mo aite imasu ka]

▸ is the museum open all day? 博物館は一日中、開いていますか [hakubutsukan wa ichi nichi jû aite imasu ka]

▸ at what time is … open? …は何時に開きますか [...wa nan ji ni akimasu ka]

▸ can I open the window? 窓を開けてもいいですか [mado o akete mo î desu ka]

▸ what time do you open? 何時に開きますか [nan ji ni akimasu ka]

open-air 野外の [yagai no]

▸ are there open-air concerts? 野外コンサートはありますか [yagai konsâto wa arimasu ka]

operating room 手術室 [shujutsu shitsu]

▸ is she still in the operating room? まだ手術室の中ですか [mada shujutsu shitsu no naka desu ka]

opinion 意見 [iken]

▸ in my opinion, … 私の意見としては… [watashi no iken toshite wa …]

orange オレンジ色の [orenji iro no] ✦ *(fruit)* オレンジ [orenji]

▸ I'd like seven oranges オレンジが七つほしいんですが [orenji ga nanatsu hoshî n desu ga]

orange juice オレンジジュース [orenji jûsu]

▸ I'll have a glass of orange juice オレンジジュースを一杯、お願いします [orenji jûsu o ippai onegai shimasu]

▸ I'd like a freshly squeezed orange juice 絞りたてのオレンジジュースがほしいんですが [shiboritate no orenji jûsu ga hoshî n desu ga]

order *(in a restaurant, a café)* 注文 [chûmon] ✦ *(in a restaurant, a café)* 注文する [chûmon suru]

▸ this isn't what I ordered: I asked for… 注文したものと違います：…を頼みました [chûmon shita mono to chigaimasu. … o tanomimashita]

▸ I ordered a coffee コーヒーを注文しました [kôhî o chûmon shimashita]

▸ we'd like to order now 注文したいんですが [chûmon shitai n desu ga]

organize 手配する [tehai suru]

▸ can you organize the whole trip for us? 旅行全部の手配をしてもらえますか [ryokô zembu no tehai o shite moraemasu ka]

other *(different)* 他の [hoka no]; *(second of two)* もう一つの [mô hitotsu no] ✦ 他のもの [hoka no mono]

▸ I'll have the other one もう一つのほうをもらいます [mô hitotsu no hô o moraimasu]

▸ on the other side of the street 道の反対側 [michi no hantai gawa]

▸ go ahead; I'm going to wait for the others 先に行ってください；他の人たちを待っています [saki ni itte kudasai. hoka no hitotachi o matte imasu]

---

opinions

▸ personally, I don't think it's fair 個人的には、あまり公平じゃないと思います [kojinteki ni wa, amari kôhê ja nai to omoimasu]

▸ I think he's right あの人の言うことは正しいと思います [ano hito no yû koto wa tadashî to omoimasu]

▸ I don't want to say 言いたくありません [itaku arimasen]

▸ I'm not sure よく分かりません [yoku wakarimasen]

▸ no idea! 見当もつきません [kentô mo tsukimasen]

▸ it depends 時と場合によるでしょう [toki to bâi ni yoru deshô]

out-of-date 期限切れ [kigen gire]
- ▸ I think my passport is out-of-date パスポートは期限が切れていると思います [pasupôto wa kigen ga kirete iru to omoimasu]

outside call 外線 (電話) [gaisen (denwa)]
- ▸ I'd like to make an outside call 外線をかけたいんですが [gaisen o kaketai n desu ga]

outside line 外線 [gaisen]
- ▸ how do you get an outside line? 外線はどうやってかけますか [gaisen wa dô yatte kakemasu ka]

overheat 過熱する [kanetsu suru]
- ▸ the engine is overheating エンジンが過熱してしまいました [enjin ga kanetsu shite shimaimashita]

owner 持ち主 [mochinushi]
- ▸ do you know who the owner is? 持ち主は誰か知っていますか [mochinushi wa dare ka shitte imasu ka]

pack *(of cigarettes, chewing gum)* 箱 [hako] ◆ *(for a trip)* 荷造りする [nizukuri suru]
- ▸ how much is a pack of cigarettes? タバコは一箱いくらですか [tabako wa hito hako ikura desu ka]
- ▸ I need to pack 荷造りしなければなりません [nizukuri shinakereba narimasen]

package *(wrapped object)* 包み [tsutsumi]; *(vacation deal)* パッケージ [pakkêji]
- ▸ I'd like to send this package to San Francisco by airmail サンフランシスコにこの小包を航空便で送りたいんですが [sanfuranshisuko ni kono kozutsumi o kôkûbin de okuritai n desu ga]
- ▸ do you have weekend packages? 週末のパッケージツアーはありますか [shûmatsu no pakkêji tsuâ wa arimasu ka]

package tour パッケージツアー [pakkêji tsuâ]
- ▸ it's my first time on a package tour パッケージツアーは初めてです [pakkêji tsuâ wa hajimete desu]

padlock 錠前 [jômae]
- ▸ I'd like to buy a padlock for my bike バイクにつける錠前を買いたいんですが [baiku ni tsukeru jômae o kaitai n desu ga]

pain *(physical)* 痛み [itami]
- I'd like something for pain 痛みに効くものがほしいんですが [itami ni kiku mono ga hoshî n desu ga]
- I have a pain here ここが痛いです [koko ga itai desu]

painkiller 鎮痛剤 [chintsûzai], 痛み止め [itamidome]
- I have a really bad toothache: can you give me a painkiller, please? 歯がすごく痛みます；鎮痛剤をください [ha ga sugoku itamimasu. chintsûzai o kudasai]

pair *(of gloves, socks)* 組 [kumi]
- a pair of shoes 靴一足 [kutsu issoku]
- a pair of pants ズボン一本 [zubon ippon]
- do you have a pair of scissors? はさみはありますか [hasami wa arimasu ka]

pants ズボン [zubon]
- a pair of pants ズボン一本 [zubon ippon]
- there is a hole in these pants このズボンには穴が開いています [kono zubon ni wa ana ga aite imasu]

pantyhose パン（ティー）スト（ッキング） [pan(tî)suto(kkingu)]
- I got a run in my pantyhose パンストが伝線しました [pansuto ga densen shimashita]

paper *(for writing on)* 紙 [kami]; *(newspaper)* 新聞 [shimbun] ◆ **papers** *(official documents)* 書類 [shorui]
- a piece of paper 紙一枚 [kami ichi mai]
- here are my papers はい、私の書類です [hai, watashi no shorui desu]

parasol *(on beach)* ビーチパラソル [bîchi parasoru]; *(traditional Japanese oiled paper)* 番傘 [bangasa]
- can you rent parasols? ビーチパラソルを貸してもらえますか [bîchi parasoru o kashite moraemasu ka]

pardon *(forgiveness)* 許し [yurushi] ◆ *(forgive)* 許す [yurusu]
- I beg your pardon?/pardon me? *(asking for repetition)* もう一度言ってもらえますか [mô ichi do itte moraemasu ka]
- I beg your pardon!/pardon me! *(to apologize)* すみません [sumimasen]; *(showing disagreement)* えっ、何ですって！ [e, nan desutte]

park 駐車する [chûsha suru]
- can we park our trailer here? トレーラーをここに駐車してもいいですか [torêrâ o koko ni chûsha shite mo î desu ka]
- am I allowed to park here? ここに駐車しても大丈夫ですか [koko ni chûsha shite mo daijôbu desu ka]

parking 駐車場 [chûshajô]
- is there any parking near the hostel? ホステルの近くに駐車場はありますか [hosuteru no chikaku ni chûshajô wa arimasu ka]

parties

Formal parties (宴会 [enkai]) at certain times of year or to mark particular events are an important part of working life and of various other social groups. They usually take place in private function rooms at Japanese-style restaurants. They begin early, around 6–6.30 p.m. and it is important to be punctual. Such parties also often finish at a set time, although some people may go on to drink somewhere else (二次会 [nijikai]).

parking lot 駐車場 [chûshajô]
- is there a parking lot nearby? 近くに駐車場はありますか [chikaku ni chûshajô wa arimasu ka]

parking space 駐車スペース [chûsha supêsu]
- is it easy to find a parking space in town? 町の中で駐車スペースは簡単に見つかりますか [machi no naka de chûsha supêsu wa kantan ni mitsukarimasu ka]

part *(piece)* 部分 [bubun]; *(area)* 地方 [chihô]
- what part of Japan are you from? 日本のどの地方の出身ですか [nihon no dono chihô no shusshin desu ka]
- I've never been to this part of Japan before 日本のこの地方には来たことがありません [nihon no kono chihô ni wa kita koto ga arimasen]

party パーティー [pâtî] ◆ パーティーをする [pâtî o suru]
- I'm planning a little party tomorrow 明日ちょっとしたパーティーをしようと思っています [ashita chotto shita pâtî o shiyô to omotte imasu]

pass *(hand)* まわす [mawasu]; *(in a car)* 通る [tôru] ◆ *(in a car)* 追い越す [oikosu] ◆ *(mountain)* 峠 [tôge]
- can you pass me the salt? 塩をまわしてくれませんか [shio o mawashite kuremasen ka]
- can you pass on this road? この道は追い越しができますか [kono michi wa oikoshi ga dekimasu ka]

passage *(corridor)* 廊下 [rôka]
- I heard someone outside in the passage 外の廊下で誰かの物音を聞きました [soto no rôka de dare ka no mono-oto o kikimashita]

passenger 乗客 [jôkyaku]
- is this where the passengers from the New York flight arrive? ニューヨークからの便の乗客が到着するのはここですか [nyûyôku kara no bin no jôkyaku ga tôchaku suru no wa koko desu ka]

passport パスポート [pasupôto]
- I've lost my passport パスポートを失くしました [pasupôto o nakushimashita]

- I forgot my passport パスポートを忘れました [pasupôto o wasuremeshita]
- my passport has been stolen パスポートを盗まれました [pasupôto o nusumaremashita]

past 過ぎて [sugite]
- twenty past twelve １２時２０分 [jûni ji nijippun]

path *(track)* 遊歩道 [yûho dô]
- is the path well-marked? 遊歩道は標識がついていますか [yûho dô wa hyôshiki ga tsuite imasu ka]

pay 払う [harau]
- do I have to pay a deposit? 保証金を払わなければなりませんか [hoshôkin o harawanakereba narimasen ka]
- do you have to pay to get in? 入るのにお金がいりますか [hairu no ni okane ga irimasu ka]
- can you pay by credit card? クレジットカードで払えますか [kurejitto kâdo de haraemasu ka]
- we're going to pay separately 別々に払います [betsubetsu ni haraimasu]

pay-per-view channel 有料チャンネル [yûryô channeru]
- are there any pay-per-view channels? 有料チャンネルはついていますか [yûryô channeru wa tsuite imasu ka]

pedestrian 歩行者 [hokôsha] ◆ 歩行者専用の [hokôsha sen'yô no]
- is this just a pedestrian street? この道は歩行者専用ですか [kono michi wa hokôsha sen'yô desu ka]

pedestrian mall 歩行者専用道路 [hokôsha sen'yô dôro]
- can you direct me to the pedestrian mall? 歩行者専用道路への行き方を教えてくれますか [hokôsha sen'yô dôro e no ikikata o oshiete kuremasu ka]

pen ペン [pen]
- can you lend me a pen? ペンを貸してくれますか [pen o kashite kuremasu ka]

pencil 鉛筆 [empitsu]
- can you lend me a pencil? 鉛筆を貸してくれますか [empitsu o kashite kuremasu ka]

penicillin ペニシリン [penishirin]
- I'm allergic to penicillin ペニシリンにアレルギーがあります [penishirin ni arerugî ga arimasu]

pepper こしょう [koshô]
- pass the pepper, please こしょうをまわしてください [koshô o mawashite kudasai]

percent パーセント [pâsento]
- could you knock 10 percent off the price? １０パーセント、引いてくれませんか [jippâsento hîte kuremasen ka]

pets

Cats and dogs have become very popular in recent years, as the birthrate has declined and living circumstances have changed. Crickets and other singing insects have been kept as pets for many centuries.

performance *(show)* ショー [shô]; *(in a movie theater)* 上演 [jôen]
- what time does the performance begin? ショーは何時に始まりますか [shô wa nan ji ni hajimarimasu ka]

perfume 香水 [kôsui]
- how much is this perfume? この香水はいくらですか [kono kôsui wa ikura desu ka]

perhaps もしかしたら [moshikashitara]
- perhaps you can help me? もしかしたら手伝ってもらえますか [moshikashitara tetsudatte moraemasu ka]

person 人 [hito]
- how much is it per person and per hour? 一人一時間に付きいくらですか [hitori ichi jikan ni tsuki ikura desu ka]

pet ペット [petto]
- are pets allowed? ペットも大丈夫ですか [petto mo daijôbu desu ka]

phone 電話 [denwa] ◆ 電話する [denwa suru]
- can I use the phone? 電話を貸してもらえますか [denwa o kashite moraemasu ka]

on the phone
- hello? もしもし [moshimoshi]
- Joe Stewart speaking ジョー・スチュアートです [jô suchuâto desu]
- I'd like to speak to Jack Adams ジャック・アダムスさんをお願いしたいんですが [jakku adamusu san o onegai shitai n desu ga]
- hold the line しばらくお待ちください [shibaraku omachi kudasai]
- can you call back in ten minutes? 10分後にかけなおしてもらえますか [jippun go ni kakenaoshite moraemasu ka]
- would you like to leave a message? 何か伝言はありませんか [nani ka dengon wa arimasen ka]
- you have the wrong number 番号をお間違えだと思いますが [bangô o omachigae da to omoimasu ga]

phone booth 電話ボックス [denwa bokkusu]
▸ is there a phone booth near here? この近くに電話ボックスはあります
か [kono chikaku ni denwa bokkusu wa arimasu ka]

phone call 電話 [denwa]
▸ I'd like to make a phone call 電話をかけたいんですが [denwa o kaketai n
desu ga]

phonecard テレホンカード [terehon kâdo]
▸ where can I buy a phonecard? テレホンカードはどこで買えますか
[terehon kâdo wa doko de kaemasu ka]

photo 写真 [shashin]
▸ can I take photos in here? ここで写真を撮ってもいいですか [koko de
shashin o totte mo î desu ka]
▸ could you take a photo of us? 写真を撮ってくれませんか [shashin o totte
kuremasen ka]
▸ I'd like copies of some photos 写真の焼き増しをお願いします [shashin no
yakimashi o onegai shimasu]

photography 写真を撮ること [shashin o toru koto]
▸ is photography allowed in the museum? 博物館の中で写真を撮ってもい
いですか [hakubutsukan no naka de shashin o totte mo î desu ka]

picnic ピクニック [pikunikku]
▸ could we go for a picnic by the river? 川のそばでピクニックをしません
か [kawa no soba de pikunikku o shimasen ka]

piece (of paper) 枚 [mai]; (of chocolate, cake, wood) 個 [ko]
▸ a piece of cake, please ケーキを一個ください [kêki o ikko kudasai]
▸ a piece of advice アドバイスを少し [adobaisu o sukoshi]
▸ a piece of news 知らせ [shirase]

pill 錠剤 [jôzai]
▸ a bottle of pills 錠剤を一ビン [jôzai o hito bin]
▸ the Pill (contraceptive) ピル [piru]

pillow 枕 [makura]
▸ could I have another pillow? 枕をもうひとつもらえませんか [makura o
mô hitotsu moraemasen ka]

pizza ピザ [piza]
▸ I'd like a large mushroom pizza マッシュルームピザの大をお願いします
[masshurûmu piza no dai o onegai shimasu]

place (area) 場所 [basho]、ところ [tokoro]; (house) 家 [ie/uchi]; (seat) 席 [seki]
▸ can you recommend a nice place to eat? いいレストランを紹介してくれ
ますか [î resutoran o shôkai shite kuremasu ka]
▸ do you want to change places with me? 席を替わりましょうか [seki o
kawarimashô ka]

plain *(clear)* はっきりした [hakkiri shita]; *(with nothing added)* 無添加の [mutenka no]

▸ do you have any plain yogurt? プレーンヨーグルトはありますか [purên yôguruto wa arimasu ka]

plan *(strategy)* 計画 [kêkaku]; *(intention, idea)* 予定 [yotê]; *(street, buildings)* 設計 [sekkê] ◆ *(organize)* 計画を立てる [kêkaku o tateru]; *(intend)* つもりだ [tsumori da]

▸ do you have plans for tonight? 今晩、なにか予定はありますか [kom ban nani ka yotê wa arimasu ka]

▸ I'm planning to stay for just one night 一泊だけするつもりです [ippaku dake suru tsumori desu]

plane 飛行機 [hikôki]

▸ which gate does the plane depart from? どのゲートから飛行機は出ますか [dono gêto kara hikôki wa demasu ka]

▸ when's the next plane to New York? ニューヨーク行きの次の飛行機はいつですか [nyûyôku yuki no tsugi no hikôki wa itsu desu ka]

plate 皿 [sara]

▸ this plate's got a crack in it この皿はひびが入っています [kono sara wa hibi ga haitte imasu]

platform *(at a station)* ホーム [hômu]

▸ which platform does the train leave from? どのホームから列車は出ますか [dono hômu kara ressha wa demasu ka]

play *(at a theater)* 劇 [geki] ◆ 遊ぶ [asobu]; *(sport, game)* する [suru]; *(instrument, music)* 演奏する [ensô suru]

▸ do you play tennis? テニスはしますか [tenisu wa shimasu ka]

▸ I play the cello チェロを演奏します [chero o ensô shimasu]

please *(offering something)* どうぞ [dôzo]; *(asking for something)* ...をください [...o kudasai]; *(asking someone to do something)* ...てください [...te kudasai]

▸ water, please 水をください [mizu o kudasai]

▸ please sit down どうぞ座ってください [dôzo suwatte kudasai]

▸ can I come in? – please do 入ってもいいですか–どうぞ [haitte mo î desu ka – dôzo]

pleased うれしい [ureshî]

▸ pleased to meet you どうぞよろしく [dôzo yoroshiku]

pleasure 喜び [yorokobi]

▸ with pleasure! 喜んで [yorokonde]

▸ it's a pleasure/my pleasure どういたしまして [dô itashimashite]

plug *(on electrical equipment)* プラグ [puragu]

▸ where can I find an adaptor for the plug on my hairdryer? ドライヤーのプ

pointing and gestures

Many gestures are different in Japan. For example, to beckon someone toward you, move your fingers in your usual gesture but with your palm facing downward. To indicate yourself, point toward the tip of your nose with your index finger. Pointing at someone is rude; instead, use your whole hand, palm uppermost.

ラグのアダプターはどこにありますか [doraiyâ no puragu no adaputâ wa doko ni arimasu ka]

plug in プラグを差し込む [puragu o sashikomu]

▶ can I plug my cellphone in here to recharge it? 携帯の充電はここでできますか [kêtai no jûden wa koko de dekimasu ka]

point *(moment)* 瞬間 [shunkan]; *(spot, location)* 地点 [chiten] ◆ *(direct)* 示す [shimesu]

▶ point of view 見方 [mikata]

▶ can you point me in the direction of the freeway? 高速道路の方向を示してくれますか [kôsoku dôro no hôkô o shimeshite kuremasu ka]

police 警察 [kêsatsu]

▶ call the police! 警察を呼んでください！ [kêsatsu o yonde kudasai]

▶ what's the number for the police? 警察は何番ですか [kêsatsu wa nam ban desu ka]

police box 交番 [kôban]

▶ is there a police box around here? この辺に交番はありますか [kono hen ni kôban wa arimasu ka]

police station 警察署 [kêsatsu sho]

▶ where is the nearest police station? 一番近い警察署はどこですか [ichiban chikai kêsatsu sho wa doko desu ka]

pool *(for swimming)* プール [pûru]

▶ main pool メインプール [mên pûru]

▶ children's pool 子供用プール [kodomo yô pûru]

▶ is the pool heated? 温水プールですか [onsui pûru desu ka]

▶ is there an indoor pool? 室内プールはありますか [shitsunai pûru wa arimasu ka]

pork 豚肉 [butaniku], ポーク [pôku]

▶ I don't eat pork 豚肉は食べません [butaniku wa tabemasen]

port 港 [minato]

▶ what time will we reach port? 何時に港に着きますか [nan ji ni minato ni tsukimasu ka]

post office

Post offices (郵便局 [yûbinkyoku]) can be recognised by the symbol 〒, and are open Monday through Friday from 9 a.m. to 5 p.m. Mailboxes are red, and those marked (手紙/はがき [tegami/hagaki]) are for regular mail and domestic deliveries, while those marked (その他の郵便 [sono ta no yûbin]) are for international and urgent mail.

portable ポータブルの [pôtaburu no]
▸ do you have a portable heater we could borrow? ポータブルヒーターを貸してもらえませんか [pôtaburu hîtâ o kashite moraemasen ka]

portion 一人分の分量 [hitori bun no bunryô]
▸ the portions at that restaurant are just right あのレストランの食事の分量はちょうどいいです [ano resutoran no shokuji no bunryô wa chôdo î desu]

possible できる [dekiru]
▸ without sauce, if possible できればソースなしで [dekireba sôsu nashi de]

postcard はがき [hagaki]; *(with picture)* 絵はがき [ehagaki]
▸ where can I buy postcards? 絵はがきはどこで買えますか [ehagaki wa doko de kaemasu ka]
▸ how much are stamps for postcards to the States? アメリカへのはがきはいくらの切手がいりますか [amerika e no hagaki wa ikura no kitte ga irimasu ka]

post office 郵便局 [yûbinkyoku]
▸ where is the nearest post office? 一番近い郵便局はどこですか [ichiban chikai yûbinkyoku wa doko desu ka]

power *(electricity)* 電気 [denki]
▸ there's no power 電気が来ていません [denki ga kite imasen]

power failure 停電 [têden]
▸ there's a power failure 停電です [têden desu]
▸ how long is the power failure expected to last? どれぐらい停電は続きますか [dore gurai têden wa tsuzukimasu ka]

prawn えび [ebi]
▸ I'd like to try a dish with shrimp or prawns えびの入った料理を食べてみたいんですが [ebi no haitta ryôri o tabete mitai n desu ga]

prefer ほうがいい [...hô ga î]
▸ I'd prefer black tea ミルクなしの紅茶のほうがいいです [miruku nashi no kôcha no hô ga î desu]
▸ I'd prefer you not smoke タバコを吸わないでくれたほうがいいです [tabako o suwanaide kureta hô ga î desu]; see box on p. 118

prescription *(medicine)* 処方箋 [shohôsen]
- is it only available by prescription? 処方箋がないと買えませんか [shohôsen ga nai to kaemasen ka]

present プレゼント [purezento]
- where can we buy presents around here? この辺でプレゼントが買えるところはどこですか [kono hen de purezento ga kaeru tokoro wa doko desu ka]

pretty きれいな [kirê na]
- she's a very pretty girl とてもきれいな女の子ですね [totemo kirê na onna no ko desu ne]

price *(cost)* 値段 [nedan]
- what's the price of gas just now? 今、ガソリンの値段はいくらですか [ima gasorin no nedan wa ikura desu ka]
- if the price is right もし値段が合えば [moshi nedan ga aeba]

price list 値段表 [nedan hyô]
- do you have a price list? 値段表はありますか [nedan hyô wa arimasu ka]

print *(photograph)* 焼付け [yakitsuke]
- could I have another set of prints? もう一組写真を焼いてほしいんですが [mô hito kumi shashin o yaite hoshî n desu ga]

problem 問題 [mondai]
- there's a problem with the heating 暖房に問題があります [dambô ni mondai ga arimasu]
- no problem 大丈夫です [daijôbu desu]

program *(for an event)* プログラム [puroguramu]; *(TV, radio)* 番組 [bangumi]
- could I see a program? プログラムを見せてもらえませんか [puroguramu o misete moraemasen ka]

pronounce *(word)* 発音する [hatsuon suru]
- how is that pronounced? どう発音しますか [dô hatsuon shimasu ka]

---

expressing a preference

- I prefer red wine to white wine 白ワインより赤のほうがいいです [shiro wain yori aka no hô ga î desu]
- I'd rather fly than go by train 列車で行くより飛行機のほうがいいです [ressha de iku yori hikôki no hô ga î desu]
- Saturday would suit me better 土曜日のほうが都合がいいです [doyôbi no hô ga tsugô ga î desu]

public *(state)* 公立の [kôritsu no]; *(open to all)* 公開の [kôkai no] ◆ 人々 [hitobito]

▸ let's go somewhere less public どこか静かなところに行きましょう [doko ka shizuka na tokoro ni ikimashô]

▸ is the temple open to the public? このお寺は一般に公開されていますか [kono otera wa ippan ni kôkai sarete imasu ka]

public holiday 祝日 [shukujitsu]

▸ is tomorrow a public holiday? 明日は祝日ですか [ashita wa shukujitsu desu ka]

public transportation 公共交通機関 [kôkyô kôtsû kikan]

▸ can you get there by public transportation? そこに公共交通機関を使って行けますか [soko ni kôkyô kôtsû kikan o tsukatte ikemasu ka]

pull *(opposite of push)* 引く [hiku]; *(muscle)* 痛める [itameru]; *(tooth)* 抜く [nuku]

▸ I've pulled a muscle 筋肉を痛めました [kinniku o itamemashita]

puncture パンク [panku]

▸ we've got a puncture パンクしました [panku shimashita]

purpose 目的 [mokuteki] ◆ **on purpose** わざと [waza to]

▸ sorry, I didn't do it on purpose すみません、わざとやったわけじゃありません [sumimasen, waza to yatta wake ja arimasen]

purse *(handbag)* ハンドバッグ [handobaggu]; *(change purse)* 財布 [saifu]

▸ my purse was stolen ハンドバッグを盗まれました [handobaggu o nusumaremashita]

push 押す [osu]

▸ can you help us push the car? 車を押すのを手伝ってもらえますか [kuruma o osu no o tetsudatte moraemasu ka]

put *(into place, position)* 置く [oku]

▸ is there somewhere I can put my bags? どこか荷物を置けるところはありますか [doko ka nimotsu o okeru tokoro wa arimasu ka]

put down *(set down)* 置く [oku]

▸ can we put our things down in the corner? その隅に物を置いてもいいですか [sono sumi ni mono o oite mo î desu ka]

put on *(clothes)* 着る [kiru]; *(TV, radio, heating)* つける [tsukeru]; *(on telephone)* つなぐ [tsunagu]

▸ can you put the heat on? 暖房をつけてもらえますか [dambo o tsukete moraemasu ka]

▸ can you put Mrs. Martin on, please? マーティンさんにつないでもらえますか [mâtin san ni tsunaide moraemasu ka]

put out (cigarette, fire) 消す [kesu]

▸ can you please put your cigarette out? すみませんが、タバコを消して
もらえますか [sumimasen ga, tabako o keshite moraemasu ka]

put up (erect) たてる [tateru]; (provide accommodation for) 泊める [tomeru]

▸ can we put up our tent here? ここにテントを張ってもいいですか [koko
ni tento o hatte mo î desu ka]

q

quarter (fourth) 四分の一 [yom bun no ichi]

▸ I'll be back in a quarter of an hour １５分で戻って来ます [jûgo fun de
modotte kimasu]

▸ a quarter past/after one １時１５分 [ichi ji jûgo fun]

▸ a quarter to/of one １２時４５分 [jûni ji yonjûgo fun]

quay 波止場 [hatoba]

▸ is the boat at the quay? 船は波止場にありますか [fune wa hatoba ni arimasu
ka]

question 質問 [shitsumon]

▸ can I ask you a question? 質問してもいいですか [shitsumon shite mo î desu
ka]

quickly 速く [hayaku]

▸ everyone speaks so quickly みんなすごく速く話します [minna sugoku
hayaku hanashimasu]

quiet 静かな [shizuka na]

▸ is it a quiet beach? 静かな浜辺ですか [shizuka na hamabe desu ka]

▸ do you have a quieter room? もっと静かな部屋はありますか [motto
shizuka na heya wa arimasu ka]

quite (rather) かなり [kanari]

▸ it's quite expensive around here この辺はかなり高いです [kono hen wa
kanari takai desu]

r

racket *(for tennis)* ラケット [raketto]
  ▸ can you rent rackets? ラケットを貸しますか [raketto o kashimasu ka]

radiator *(car)* ラジエーター [rajiêtâ]
  ▸ the radiator's leaking ラジエーターが漏れています [rajiêtâ ga morete imasu]

radio *(set)* ラジオ [rajio]
  ▸ the radio doesn't work ラジオが壊れています [rajio ga kowarete imasu]

radio station ラジオ局 [rajio kyoku]
  ▸ can you get any English-language radio stations here? ここで英語のラジオ局は聞けますか [koko de êgo no rajio kyoku wa kikemasu ka]

railroad *(system)* 鉄道 [tetsudô]; *(organization)* 鉄道会社 [tetsudô gaisha]; *(track)* 線路 [senro]
  ▸ what region does this railroad cover? この鉄道会社はどの地域を走っていますか [kono tetsudô gaisha wa dono chi-iki o hashitte imasu ka]

rain 雨 [ame]
  ▸ it's raining 雨です [ame desu]

random
  ▸ at random でたらめに [detarame ni]

rare *(meat)* レア [rea]; *(unusual)* 珍しい [mezurashî]
  ▸ rare, please レアでお願いします [rea de onegai shimasu]

rate *(price)* 料金 [ryôkin]
  ▸ what's your daily rate? 一日の料金はいくらですか [ichi nichi no ryôkin wa ikura desu ka]

rate of exchange 両替率 [ryôgae ritsu]
  ▸ they offer a good rate of exchange 両替率がいいです [ryôgae ritsu ga î desu]

razor *(for wet shaving)* かみそり [kamisori]; *(electric)* 電気かみそり [denki kamisori]
  ▸ where can I buy a new razor? かみそりはどこで買えますか [kamisori wa doko de kaemasu ka]

razor blade かみそりの刃 [kamisori no ha]
  ▸ I need to buy some razor blades かみそりの刃を買わなければなりません [kamisori no ha o kawanakereba narimasen]

red and white

Red and white together symbolize happiness and celebration, as in the decorated envelopes used to give money at weddings and other happy occasions.

read 読む [yomu]
- ▸ I enjoy reading 本を読むのが好きです [hon o yomu no ga suki desu]
- ▸ I read about it in the guidebook それについてガイドブックで読みました [sore ni tsuite gaidobukku de yomimashita]

ready *(prepared)* 準備のできた [jumbi no dekita]; *(willing)* 喜んでする [yorokonde suru]
- ▸ when will it be ready? いつできますか [itsu dekimasu ka]

really *(actually)* 本当に [hontô ni]; *(very)* とても [totemo]
- ▸ really? 本当？ [hontô]

rear *(of a train)* 後ろ [ushiro]
- ▸ your seats are in the rear of the train 席は列車の後ろのほうです [seki wa ressha no ushiro no hô desu]

rec center, recreation center レクリエーションセンター [rekuriêshon sentâ]
- ▸ what kinds of activities does the recreation center offer? レクリエーションセンターではどんなことができますか [rekuriêshon sentâ de wa donna koto ga dekimasu ka]

receipt レシート [reshîto], 領収書 [ryôshûsho]
- ▸ can I have a receipt, please? 領収書をください [ryôshûsho o kudasai]

receive *(package, letter)* 受け取る [uketoru]
- ▸ I should have received the package this morning 今朝、小包を受け取るはずだったんですが [kesa kozutsumi o uketoru hazu datta n desu ga]

reception *(of company, hospital)* 受付 [uketsuke]; *(party)* 宴会 [enkai]; *(for TV, radio, cell phone)* 受信状態 [jushin jôtai]
- ▸ there's no reception 受信できません [jushin dekimasen]
- ▸ I'm looking for the Mackenzie wedding reception マッケンジー家の披露宴の会場を探しています [makkenjî ke no hirôen no kaijô o sagashite imasu]

reception desk *(at hotel)* フロント [furonto]
- ▸ can I leave my backpack at the reception desk? バックパックをフロントに預けられますか [bakkupakku o furonto ni azukeraremasu ka]

recline 倒す [taosu]
- ▸ do you mind if I recline my seat? 椅子を倒してもかまいませんか [isu o taoshite mo kamaimasen ka]

recommend 推薦する [suisen suru], 勧める [susumeru]
- could you recommend another hotel? 別のホテルを推薦してくれません
  か [betsu no hoteru o suisen shite kuremasen ka]
- could you recommend a restaurant? レストランを推薦してくれません
  か [resutoran o suisen shite kuremasen ka]
- what do you recommend? 何がお勧めですか [nani ga osusume desu ka]

record store レコード屋 [rekôdo ya]
- I'm looking for a record store レコード屋を探しています [rekôdo ya o
  sagashite imasu]

red (dress, hair) 赤い [akai] ◆ (color, wine) 赤 [aka]
- dressed in red 赤い服を着て [akai fuku o kite]
- what kinds of red wine do you have? 赤ワインはどんなものがあります
  か [aka wain wa donna mono ga arimasu ka]

redhead 赤毛の人 [akage no hito]
- a tall redhead wearing glasses メガネをかけて背の高い赤毛の人
  [megane o kakete se no takai akage no hito]

red light 赤信号 [aka shingô]
- you failed to stop at a red light 赤信号で止まりませんでした [aka shingô
  de tomarimasen deshita]

reduced (price, rate) 割引した [waribiki shita]
- is there a reduced rate for students? 学生割引はありますか [gakusê
  waribiki wa arimasu ka]

reduced-price (ticket) 割引の [waribiki no]
- two reduced-price tickets and one full-price 割引チケットを２枚と正規
  料金１枚 [waribiki chiketto o ni mai to sêki ryôkin ichi mai]

reduction 割引 [waribiki]
- do you have reductions for groups? 団体割引はありますか [dantai waribiki
  wa arimasu ka]

red wine 赤ワイン [aka wain]
- a bottle of red wine 赤ワイン一本 [aka wain ippon]

refund 払い戻し [haraimodoshi]
- this skirt has a stain; can you give me a refund? このスカートはしみがつ
  いています。払い戻してもらえますか [kono sukâto wa shimi ga tsuite
  imasu. haraimodoshite moraemasu ka]

refundable 払い戻しのきく [haraimodoshi no kiku]
- are the tickets refundable? チケットは払い戻しがききますか [chiketto wa
  haraimodoshi ga kikimasu ka]

regard (respect) 敬意 [kêi]; (greeting) よろしく [yoroshiku] ◆ **with regard
to** ...に関して... [ni kanshite]

▸ give my regards to your parents! ご両親によろしくお伝えください
[goryôshin ni yoroshiku otsutae kudasai]

▸ I'm calling you with regard to... ...に関して電話をしています [...ni kanshite
denwa o shite imasu]

region 地方 [chihô]

▸ in the North East region of Japan 日本の東北地方に [nihon no tôhoku chihô
ni]

registered mail 書留 [kakitome]

▸ I would like to send a letter by registered mail 書留で送りたいんですが
[kakitome de okuritai n desu ga]

registration (of car) ナンバープレートの番号 [nambâ purêto no bangô]

▸ here's the car's registration これがナンバープレートの番号です [kore ga
nambâ purêto no bangô desu]

relative 親戚 [shinseki]

▸ I have relatives in Osaka 大阪に親戚がいます [ôsaka ni shinseki ga imasu]

remember (know) 覚えている [oboete iru]; (recall) 思い出す [omoidasu]

▸ do you remember me? わたしのことを覚えていますか [watashi no koto o
oboete imasu ka]

▸ I can't remember his name 名前が思い出せません [namae ga omoidasemasen]

remote (control) リモコン [rimokon]

▸ I can't find the remote for the TV テレビのリモコンが見つかりません
[terebi no rimokon ga mitsukarimasen]

rent 使用料 [shiyô ryô]; (for house) 家賃 [yachin] ◆ 借りる [kariru]

▸ how much is the rent per week? 一週間の使用料はいくらですか
[isshûkan no shiyô ryô wa ikura desu ka]

▸ I'd like to rent a car for a week 車を一週間借りたいんですが [kuruma o
isshûkan karitai n desu ga]

▸ I'd like to rent a boat ボートを借りたいんですが [bôto o karitai n desu ga]

▸ does it work out cheaper to rent the equipment by the week? 道具は週単
位で借りたほうが安いですか [dôgu wa shû tan'i de karita hô ga yasui desu ka]

rental (renting, apartment, house) 賃貸 [chintai]; (equipment, car) レンタル
[rentaru]

▸ we have the rental for two weeks 二週間借りています [ni shûkan karite
imasu]

repair 修理 [shûri] ◆ 修理する [shûri suru]

▸ will you be able to make the repairs today? 今日、修理できますか [kyô
shûri dekimasu ka]

▸ how long will it take to repair? 修理するのにどれぐらい時間がかかりま
すか [shûri suru no ni dore gurai jikan ga kakarimasu ka]

restaurants

Japanese people enjoy eating out and there is a vast range of places to eat, from cheap family noodle-shops, found almost everywhere, to high-class expensive restaurants serving exquisitely presented traditional formal cuisine. As well as McDonalds® and Japanese fast-food chains, Chinese and Italian food is also very popular, and Korean food is currently enjoying a boom. You can find cuisine from almost anywhere in the world somewhere in Tokyo.

repeat 繰り返す [kurikaesu]

▸ can you repeat that, please? 繰り返してもらえますか [kurikaeshite moraemasu ka]

report *(theft)* 届け出る [todokederu]

▸ I'd like to report something stolen 盗難を届け出たいんですが [tônan o todokodetai n desu ga]

▸ I'd like to report the loss of my credit cards クレジットカードの紛失を届け出たいんですが [kurejitto kâdo no funshitsu o todokedetai n desu ga]

reservation 予約 [yoyaku]

▸ do you have to make a reservation? 予約が必要ですか [yoyaku ga hitsuyô desu ka]

▸ I have a reservation in the name of Jones ジョーンズの名前で予約してあります [jônzu no namae de yoyaku shite arimasu]

reserve *(ticket, room)* 予約する [yoyaku suru]

▸ (on phone) hello, I'd like to reserve a table for two for tomorrow night at 8 もしもし、明日の夜8時に二人分のテーブルを予約したいんですが [moshimoshi, ashita no yoru hachi ji ni futari bun no têburu o yoyaku shitai n desu ga]

at the restaurant

▸ I'd like to reserve a table for tonight 今夜の予約をしたいんですが [kon ya no yoyaku o shitai n desu ga]

▸ can we see the menu? メニューを見せてもらえますか [menyû o misete moraemasu ka]

▸ do you have a set menu? セットメニューはありますか [setto menyû wa arimasu ka]

▸ rare/medium/well done, please レア/ミディアム/ウェルダンでお願いします [rea/midiamu/werudan de onegai shimasu]

▸ can I have the check, please? お勘定、お願いします [okanjô onegai shimasu]

rice

Rice is the staple food in Japan. You will be served a bowl of rice with every meal, except for noodle dishes. The rice is white and quite sticky, so relatively easy to pick up with chopsticks. You can also find it pressed into triangular shapes (おにぎり [onigiri]), often wrapped in 海苔 [nori] seaweed, or in 寿司 [sushi]. The suffix 丼 [don] at the end of the name of a dish means that it will be served on a bowl of plain white rice.

reserved *(booked)* 予約された [yoyaku sareta]
  ▸ is this table reserved? このテーブルは予約席ですか [kono têburu wa yoyaku seki desu ka]

rest *(relaxation)* 休息 [kyûsoku] ◆ *(relax)* 休む [yasumu]
  ▸ I've come here to get some rest 休息を取るためにここに来ました [kyûsoku o toru tame ni koko ni kimashita]

restaurant レストラン [resutoran]
  ▸ are there any good restaurants around here? この辺にいいレストランは ありますか [kono hen ni î resutoran wa arimasu ka]; see boxes on p. 125

restriction 制限 [sêgen]
  ▸ are there restrictions on how much luggage you can take? 荷物の制限はあ りますか [nimotsu no sêgen wa arimasu ka]

restroom トイレ [toire], お手洗い [otearai]
  ▸ is there a restroom on the bus? バスにトイレはついていますか [basu ni toire wa tsuite imasu ka]

retired 退職した [taishoku shita]
  ▸ I'm retired now 退職しました [taishoku shimashita]

return *(arrival back)* 帰り [kaeri] ◆ *(go back)* 戻る [modoru]; *(home)* 帰る [kaeru] ◆ *(rental car)* 返す [kaesu]
  ▸ when do we have to return the car? 車はいつ返さなければなりませんか [kuruma wa itsu kaesanakereba narimasen ka]

return trip 帰り [kaeri]
  ▸ the return trip is scheduled for 6 o'clock 帰りは6時に出発の予定です [kaeri wa roku ji ni shuppatsu no yotê desu]

rice *(uncooked)* 米 [kome]; *(cooked)* ご飯 [gohan]
  ▸ I'd like steamed/boiled rice, please ご飯をお願いします [gohan o onegai shimasu]

ride *(trip in a car)* ドライブ [doraibu]; *(lift, on a bike, motorcycle)* 乗ること [noru koto]

▸ do you want a ride? 車で送りましょうか [kuruma de okurimashô ka]

▸ where can we go for a ride around here? このあたりではどこへドライブ に行ったらいいでしょうか [kono atari de wa doko e doraibu ni ittara î deshô ka]

riding (on horseback) 乗馬 [jôba]

▸ to go riding 乗馬をする [jôba o suru]

right (correct) 正しい [tadashî]; (not left) 右の [migi no] ◆ 右 [migi] ◆ 正しく [tadashiku]

▸ to the right (of) の右側に [...no migi gawa ni]

▸ that's right そうです [sô desu]

▸ I don't think the check's right 勘定が正しくないと思うんですが [kanjô ga tadashiku nai to omou n desu ga]

▸ is this the right train for Kyoto? 京都行きはこの列車でいいですか [kyôto yuki wa kono ressha de î desu ka]

▸ is this the right number? この番号は正しいですか [kono bangô wa tadashî desu ka]

▸ take the next right 次を右です [tsugi o migi desu]

▸ you have to turn right 右に曲がりなさい [migi ni magarinasai]

right-hand 右側の [migi gawa no]

▸ it's on the right-hand side of the steering column ハンドルの付け根の右 にあります [handoru no tsukene no migi ni arimasu]

right of way 通行優先 [tsûkô yûsen]

▸ who has the right of way here? どちらが通行優先ですか [dochira ga tsûkô yûsen desu ka]

road 道路 [dôro]

▸ which road do I take for Nara? 奈良へはどの道路を行ったらいいですか [nara e wa dono dôro o ittara î desu ka]

▸ what is the speed limit on this road? この道路の制限速度は何キロです か [kono dôro no sêgen sokudo wa nan kiro desu ka]

rob (person) 物を盗む [mono o nusumu]

▸ I've been robbed 物を盗まれました [mono o nusumaremashita]

rock climbing ロッククライミング [rokku kuraimingu]

▸ can you go rock climbing here? ここでロッククライミングはできます か [koko de rokku kuraimingu wa dekimasu ka]

roller skate ローラースケートの靴 [rôrâ sukêto no kutsu]

▸ where can we rent roller skates? ローラースケートの靴はどこで借りら れますか [rôrâ sukêto no kutsu wa doko de kariraremasu ka]

room (bedroom) 部屋 [heya]; (space) 空間 [kûkan]

▸ do you have any rooms available? 空室はありますか [kûshitsu wa arimasu ka]

- how much is a room with a bathroom? 風呂付きの部屋はいくらですか [furo tsuki no heya wa ikura desu ka]
- I've reserved a room for tonight under the name Pearson ピアソンの名前で今夜、部屋を予約してあります [piason no namae de kon ya heya o yoyaku shite arimasu]
- can I see the room? 部屋を見せてもらえますか [heya o misete moraemasu ka]

rosé *(wine)* ロゼの [roze no] ◆ ロゼ [roze]
- could you recommend a good rosé? いいロゼワインを推薦してくれませんか [i roze wain o suisen shite kuremasen ka]

round trip 往復 [ôfuku]
- how long will the round trip take? 往復でどれぐらい時間がかかりますか [ôfuku de dore gurai jikan ga kakarimasu ka]

route *(itinerary)* 道 [michi]
- is there an alternative route we could take? 代わりに通れる道はありますか [kawari ni tôreru michi wa arimasu ka]

row *(of seats)* 列 [retsu]
- can we have seats in the front row? 最前列の席をもらえますか [saizen retsu no seki o moraemasu ka]

rowboat ボート [bôto]
- can we rent a rowboat? ボートを借りられますか [bôto o kariraremasu ka]

rubber ring 輪ゴム [wa gomu]
- where can I buy a rubber ring? 輪ゴムはどこで買えますか [wa gomu wa doko de kaemasu ka]

run 走り [hashiri]; *(for skiing)* すべり [suberi] ◆ *(on foot)* 走る [hashiru]; *(bus, train)* 運行する [unkô suru]; *(engine)* 動く [ugoku] ◆ *(traffic light)* 無視する [mushi suru]
- I'm going for a run 走りに行くつもりです [hashiri ni iku tsumori desu]
- the bus runs every half hour バスは３０分ごとに運行しています [basu wa sanjippun goto ni unkô shite imasu]

running ランニング [ranningu]
- where can you go running here? どこでランニングができますか [doko de ranningu ga dekimasu ka]

run out of 切らす [kirasu]
- I've run out of gas ガソリンが切れてしまいました [gasorin ga kirete shimaimashita]

s

safe 安全な [anzen na] ◆ *(for valuables)* 金庫 [kinko]
▸ is it safe to swim here? ここで泳いでも安全ですか [koko de oyoide mo anzen desu ka]
▸ is it safe to camp here? ここでキャンプしても安全ですか [koko de kyampu shite mo anzen desu ka]
▸ can I leave this in the safe? これを金庫に預けられますか [kore o kinko ni azukeraremasu ka]

sail *(of a boat)* 帆 [ho]
▸ we need to adjust that sail 帆を調節しなければなりません [ho o chôsetsu shinakereba narimasen]

sailboat ヨット [yotto]
▸ can we rent a sailboat? ヨットを借りられますか [yotto o kariraremasu ka]

sailing ヨット [yotto]
▸ to go sailing ヨットに乗る [yotto ni noru]
▸ I'd like to take beginners' sailing classes ヨットの初心者コースを取りたいんですが [yotto no shoshinsha kôsu o toritai n desu ga]

salad サラダ [sarada]
▸ can I just have a salad? サラダだけもらえますか [sarada dake moraemasu ka]

sale *(selling)* 販売 [hambai]; *(at reduced prices)* セール [sêru]
▸ is it for sale? これは売り物ですか [kore wa urimono desu ka]
▸ can you get your money back on sale items? セール商品の払い戻しはできますか [sêru shôhin no haraimodoshi wa dekimasu ka]

sales tax 消費税 [shôhizê]
▸ is sales tax included? 消費税は含まれていますか [shôhizê wa fukumarete imasu ka]
▸ can you deduct the sales tax? 消費税の分を引いてくれませんか [shôhizê no bun o hîte kuremasen ka]

salt 塩 [shio] ◆ 塩をかける [shio o kakeru]
▸ can you pass me the salt? 塩をまわしてくれますか [shio o mawashite kuremasu ka]
▸ it doesn't have enough salt 塩が足りません [shio ga tarimasen]

salty 塩辛い [shiokarai]
▸ it's too salty 塩辛すぎます [shiokarasugimasu]

same 同じ [onaji]
- I'll have the same 同じものにします [onaji mono ni shimasu]
- the same (as) と同じ [...to onaji]
- it's the same as yours あなたのものと同じです [anata no mono to onaji desu]

sandwich サンド(イッチ) [sando(itchi)]
- a chicken sandwich, please チキンサンドをください [chikin sando o kudasai]

Saturday 土曜日 [doyôbi]
- Saturday, September 13th 9月13日、土曜日 [kugatsu jûsan nichi doyôbi]
- it's closed on Saturdays 土曜日は閉まります [doyôbi wa shimarimasu]

sauce ソース [sôsu]
- what kind of sauce is this? これは何のソースですか [kore wa nan no sôsu desu ka]

sauna サウナ [sauna]
- is there a sauna? サウナはありますか [sauna wa arimasu ka]

say 言う [yû]
- how do you say 'good luck' in Japanese? good luckは日本語で何と言いますか [good luck wa nihongo de nan to îmasu ka]

scared
- to be scared 怖い [kowai]
- I'm scared of spiders くもが怖いです [kumo ga kowai desu]

scheduled flight 定期便 [têki bin]
- when is the next scheduled flight to Sapporo? 次の札幌行きの定期便はいつですか [tsugi no sapporo yuki no têki bin wa itsu desu ka]

school *(for children)* 学校 [gakkô]; *(college, university)* 大学 [daigaku]
- are you still in school? まだ学生ですか [mada gakusê desu ka]

scooter スクーター [sukûtâ]
- I'd like to rent a scooter スクーターを借りたいんですが [sukûtâ o karitai n desu ga]

Scotch *(whiskey)* スコッチ [sukotchi]
- a Scotch on the rocks, please スコッチのオンザロックをお願いします [sukotchi no on za rokku o onegai shimasu]

Scotch tape® セロテープ [serotêpu]
- do you have any Scotch tape®? セロテープはありますか [serotêpu wa arimasu ka]

scrambled eggs スクランブルエッグ [sukuramburu eggu]
- I'd like scrambled eggs for breakfast 朝食にスクランブルエッグがほしいんですが [chôshoku ni sukuramburu eggu ga hoshî n de gasu]

seasons

Japan prides itself on having four seasons, and dressing and behaving appropriately to each of them is important. As well as spring, summer, fall and winter, there is a rainy season (梅雨 [tsuyu]), which lasts from around early June through mid-July over most of Japan, except for Hokkaido.

screen *(room in a movie theater)* スクリーン [sukurîn]
▸ how many screens does the movie theater have? 映画館にはスクリーンがいくつありますか [êgakan ni wa sukurîn ga ikutsu arimasu ka]

scuba diving スキューバダイビング [sukyûba daibingu]
▸ can we go scuba diving? スキューバダイビングはできますか [sukyûba daibingu wa dekimasu ka]

sea 海 [umi]
▸ the sea is rough 海は荒れています [umi wa arete imasu]
▸ how long does it take to walk to the sea? 海まで歩いてどれぐらいかかりますか [umi made aruite dore gurai kakarimasu ka]

seasick 船酔いの [funayoi no]
▸ I feel seasick 船に酔いました [fune ni yoimashita]

seasickness 船酔い [funayoi]
▸ can you give me something for seasickness, please? 船酔いに効くものをください [funayoi ni kiku mono o kudasai]

seaside resort 海辺のリゾート地 [umibe no rizôto chi]
▸ what's the nearest seaside resort? 一番近い海辺のリゾート地はどこですか [ichiban chikai umibe no rizôto chi wa doko desu ka]

season *(of the year)* 季節 [kisetsu]
▸ what is the best season to come here? ここに来る一番いい季節はいつですか [koko ni kuru ichiban î kisetsu wa itsu desu ka]

season ticket 定期(券) [têki(ken)]
▸ how much is a season ticket? 定期はいくらですか [têki wa ikura desu ka]

seat 席 [seki]
▸ is this seat taken? この席は誰か座っていますか [kono seki wa dare ka suwatte imasu ka]
▸ excuse me, I think you're (sitting) in my seat すみません、そこは私の席なんですが [sumimasen, soko wa watashi no seki na n desu ga]

seaweed 海草 [kaisô]
▸ how can I cook this seaweed? この海草はどうやって料理したらいいですか [kono kaisô wa dô yatte ryôri shitara î desu ka]; see box on p. 132

seaweed

Seaweed is a very common food, rich in minerals, and each variety is used in different ways. のり [nori] is usually used in dried sheets to wrap sushi or shredded on top of rice dishes; わかめ [wakame] is mainly used in miso soup, stews, or served with ラーメン [râmen] (Chinese noodles); and 昆布 [kombu] is used to make stock, together with bonito fish flakes.

second *(unit of time)* 秒 [byô]; *(gear)* 二速 [ni soku] ◆ 二番目の [ni bam me no]
▸ wait a second! ちょっと待ってください [chotto matte kudasai]
▸ is it in second? ２速ですか [ni soku desu ka]
▸ it's the second street on your right 右側の二番目の通りです [migi gawa no ni bam me no tôri desu]

see *(to meet)* 会う [au]; *(to look)* 見る [miru]
▸ I'm here to see Dr. Brown ブラウン先生に会いに来ました [buraun sensê ni ai ni kimashita]
▸ can I see the room? 部屋を見てもいいですか [heya o mite mo î desu ka]
▸ I'd like to see the dress in the window ショーウィンドーのワンピースを見たいんですが [shô windô no wanpîsu o mitai n desu ga]
▸ see you! じゃ、また [ja mata]
▸ see you later また後で [mata ato de]
▸ see you (on) Thursday! 木曜日に会いましょう [mokuyôbi ni aimashô]

self-service *(restaurant)* セルフサービスの [serufu sâbisu no] ◆ セルフサービス [serufu sâbisu]
▸ is it self-service? セルフサービスですか [serufu sâbisu desu ka]

sell 売る [uru]
▸ do you sell stamps? 切手は売っていますか [kitte wa utte imasu ka]
▸ the radio I was sold is defective 買ったラジオは不良品でした [katta rajio wa furyôhin deshita]

send 送る [okuru]
▸ I'd like to send this package to Boston by airmail この小包をボストンに航空便で送りたいんですが [kono kozutsumi o bosuton ni kôkûbin de okuritai n desu ga]
▸ could you send a tow truck? 牽引車を送ってくれませんか [ken'insha o okutte kuremasen ka]

separately *(individually)* 別々に [betsubetsu ni]
▸ is it sold separately? 別々に売っていますか [betsubetsu ni utte imasu ka]

September 九月 [kugatsu]
▸ September 9th ９月９日 [kugatsu kokonoka]

---

customer service

Customer service is highly valued in Japan, and staff in stores, restaurants, hotels, banks etc. will go to great lengths to ensure the customer is happy. You will hear the word いらっしゃいませ [irasshaimase] (welcome! can I help you?) constantly, and department stores are full of smartly uniformed staff, including an information desk at the main entrance and elevator ladies.

---

serve *(meal, drink)* 出す [dasu]; *(town, station)* 受け持つ [ukemotsu]
- when is breakfast served? 朝食は何時からですか [chôshoku wa nan ji kara desu ka]
- are you still serving lunch? 昼食はまだ出していますか [chûshoku wa mada dashite imasu ka]
- does the train company serve the Kansai area? その鉄道会社は関西地方を受け持っていますか [sono tetsudô gaisha wa kansai chihô o ukemotte imasu ka]

service *(in a restaurant)* 接客 [sekkyaku] ◆ *(car)* 点検 [tenken]
- the service was terrible 接客態度がひどかったです [sekkyaku taido ga hidokatta desu]
- we have to have the car serviced 車を点検に出さなければなりません [kuruma o tenken ni dasanakereba narimasen]

service charge サービス料 [sâbisu ryô]
- is the service charge included? サービス料は含まれていますか [sâbisu ryô wa fukumarete imasu ka]

set *(of plates)* セット [setto] ◆ *(sun)* 沈む [shizumu]
- do you have a spare set of keys? 予備の鍵のセットはありますか [yobi no kagi no setto wa arimasu ka]
- what time does the sun set? 何時に日が沈みますか [nan ji ni hi ga shizumimasu ka]

seven 七 [shichi/nana]
- there are seven of us 全部で七人です [zembu de nana nin desu]

several いくつかの [ikutsu ka no] ◆ いくつか [ikutsu ka]
- I've been before, several years ago 何年か前に行ったことがあります [nan nen ka mae ni itta koto ga arimasu]

shade *(shadow)* 影 [kage]
- can we have a table in the shade? 影になっているところのテーブルをお願いできますか [kage ni natte iru tokoro no têburu o onegai dekimasu ka]

shake *(bottle)* 振る [furu] ◆ *(in agreement)* 同意する [dôi suru]
- to shake hands 握手する [akushu suru]

shoes

Japanese distinguish very clearly between inside and outside, and shoes are never worn in the house. There is always a step, even if only a very shallow one, in the entrance (玄関 [genkan]), and this is where you take your shoes off. You will be given slippers to wear on wooden or carpeted floors, but even these need to be removed before walking on 畳 [tatami] matted floors. There may also be special plastic slippers to wear in the bathroom (toilet). You may need to take your shoes off to go inside temples and shrines.

shame *(remorse, humiliation)* 恥 [haji]; *(pity)* 残念なこと [zannen na koto]
  ▸ (what a) shame! 残念ですね [zannen desu ne]

shampoo シャンプー [shampû]
  ▸ do you have any shampoo? シャンプーはありますか [shampû wa arimasu ka]

share 分ける [wakeru]
  ▸ we're going to share it: can you bring us two plates? 分けるので、皿を二枚もらえますか [wakeru node, sara o ni mai moraemasu ka]

shared *(bathroom, kitchen)* 共用の [kyôyô no]
  ▸ is the bathroom shared? トイレは共用ですか [toire wa kyôyô desu ka]

shaver 電気かみそり [denki kamisori]
  ▸ where can I buy a new shaver? 電気かみそりはどこで買えますか [denki kamisori wa doko de kaemasu ka]

sheet *(for a bed)* シーツ [shîtsu]; *(of paper)* 紙 [kami]
  ▸ could you change the sheets? シーツを換えてくれませんか [shîtsu o kaete kuremasen ka]

ship 船 [fune]
  ▸ when does the ship dock? いつ船は港に着きますか [itsu fune wa minato ni tsukimasu ka]

shoe 靴 [kutsu]
  ▸ what sort of shoes should you wear? どんな靴を履いたらいいですか [donna kutsu o haitara î desu ka]

shoe size 靴のサイズ [kutsu no saizu]
  ▸ what's your shoe size? 靴のサイズはいくつですか [kutsu no saizu wa ikutsu desu ka]

shop *(store)* 店 [mise]
  ▸ what time do the shops downtown close? 町の店は何時に閉まりますか [machi no mise wa nan ji ni shimarimasu ka]

shopping 買い物 [kaimono]
- where can you go shopping around here? この辺で買い物に行けるところはどこですか [kono hen de kaimono ni ikeru tokoro wa doko desu ka]

shopping bag (plastic) ビニール袋 [binîru bukuro]
- can I have a shopping bag, please? ビニール袋をもらえますか [binîru bukuro o moraemasu ka]

shopping center ショッピングセンター [shoppingu sentâ]
- I'm looking for a shopping center ショッピングセンターを探しています [shoppingu sentâ o sagashite imasu]

shop window ショーウィンドー [shô windô]
- we've been looking in the shop windows ショーウィンドーを見ています [shô windô o mite imasu]

short (time, in length) 短い [mijikai]; (in height) 背が低い [se ga hikui]; (of funds) 足りない [tarinai]
- we're only here for a short time ここには短い間いるだけです [koko ni wa mijikai aida iru dake desu]
- we'd like to do a shorter trip もっと短い旅行のほうがいいんですが [motto mijikai ryokô no hô ga î n desu ga]
- I'm 200 yen short ２００円足りません [nihyaku en tarimasen]

shortcut 近道 [chikamichi]
- is there a shortcut? 近道はありますか [chikamichi wa arimasu ka]

short wave 短波 [tampa]
- can you get any English stations on short wave? 短波放送で英語の局は聞けますか [tampa hôsô de êgo no kyoku wa kikemasu ka]

should べき [...beki]
- you should go to hospital 病院に行くべきです [byôin ni iku beki desu]

show (at the theater) ショー [shô]; (at the movies) 映画 [êga]; (on TV) テレビ番組 [terebi bangumi] ◆ (let see) 見せる [miseru]
- what time does the show begin? ショーは何時に始まりますか [shô wa nan ji ni hajimarimasu ka]
- could you show me where that is on the map? それがどこか地図で見せてくれませんか [sore ga doko ka chizu de misete kuremasen ka]
- could you show me the room? 部屋を見せてくれませんか [heya o misete kuremasen ka]

shower (device, act) シャワー [shawâ]; (of rain) にわか雨 [niwaka ame]
- I'd like a room with a shower, please シャワー付きの部屋をお願いします [shawâ tsuki no heya o onegai shimasu]
- how does the shower work? シャワーはどうやって使ったらいいですか [shawâ wa dô yatte tsukattara î desu ka]
- the shower is leaking シャワーが漏れています [shawâ ga morete imasu]

shower head シャワーヘッド [shawâ heddo]
- ▸ the shower head is broken シャワーヘッドが壊れています [shawâ heddo ga kowarete imasu]

shrimp えび [ebi]
- ▸ I'm allergic to shrimp えびにアレルギーがあります [ebi ni arerugî ga arimasu]

shut 閉める [shimeru] ◆ 閉まる [shimaru]
- ▸ the window won't shut 窓が閉まりません [mado ga shimarimasen]

shutter シャッター [shattâ]
- ▸ the shutters on the shop are closed 店のシャッターが閉まっています [mise no shattâ ga shimatte imasu]

shuttle (vehicle) シャトルバス [shatoru basu]
- ▸ is there a shuttle to the airport? 空港へのシャトルバスはありますか [kûkô e no shatoru basu wa arimasu ka]

sick (unwell) 病気の [byôki no]
- ▸ I feel sick 吐き気がします [hakike ga shimasu]
- ▸ to be sick (be unwell) 病気だ [byôki da]; (vomit) 吐く [haku]

side (of the body) わき腹 [wakibara]; (of an object) 横 [yoko]; (edge, opposing part) 側 [gawa]
- ▸ I have a pain in my right side 右のわき腹が痛いです [migi no wakibara ga itai desu]
- ▸ could we have a table on the other side of the room? 部屋の反対側の席に座ってもいいですか [heya no hantai gawa no seki ni suwatte mo î desu ka]
- ▸ you drive on the left in Japan, don't you? 日本では車は左側通行ですね [nihon de wa kuruma wa hidari gawa tsûkô desu ne]

sidewalk 歩道 [hodô]
- ▸ the sidewalks are very clean here ここの歩道はとてもきれいですね [koko no hodô wa totemo kirê desu ne]

sight (seeing) 視力 [shiryoku] ◆ **sights** (of a place) 見物 [kembutsu]
- ▸ I'm having problems with my sight 視力に問題があります [shiryoku ni mondai ga arimasu]
- ▸ what are the sights that are most worth seeing? 一番見物する価値のあるものは何ですか [ichban kembutsu suru kachi no aru mono wa nan desu ka]

sign サインする [sain suru] ◆ (gesture) 合図する [aizu suru]
- ▸ do I sign here? ここにサインするんですか [koko ni sain suru n desu ka]

signpost 道しるべ [michi shirube]
- ▸ does the route have good signposts? 道しるべがちゃんとありますか [michi shirube ga chanto arimasu ka]

silver *(metal)* 銀 [gin]
- is it made of silver? 銀製ですか [gin sê desu ka]

since 以来 [irai] ◆ *(in time)* から [kara]; *(because)* ...ので [...node]
- I've been here since Tuesday 火曜日からここにいます [kayôbi kara koko ni imasu]
- it hasn't rained once since we've been here ここに来てから一度も雨が降っていません [koko ni kite kara ichi do mo ame ga futte imasen]

single *(only one)* たった一つの [tatta hitotsu no]; *(unmarried)* 独身の [dokushin no] ◆ *(CD)* シングル [shinguru]
- I'm single 独身です [dokushin desu]
- she's a single woman in her thirties ３０代で独身の女性です [sanjû dai de dokushin no josê desu]

single bed シングルベッド [shinguru beddo]
- we'd prefer two single beds シングルベッド二つのほうがいいんですが [shinguru beddo futatsu no hô ga î n desu ga]

single room シングルルーム [shinguru rûmu]
- I'd like to book a single room for five nights, please シングルルームを五泊、予約したいんですが [shinguru rûmu o go haku yoyaku shitai n desu ga]

sister *(one's own elder sister)* 姉 [ane]; *(someone else's elder sister)* お姉さん [onê-san]; *(one's own younger sister)* 妹 [imôto]; *(someone else's younger sister)* 妹さん [imôto-san]
- I have two elder sisters 姉が二人います [ane ga futari imasu]

sit 座る [suwaru]
- may I sit at your table? そちらのテーブルに座ってもいいですか [sochira no têburu ni suwatte mo î desu ka]
- is anyone sitting here? ここに誰か座っていますか [koko ni dare ka suwatte imasu ka]

site *(of a town, a building)* 場所 [basho]; *(archeological)* 遺跡 [iseki]
- can we visit the building site? その建設場所に行くことができますか [sono kensetsu basho ni iku koto ga dekimasu ka]

six 六 [roku]
- there are six of us 全部で六人です [zembu de roku nin desu]

sixth 六番目の [roku bam me no] ◆ 六番目 [roku bam me]
- our room is on the sixth floor 部屋は六階です [heya wa rokkai desu]

size *(of a person, clothes)* サイズ [saizu]
- do you have another size? 他のサイズはありますか [hoka no saizu wa arimasu ka]
- do you have it in a smaller size? もっと小さいサイズはありますか [motto chîsai saizu wa arimasu ka]; see box on p. 138

sizes

Japanese are generally smaller than Americans, so larger sizes of clothes and shoes are not widely available, although the younger generations are becoming much taller. Women's clothes are sized 5–15 (US 6–14) or S, M, L and XL, and men's clothes sizes are given in centimeters. Shoe sizes are given in centimeters. The largest size generally available for men is 27 cm and for women 25 cm.

▸ I take or I'm an American size 7 *(shoes, clothes)* アメリカのサイズで7です [amerika no saizu de nana desu]

skate スケートをする [sukêto o suru] ◆ スケート靴 [sukêto gutsu]

▸ can you skate? スケートはできますか [sukêto wa dekimasu ka]

▸ how much is it to rent skates? スケート靴を借りるのはいくらですか [sukêto gutsu o kariru no wa ikura desu ka]

skating スケート [sukêto]

▸ where can we go skating? スケートはどこでできますか [sukêto wa doko de dekimasu ka]

ski boots スキー靴 [sukî gutsu]

▸ I'd like to rent ski boots スキー靴を借りたいんですが [sukî gutsu o karitai n desu ga]

skiing スキー [sukî]

▸ where can we go skiing near here? この近くでスキーのできるところはどこですか [kono chikaku de sukî no dekiru tokoro wa doko desu ka]

skis スキー板 [sukî ita]

▸ I'd like to rent a pair of skis for the week, please スキー板を一週間、借りたいんですが [sukî ita o isshûkan karitai n desu ga]

sleep *(be asleep)* 眠る [nemuru]; *(spend night)* 寝る [neru]

▸ I slept well よく寝ました [yoku nemashita]

▸ I can't sleep 眠れません [nemuremasen]

sleeping bag 寝袋 [nebukuro]

▸ where can I buy a new sleeping bag? 寝袋はどこで買えますか [nebukuro wa doko de kaemasu ka]

slice *(of bread, ham)* 薄切り [usugiri] ◆ 薄く切る [usuku kiru]

▸ a thin slice of ham ハム一枚 [hamu ichi mai]

slim *(person)* 細い [hosoi]

▸ she's slim 細いです [hosoi desu]

smoking

Cigarettes are relatively cheap and can easily be bought from vending machines. Smoking is still very popular in Japan, and it is only in recent years that non-smoking areas have become more common in stations, restaurants and other public places. Local trains are all non-smoking, and express and bullet trains (新幹線 [shinkansen]) are gradually following suit, although many still have smoking carriages.

slow *(speed)* 遅い [osoi]; *(behind time)* 遅れている [okurete iru]
▸ the fog was slow to clear 霧が晴れるのが遅かったです [kiri ga hareru no ga osokatta desu]
▸ is that clock slow? あの時計は遅れていますか [ano tokê wa okurete imasu ka]

slowly ゆっくりと [yukkuri to]
▸ could you speak more slowly, please? もっとゆっくり話してくれませんか [motto yukkuri hanashite kuremasen ka]

small 小さい [chîsai]
▸ do you have anything smaller? もっと小さいのはありますか [motto chîsai no wa arimasu ka]

smell *(notice a smell of)* におう [niou] ◆ *(have a smell)* においがする [nioi ga suru]; *(have a bad smell)* ひどいにおいがする [hidoi nioi ga suru]
▸ can you smell something burning? 何か焦げているにおいがしませんか [nani ka kogete iru nioi ga shimasen ka]
▸ it smells in here ここがにおいます [koko ga nioimasu]

smoke 煙 [kemuri] ◆ *(person)* タバコを吸う [tabako o su-u]
▸ is the smoke bothering you? 煙が気になりますか [kemuri ga ki ni narimasu ka]
▸ do you mind if I smoke? タバコを吸ってもいいですか [tabako o sutte mo î desu ka]
▸ no thanks, I don't smoke 結構です、吸いません [kekkô desu, suimasen]

smoker 喫煙者 [kitsuensha]
▸ are you smokers or nonsmokers? タバコを吸いますか、吸いませんか [tabako o suimasu ka, suimasen ka]

smoking タバコを吸うこと [tabako o su-u koto]
▸ is smoking allowed here? ここでタバコを吸ってもいいですか [koko de tabako o sutte mo î desu ka]
▸ I can't stand smoking タバコには耐えられません [tabako ni wa taeraremasen]

smoking carriage 喫煙車 [kitsuen sha]
▸ I'd like a seat in a smoking carriage 喫煙車の席をお願いします [kitsuen sha no seki o onegai shimasu]
▸ is there a smoking carriage? 喫煙車はありますか [kitsuen sha wa arimasu ka]

smoking section 喫煙コーナー [kitsuen kônâ]
▸ I'd like a table in the smoking section 喫煙コーナーのテーブルがいいんですが [kitsuen kônâ no têburu ga î n desu ga]

sneaker スニーカー [sunîkâ]
▸ your sneakers are really trendy! そのスニーカー、かっこいいですね [sono sunîkâ kakkoî desu ne]

snorkel シュノーケル [shunôkeru]
▸ I'd like to rent a snorkel and mask, please シュノーケルとマスクを借りたいんですが [shunôkeru to masuku o karitai n desu ga]

snow 雪 [yuki] ◆ 雪が降る [yuki ga furu]
▸ it's snowing 雪が降っています [yuki ga futte imasu]

snowboard スノーボード [sunôbôdo]
▸ I'd like to rent a snowboard スノーボードを借りたいんですが [sunôbôdo o karitai n desu ga]

snowboarding スノーボード [sunôbôdo]
▸ where can we go snowboarding near here? この近くでスノーボードができるところはどこですか [kono chikaku de sunôbôdo ga dekiru tokoro wa doko desu ka]

snow tire スノータイヤ [sunô taiya]
▸ do I need snow tires? スノータイヤが必要ですか [sunô taiya ga hitsuyô desu ka]

so *(to such a degree)* こんなに [konna ni]; *(also)* も [mo]; *(consequently)* だから [da kara]
▸ it's so big! とても大きいですね [totemo ôkî desu ne]
▸ there's so many choices I don't know what to have 選択の余地が多すぎて何を選んでいいのか分かりません [sentaku no yochi ga ôsugite nani o erande î ka wakarimasen]
▸ I'm hungry – so am I! おなかが空きました–私もです [onaka ga sukimashita – watashi mo desu]

soap 石鹸 [sekken]
▸ there's no soap 石鹸がありません [sekken ga arimasen]

socket *(electric)* コンセント [konsento]
▸ is there a socket I can use to recharge my cell? 携帯の充電に使えるコンセントはありますか [kêtai no jûden ni tsukaeru konsento wa arimasu ka]

sorry

Japanese apologize frequently. The most widely used word for 'sorry' is
すみません [sumimasen]. Note that this word can also be used to mean
'thank you,' particularly for an unexpected kindness or gift.

solution *(to a problem)* 解決 [kaiketsu]; *(liquid)* 溶液 [yôeki]
- that seems to be the best solution それが最上の解決策のようです [sore
  ga saijô no kaiketsu saku no yô desu]
- I'd like some rinsing solution for soft lenses ソフトコンタクトの洗浄液が
  ほしいんですが [sofuto kontakuto no senjôeki ga hoshî n desu ga]

some *(an amount of)* 多少の [tashô no]; *(a number of)* いくつかの [ikutsu ka no]
- some shops are open on Sunday いくつかの店は日曜日に開いています
  [ikutsu ka no mise wa nichiyôbi ni aite imasu]
- can I have some? 少しもらえますか [sukoshi moraemasu ka]

somebody, someone 誰か [dare ka]
- somebody left this for you 誰かがこれを置いていってくれました [dare
  ka ga kore o oite itte kuremashita]

something 何か [nani ka]
- is something wrong? どうかしたんですか [dô ka shita n desu ka]

somewhere どこか [doko ka]
- I'm looking for somewhere to stay どこか泊まるところを探しています
  [doko ka tomaru tokoro o sagashite imasu]
- somewhere near here この近く [kono chikaku]
- somewhere else 他のどこか [hoka no doko ka]

son *(one's own)* 息子 [musuko]; *(someone else's)* 息子さん [musuko-san]
- this is my son 息子です [musuko desu]

soon 近いうちに [chikai uchi ni]
- see you soon! 近いうちに会いましょう [chikai uchi ni aimashô]
- as soon as possible できるだけ早く [dekiru dake hayaku]

sore throat のどの痛み [nodo no itami]
- I have a sore throat のどが痛いです [nodo ga itai desu]

sorry すみません [sumimasen]
- I'm sorry すみません [sumimasen]
- sorry I'm late 遅れてすみません [okurete sumimasen]
- I'm sorry, but this seat is taken すみません、この席は人がいます
  [sumimasen, kono seki wa hito ga imasu]
- sorry to bother you ご迷惑をおかけしてすみません [gomêwaku o okake
  shite sumimasen]

soya

Soya is an essential part of the Japanese diet, and a very healthy one, as it is low in calories and high in protein. It is the basis of Buddhist vegetarian dishes (精進料理 [shôjin ryôri]). It comes in many forms: as a sauce (しょうゆ [shôyu]), as fermented beans (納豆 [nattô]), as blocks of bean curd (豆腐 [tôfu]), or as a thick paste of fermented beans (味噌 [miso]). Tôfu is eaten either as it is or in soup, depending on the season. It is also served cold, sprinkled with ginger and garnished with finely chopped spring onion and soya sauce, or deep-fried.

- sorry? *(asking for repetition)* 何ですか [nan desu ka]
- no, sorry いいえ、すみません [îe, sumimasen]

sound 音 [oto]; *(of a voice)* 声 [koe]
- can you turn the sound down? 音を小さくしてもらえますか [oto o chîsaku shite moraemasu ka]

souvenir 土産 [miyage]
- where can I buy souvenirs? 土産はどこで買えますか [miyage wa doko de kaemasu ka]

souvenir shop 土産物屋 [miyagemono ya]
- I'm looking for a souvenir shop 土産物屋を探しています [miyagemono ya o sagashite imasu]

soya 大豆 [daizu]
- soya sauce しょうゆ [shôyu]

spa *(town (hot springs))* 温泉 [onsen]; *(health club)* スパ [supa]
- we want to go to a quiet spa town 静かな温泉に行きたいです [shizukana onsen ni ikitai desu]

space *(room)* スペース [supêsu]; *(for parking)* 駐車スペース [chûsha supêsu]; *(for a tent, a trailer)* 場所 [basho]
- is there space for another bed in the room? 部屋にはもう一つベッドを入れるスペースがありますか [heya ni wa mô hitotsu beddo o ireru supêsu ga arimasu ka]
- I'd like a space for one tent for two days テント一つ分の場所を二日間借りたいんですが [tento hitotsu bun no basho o futsuka kan karitai n desu ga]
- do you have any spaces farther from the road? 道路からもっと離れたところにスペースがありますか [dôro kara motto hanareta tokoro ni supêsu ga arimasu ka]

spade *(child's toy)* シャベル [shaberu]
- my son's left his spade at the beach 息子がシャベルを浜辺に忘れて来ました [musuko ga shaberu o hamabe ni wasurete kimashita]

spare (clothes, battery) 余分の [yobun no] ◆ (tire) スペアタイヤ [supea taiya]; (part) 交換部品 [kôkan buhin]

▸ should I take some spare clothes 余分の服を持って行ったほうがいいですか [yobun no fuku o motte itta hô ga î desu ka]

▸ I don't have any spare cash 余分なお金は全然持っていません [yobun na okane wa zenzen motte imasen]

▸ I've got a spare ticket for the game 試合のチケットを一枚余分に持っています [shiai no chiketto o ichi mai yobun ni motte imasu]

spare part 交換部品 [kôkan buhin]

▸ where can I get spare parts? 交換部品はどこで手に入りますか [kôkan buhin wa doko de te ni hairimasu ka]

spare tire スペアタイヤ [supea taiya]

▸ the spare tire's flat too スペアタイヤもパンクしています [supea taiya mo panku shite imasu]

spare wheel 車輪の替え [sharin no kae]

▸ there's no spare wheel 車輪の替えはありません [sharin no kae wa arimasen]

sparkling ガス入りの [gasu iri no]

▸ could I have a bottle of sparkling water, please? ガス入りのミネラルウォーターを一本もらえませんか [gasu iri no mineraru wôtâ o ippon moraemasen ka]

speak 話す [hanasu]

▸ I speak hardly any Japanese 日本語はほとんど何も話せません [nihongo wa hotondo nani mo hanasemasen]

▸ is there anyone here who speaks English? ここに英語が話せる人はいますか [koko ni êgo ga hanaseru hito wa imasu ka]

▸ could you speak more slowly? もっとゆっくり話してくれませんか [motto yukkuri hanashite kuremasen ka]

▸ hello, I'd like to speak to Mr...; this is... もしもし、...さんをお願いします。...と申します [moshimoshi, ...san o onegai shimasu. ...to môshimasu]

▸ who's speaking please? どちらさまでしょうか [dochira sama deshô ka]

▸ hello, Gary speaking もしもし、ギャリーです [moshimoshi, gyarî desu]

special (at restaurant) 特別料理 [tokubetsu ryôri]

▸ what's today's special? 今日の特別料理は何ですか [kyô no tokubetsu ryôri wa nan desu ka]

specialist (expert) 専門家 [semmonka]; (doctor) 専門医 [semmon'i]

▸ could you refer me to a specialist? 専門医に照会してもらえませんか [semmon'i ni shôkai shite moraemasen ka]

specialty (expertise) 専門 [semmon]; (cuisine) 名物料理 [mêbutsu ryôri]

▸ what are the local specialties? この地方の名物料理は何ですか [kono chihô no mêbutsu ryôri wa nan desu ka]

speed limit 制限速度 [sêgen sokudo]
- what's the speed limit on this road? この道路の制限速度は何キロですか [kono dôro no sêgen sokudo wa nan kiro desu ka]

speedometer 速度計 [sokudokê]
- the speedometer's broken 速度計が壊れています [sokudokê ga kowarete imasu]

speed trap ネズミ取り [nezumitori]
- are there lots of speed traps in the area? この地域にはたくさんネズミ取りがありますか [kono chi-iki ni wa takusan nezumitori ga arimasu ka]

spell つづる [tsuzuru]
- how do you spell your name? 名前はどうつづりますか [namae wa dô tsuzurimasu ka]

spend *(money)* 使う [tsukau]; *(time)* 過ごす [sugosu]
- we are prepared to spend up to 20000 yen ２万円まで使うつもりでいます [niman en made tsukau tsumori de imasu]
- I spent a month in Japan a few years ago 数年前に日本で一ヶ月過ごしました [sû nen mae ni nihon de ikka getsu sugoshimashita]

spicy 辛い [karai]
- is this dish spicy? この料理は辛いですか [kono ryôri wa karai desu ka]

spoon スプーン [supûn]
- could I have a spoon? スプーンをもらえませんか [supûn o moraemasen ka]

sport スポーツ [supôtsu]
- do you play any sports? スポーツは何かしますか [supôtsu wa nani ka shimasu ka]
- I play a lot of sports スポーツをよくします [supôtsu o yoku shimasu]

sporty *(person)* スポーツが好きな [supôtsu ga suki na]
- I'm not very sporty あまりスポーツが好きなほうじゃありません [amari supôtsu ga suki na hô ja arimasen]

sprain 捻挫する [nenza suru]
- I think I've sprained my ankle 足首を捻挫したんだと思います [ashikubi o nenza shita n da to omoimasu]
- my wrist is sprained 手首を捻挫しました [tekubi o nenza shimashita]

spring 春 [haru]
- in (the) spring 春に [haru ni]

stain 染み [shimi]
- can you remove this stain? この染みを取れますか [kono shimi o toremasu ka]

stairs 階段 [kaidan]
- where are the stairs? 階段はどこですか [kaidan wa doko desu ka]

stamps

Stamps are sold at post offices but also in convenience stores. There are different rates for letters and postcards, and for deliveries within Japan and abroad.

stall *(car, engine)* 止まる [tomaru]
- the engine keeps stalling エンジンが何度も止まってしまいます [enjin ga nan do mo tomatte shimaimasu]

stamp *(for letter, postcard)* 切手 [kitte]
- do you sell stamps? 切手を売っていますか [kitte o utte imasu ka]

stand *(stall, booth)* 屋台 [yatai]; *(in a stadium)* スタンド [sutando] ◆ *(tolerate)* 耐える [taeru] ◆ *(be upright)* 立つ [tatsu]; *(get up)* 立ち上がる [tachiagaru]
- where's stand number 5? ５番スタンドはどこですか [go ban sutando wa doko desu ka]

start *(begin)* 始まる [hajimaru]; *(function)* 動く [ugoku] ◆ 始める [hajimeru]
- when does the concert start? コンサートはいつ始まりますか [konsâto wa itsu hajimarimasu ka]
- the car won't start 車が動きません [kuruma ga ugokimasen]

starving *(very hungry)* おなかがすごく減った [onaka ga sugoku hetta]
- I'm absolutely starving おなかが死ぬほど減りました [onaka ga shinu hodo herimashita]

States
- the States アメリカ [amerika]
- I'm from the States アメリカからです [amerika kara desu]
- I live in the States アメリカに住んでいます [amerika ni sunde imasu]
- have you ever been to the States? アメリカに行ったことがありますか [amerika ni itta koto ga arimasu ka]

station *(railroad, bus, subway)* 駅 [eki]; *(TV, radio)* 局 [kyoku]; *(police)* 警察署 [kêsatsusho]
- to the train station, please! 駅へお願いします [eki e onegai shimasu]
- Is there a police station near here? この近くに警察署はありますか [kono chikaku ni kêsatsusho wa arimasu ka]
- where is the nearest subway station? 一番近い地下鉄の駅はどこですか [ichiban chikai chikatetsu no eki wa doko desu ka]

stay *(in a place)* 泊まる [tomaru] ◆ *(visit)* 滞在 [taizai]
- we're planning to stay for two nights 二晩泊まる予定です [futa ban tomaru yotê desu]
- a two-week stay ２週間の滞在 [ni shûkan no taizai]

steak ステーキ [sutêki]
- I'd like a steak and fries ステーキとフライドポテトがほしいんですが [sutêki to furaido poteto ga hoshî n desu ga]

steal 盗む [nusumu]
- my passport was stolen パスポートを盗まれました [pasupôto o nusumaremashita]
- my bicycle has been stolen 自転車を盗まれました [jitensha o nusumaremashita]

steering 運転 [unten]
- there's a problem with the steering 運転しにくいです [unten shinikui desu]

steering wheel ハンドル [handoru]
- the steering wheel is very stiff ハンドルがすごく動かしにくいです [handoru ga sugoku ugokashinikui desu]

stick shift (lever) 変速レバー [hensoku rebâ]; (car) マニュアル [manyuaru]
- is it a stick shift or an automatic? マニュアルですかオートマチックですか [manyuaru desu ka, ôtomachikku desu ka]

still (remaining) あと [ato]; (even now) まだ [mada]
- how many kilometers are there still to go? あと何キロありますか [ato nan kiro arimasu ka]
- we're still waiting to be served まだ食事が来るのを待っています [mada shokuji ga kuru no o matte imasu]

sting (insect) 刺す [sasu]
- I've been stung by a wasp スズメバチに刺されました [suzumebachi ni sasaremashita]

stomach おなか [onaka]
- my stomach hurts おなかが痛いです [onaka ga itai desu]

stomachache 腹痛 [fukutsû]
- I have a really bad stomachache 腹痛がひどいです [fukutsû ga hidoi desu]

stop (movement) 停止 [têshi]; (bus stop) バス停 [basu tê] ◆ 止める [tomeru] ◆ 止まる [tomaru]
- is this the right bus stop for...? ...はこのバス停ですか [...wa kono basu tê desu ka]
- stop it! やめなさい！ [yamenasai]
- where in town does the shuttle stop? シャトルバスは町のどこに止まりますか [shatoru basu wa machi no doko ni tomarimasu ka]
- please stop here ここで止めてください [koko de tomete kudasai]
- which stations does this train stop at? この列車はどこに止まりますか [kono ressha wa doko ni tomarimasu ka]
- do we stop at Nagoya? 名古屋に止まりますか [nagoya ni tomarimasu ka]

stores

You can usually find small stores and minimarkets near railway stations – these are open all day long but are closed on Sundays or one weekday, depending on the area. Small stores are usually open from 9 a.m to 6 or 7 p.m. Convenience stores (コンビニ [kombini]) are small local stores open 24 hours a day, selling food, toiletries, stationery and other essential items. The biggest chains are Seven/Eleven, Lawson, Family Mart and am/pm. You can also buy a vast range of items from vending machines (自動販売機 [jidôhambaiki]).

store *(place selling goods)* 店 [mise]

▸ are there any bigger stores in the area? この辺にもっと大きな店はありますか [kono hen ni motto ôki na mise wa arimasu ka]

store window ショーウィンドー [shô windô]

▸ the store windows are beautifully decorated at Christmas クリスマスにはショーウィンドーはきれいに飾られます [kurisumasu ni wa shô windô wa kirê ni kazararemasu]

storm 嵐 [arashi]

▸ is there going to be a storm? 嵐になりそうですか [arashi ni narisô desu ka]

straight まっすぐな [massugu na] ◆ *(in a straight line)* まっすぐに [massugu ni]

▸ you have to keep going straight ずっとまっすぐ行かなければなりません [zutto massugu ikanakereba narimasen]

street 通り [tôri]

▸ will this street take me to the station? この通りを行くと駅に着きますか [kono tôri o iku to eki ni tsukimasu ka]

in a store

▸ no, thanks, I'm just looking 結構です、見ているだけです [kekkô desu. mite iru dake desu]

▸ how much is this? これはいくらですか [kore wa ikura desu ka]

▸ I take a size 12/I'm a size 12 in American size アメリカのサイズで１２です [amerika no saizu de jûni desu]

▸ can I try this coat on? このコートを着てみてもいいですか [kono kôto o kite mite mo î desu ka]

▸ can it be exchanged? 交換してもらえますか [kôkan shite moraemasu ka]

subway

There are extensive subway systems in all the major cities. Fares depend on the distance you travel, and tickets are bought from machines. Although subway maps with station names in romanization are on display in the major stations, smaller ones may only have Japanese maps, so if you're not sure, buy the cheapest ticket and pay the excess when you arrive.

streetcar 市電 [shiden]
- can you buy tickets on the streetcar? 切符は市電に乗ってから買えますか [kippu wa shiden ni notte kara kaemasu ka]
- which streetcar line do we have to take? どの市電の線に乗ったらいいですか [dono shiden no sen ni nottara î desu ka]
- where is the nearest streetcar stop? 一番近い市電の乗り場はどこですか [ichiban chikai shiden no noriba wa doko desu ka]

strong 強い [tsuyoi]
- is the current very strong here? ここは潮の流れが強いですか [koko wa shio no nagare ga tsuyoi desu ka]

stuck
- to be stuck *(jammed)* 動かない [ugokanai]; *(trapped)* 閉じ込められている [tojikomerarete iru]
- someone is stuck in the elevator 誰かエレベーターに閉じ込められています [dare ka erebêtâ ni tojikomerarete imasu]

student 学生 [gakusê]
- I'm a student 学生です [gakusê desu]

student discount 学生割引 [gakusê waribiki]
- do you have student discounts? 学生割引はありますか [gakusê waribiki wa arimasu ka]

style *(manner, design)* 様式 [yôshiki]; *(elegance)* 気品 [kihin]
- she has a lot of style とても気品があります [totemo kihin ga arimasu]

subway 地下鉄 [chikatetsu]
- can I have a map of the subway? 地下鉄の路線図をもらえますか [chikatetsu no rosenzu o moraemasu ka]

subway train 地下鉄 [chikatetsu]
- when's the last subway train from this station? この駅の最後の地下鉄は何時ですか [kono eki no saigo no chikatetsu wa nan ji desu ka]

sudden 急な [kyû na]
- all of a sudden 突然 [totsuzen]

sugar 砂糖 [satô]

‣ can you pass me the sugar? 砂糖をまわしてくれますか [satô o mawashite kuremasu ka]

suggest (propose) 提案する [têan suru] (recommend) 勧める [susumeru]

‣ do you have anything else you can suggest? 他に提案することはありますか [hoka ni têan suru koto wa arimasu ka]

suit (be convenient for) 都合がいい [tsugô ga î]; (clothes, color) 似合う [niau]

‣ that arrangement suits me perfectly とても都合がいいです [totemo tsugô ga î desu]

‣ the color doesn't suit me その色は私には似合いません [sono iro wa watashi ni wa niaimasen]

suitcase スーツケース [sûtsukêsu]

‣ one of my suitcases is missing スーツケースが一つ足りません [sûtsukêsu ga hitotsu tarimasen]

‣ my suitcase was damaged in transit 輸送の途中でスーツケースに傷がつきました [yusô no tochû de sûtsukêsu ni kizu ga tsukimashita]

summer 夏 [natsu]

‣ in (the) summer 夏に [natsu ni]

summer vacation 夏休み [natsu yasumi]

‣ we've come here for our summer vacation 夏休みでここに来ました [natsu yasumi de koko ni kimashita]

sun 太陽 [taiyô]

‣ the sun's very strong at this time of day 一日のうちで今頃はとても日が強いです [ichi nichi no uchi de ima goro wa totemo hi ga tsuyoi desu]

sunburn 日焼け [hiyake]

‣ I've got a bad sunburn ひどく日焼けをしました [hidoku hiyake o shimashita]

‣ do you have cream for a sunburn? 日焼け後のクリームはありますか [hiyake go no kurîmu wa arimasu ka]

Sunday 日曜日 [nichiyôbi]

‣ where can I find a doctor on a Sunday? 日曜日にやっている医者はどこですか [nichiyôbi ni yatte iru isha wa doko desu ka]

‣ are the stores open on Sunday? 日曜日に店は開いていますか [nichiyôbi ni mise wa aite imasu ka]

sunglasses サングラス [sangurasu]

‣ I've lost my sunglasses サングラスを失くしました [sangurasu o nakushimashita]

sunny (day, weather) 晴れの [hare no]

‣ it's sunny 晴れています [harete imasu]

supermarkets

Big supermarkets and hypermarkets such as Jusco, Ito Yokado, and Seiyu are open daily 10 a.m to 10 p.m (some are open 24 hours), including Sundays. Food is usually on the basement level.

sunrise 日の出 [hi no de]
  ▸ what time is sunrise? 日の出は何時ですか [hi no de wa nan ji desu ka]

sunset 夕焼け [yûyake]
  ▸ isn't the sunset beautiful? 夕焼けがきれいですね [yûyake ga kirê desu ne]

suntan lotion 日焼けクリーム [hiyake kurîmu]
  ▸ I'd like SPF 30 suntan lotion SPF30の日焼けクリームをください [esupîefu sanjû no hiyake kurîmu o kudasai]

supermarket スーパー [sûpâ]
  ▸ is there a supermarket nearby? 近くにスーパーはありますか [chikaku ni sûpâ wa arimasu ka]

surcharge 追加料金 [tsuika ryôkin]
  ▸ do I have to pay a surcharge? 追加料金を払わなければいけませんか [tsuika ryôkin o harawanakereba ikemasen ka]

surfboard サーフボード [sâfubôdo]
  ▸ is there somewhere we can rent surfboards? サーフボードを借りられるところはありますか [sâfubôdo o karirareru tokoro wa arimasu ka]

surfing サーフィン [sâfin]
  ▸ can we go surfing around here? この辺でサーフィンはできますか [kono hen de sâfin wa dekimasu ka]

surprise びっくりすること [bikkuri suru koto]
  ▸ what a surprise! びっくりしました [bikkuri shimashita]

surrounding area 周辺 [shûhen]
  ▸ Tokyo and the surrounding area 東京とその周辺 [tôkyô to sono shûhen]

swallow 飲み込む [nomikomu]
  ▸ the ATM outside has swallowed my credit card 外のATMからクレジットカードが出てきません [soto no êtîemu kara kurejitto kâdo ga dete kimasen]
  ▸ it hurts when I swallow 飲み込むと痛みます [nomikomu to itamimasu]

swim 水泳 [suiê] ◆ 泳ぐ [oyogu]
  ▸ is it safe to swim here? ここで泳いでも安全ですか [koko de oyoide mo anzen desu ka]
  ▸ to go for a swim 水泳に行く [suiê ni iku]

swimming pool プール [pûru]
- is there an open-air swimming pool? 屋外プールはありますか [okugai pûru wa arimasu ka]

switch スイッチ [suitchi]
- the switch doesn't work スイッチが壊れています [suitchi ga kowarete imasu]

switch off *(light, radio)* 消す [kesu]; *(electricity, appliance)* 切る [kiru]
- where do you switch the light off? どうやって電気を消したらいいですか [dô yatte denki o keshitara î desu ka]
- my cell was switched off 携帯は切ってありました [kêtai wa kitte arimashita]

switch on *(light, heating, TV)* つける [tsukeru]; *(engine)* かける [kakeru]
- where do I switch this light on? どうやって電気をつけたらいいですか [dô yatte denki o tsuketara î desu ka]

synagogue シナゴーグ [shinagôgu]
- where's the nearest synagogue? 一番近いシナゴーグはどこですか [ichiban chikai shinagôgu wa doko desu ka]

table テーブル [têburu]
- I've reserved a table in the name of... ...の名前でテーブルを予約してあります [...no namae de têburu o yoyaku shite arimasu]
- a table for four, please! 四人分のテーブルをお願いします [yo nin bun no têburu o onegai shimasu]

table tennis 卓球 [takkyû]
- are there tables for table tennis? 卓球台はありますか [takkyû dai wa arimasu ka]

table wine テーブルワイン [têburu wain]
- a bottle of red table wine 赤のテーブルワイン一本 [aka no têburu wain ippon]

take *(get hold of)* 取る [toru]; *(steal)* 盗む [nusumu]; *(carry)* 持って行く [motte iku]; *(accompany)* 連れて行く [tsurete iku]; *(transport)* 乗る [noru]; *(require)* 要る [iru]; *(wear)* 着る [kiru]; *(time)* かかる [kakaru]
- someone's taken my bag 誰かにかばんを盗まれました [dare ka ni kaban o nusumaremashita]
- can you take me to this address? この住所に連れて行ってくれますか [kono jûsho ni tsurete itte kuremasu ka]

- are you taking the plane or the train to Fukuoka? 福岡まで飛行機に乗りますか、列車に乗りますか [fukuoka made hikôki ni norimasu ka, ressha ni norimasu ka]
- which road should I take? どちらの道を選んだらいいですか [dochira no michi o erandara î desu ka]
- I take a size 40 sweater in American size アメリカのサイズで４０のセーターを着ています [amerika no saizu de yonjû no sêtâ o kite imasu]
- how long does the trip take? 移動はどれぐらいかかりますか [idô wa dore gurai kakarimasu ka]
- how long does it take to get to Tokyo? 東京までどれぐらいかかりますか [tôkyô made dore gurai kakarimasu ka]
- could you take a photo of us? 写真を撮ってくれませんか [shashin o totte kuremasen ka]

take back (to a store) 返品する [hempin suru]; (to one's home) 持って帰る [motte kaeru]
- I'm looking for a present to take back to my son 息子に持って帰るプレゼントを探しています [musuko ni motte kaeru purezento o sagashite imasu]

take down (bags, luggage) 下ろす [orosu]
- could you take these bags down, please? この荷物を下ろしてもらえませんか [kono nimotsu o oroshite moraemasen ka]

take in (bags, luggage) 入れる [ireru]
- can you have someone take in my bags, please? かばんを中に入れてくれる人はいますか [kaban o naka ni irete kureru hito wa imasu ka]

taken (seat) 人が座っている [hito ga suwatte iru]
- sorry, this seat is taken すみません、ここはもう座っている人がいます [sumimasen, koko wa mô suwatte iru hito ga imasu]

take up (bags, luggage) 持ち上げる [mochiageru]
- can someone take our bags up to our room? 誰かかばんを部屋まで持って行ってくれますか [dare ka kaban o heya made motte itte kuremasu ka]

talk 話す [hanasu]
- could I talk with you for a moment? ちょっと話ができませんか [chotto hanashi ga dekimasen ka]

tall (tree, building) 高い [takai]; (person) 背が高い [se ga takai]
- what's that tall building over there? 向こうの高い建物は何ですか [mukô no takai tatemono wa nan desu ka]

tank (for gas) タンク [tanku]
- is the tank full? タンクはいっぱいですか [tanku wa ippai desu ka]

taste 味 [aji] ◆ (sense) 味が分かる [aji ga wakaru]; (try) 味見する [ajimi suru] ◆ 味がする [aji ga suru]

taxis

Taxis have a sign on the roof with the name of the taxi company, which is lit up at night to show the taxi is vacant. In the daytime, a small sign by the driver's window indicates whether the taxi is free (空車 [kûsha]). Standard taxis (中型 [chûgata]) take a maximum of four passengers, but the smaller ones (小型 [kogata]) only take three. Doors open and close automatically, so you should not try to do this yourself. Inside, the seats have white protective covers and the drivers wear white gloves. If you are going somewhere other than well-known locations, such as big hotels and tourist attractions, it is useful to have directions or a map, as taxi-drivers often don't have very detailed knowledge of their cities. There is no need to tip.

▸ I can't taste anything 味が全然しません [aji ga zenzen shimasen]

▸ would you like to taste the wine? ワインの味見はいかがですか [wain no ajimi wa ikaga desu ka]

▸ it tastes funny へんな味がします [hen na aji ga shimasu]

tax 税金 [zêkin]

▸ does this price include tax? この値段は税金が含まれていますか [kono nedan wa zêkin ga fukumarete imasu ka]

taxi タクシー [takushî]

▸ how much does a taxi cost from here to the station? ここから駅までタクシーはいくらですか [koko kara eki made takushî wa ikura desu ka]

▸ I'd like to reserve a taxi to take me to the airport, please 空港へのタクシーを予約したいんですが [kûkô e no takushî o yoyaku shitai n desu ga]

taking a taxi

▸ could you call me a taxi, please? タクシーを呼んでもらえませんか [takushî o yonde moraemasen ka]

▸ to the station/airport, please 駅/空港までお願いします [eki/kûkô made onegai shimasu]

▸ stop here/at the lights/at the corner, please ここで/信号で/角で止めてください [koko de/shingô de/kado de tomete kudasai]

▸ can you wait for me? 待っていてくれますか [matte ite kuremasu ka]

▸ how much is it? いくらですか [ikura desu ka]

▸ keep the change お釣りは取っておいてください [otsuri wa totte oite kudasai]

tea

Green tea is a true Japanese specialty. There is an enormous variety available, some of which is extremely expensive. The best tea leaves are protected from the sun as they grow, then carefully harvested and crushed to a powder for use in the tea ceremony (茶の湯 [chanoyu] or 茶道 [sadô]). In everyday life, clear green tea (お茶 [ocha]) is drunk instead of water, and is automatically served in restaurants. Only black tea is served in coffee-shops.

taxi driver タクシーの運転手 [takushî no untenshu]
▸ can you ask the taxi driver to wait? タクシーの運転手に待つように、言ってくれますか [takushî no untenshu ni matsu yô ni itte kuremasu ka]

taxi stand タクシー乗り場 [takushî noriba]
▸ where can I find a taxi stand? タクシー乗り場はどこですか [takushî noriba wa doko desu ka]

tea *(drink)* お茶 [ocha]
▸ tea with milk ミルクティー [miruku tî]
▸ tea without milk ミルクなしの紅茶 [miruku nashi no kôcha]

teach 教える [oshieru]
▸ so, you teach Japanese? maybe you could help me! 日本語を教えているんですか。ちょっと助けてもらえませんか [nihongo o oshiete iru n desu ka. chotto tasukete moraemasen ka]

teacher *(one's own occupation)* 教師 [kyôshi]; *(other's occupation)* 先生 [sensê]
▸ I'm a teacher 教師です [kyôshi desu]

tea house 茶室 [chashitsu]
▸ when does the tea house open? 茶室はいつ開いていますか [chashitsu wa itsu aite imasu ka]

tea ceremony

The tea ceremony is an aesthetic ritual strongly influenced by Zen Buddhism, and aims to develop discipline and contemplation. The powdered green tea is stirred into the water with a bamboo whisk called a chasen to make a frothy, bitter tea called 抹茶 [matcha]. Before drinking, you should turn the tea bowl around in your hands three times in order to admire its beauty.

telephone

So many people have cellphones (携帯 [kêtai]) in Japan that using public telephones has become much less common and there are far fewer than a decade or two ago. Nevertheless, public telephones are still plentiful. Telephone booths have been modernized and most now take IC cards instead of the old NTT ones. Phonecards are sold at kiosks and convenience stores, or from vending machines inside the booth itself. Payphones in cafés usually only take coins. Only certain public telephones allow you to make international calls. To call the USA or Canada from Japan, dial 010 1 followed by the phone number, including the area code.

telephone 電話 [denwa] ◆ 電話する [denwa suru]
▸ can I use the telephone? 電話を貸してもらってもいいですか [denwa o kashite moratte mo î desu ka]

telephone booth 電話ボックス [denwa bokkusu]
▸ is there a telephone booth near here? 近くに電話ボックスはありますか [chikaku ni denwa bokkusu wa arimasu ka]

telephone call 電話 [denwa]
▸ I'd like to make a telephone call 電話をかけたいんですが [denwa o kaketai n desu ga]

television *(system, set)* テレビ [terebi]; *(broadcasts)* テレビ放送 [terebi hôsô]
▸ what's on television tonight? 今夜はテレビで何がありますか [kon ya wa terebi de nani ga arimasu ka]; see box on p. 156

tell *(say)* 言う [yû]; *(time, direction)* 教える [oshieru]
▸ can you tell me the way to the museum? 博物館に行く道を教えてくれますか [hakubutsukan ni iku michi o oshiete kuremasu ka]
▸ can you tell me what time it is? 今、何時か教えてくれますか [ima nan ji ka oshiete kuremasu ka]

temperature *(meteorological)* 温度 [ondo]; *(fever)* 熱 [netsu]
▸ what's the temperature? 温度は何度ですか [ondo wa nan do desu ka]
▸ I've got a temperature 熱が出てきました [netsu ga dete kimashita]

telephone numbers

Phone numbers are read out one digit at a time. When writing a phone number, the different elements are separated by hyphens: for example, in the number 03-1234-5678, the 03 stands for Tokyo, the 1234 is the area, and 5678 the person's number. '0' is pronounced as zero or rê.

television

The public broadcasting corporation, NHK, has two channels, while commercial channels, such as TV Asahi, TBS, Fuji TV and NTV, are run by the big media companies; these have links with dozens of local television stations.

temple 寺 [tera]
- could you tell me where the temple is, please? 寺がどこにあるか教えてくれませんか [tera ga doko ni aru ka oshiete kuremasen ka]

ten 十 [jû]
- there are ten of us 全部で十人です [zembu de jû nin desu]

tennis テニス [tenisu]
- where can we play tennis? テニスはどこでできますか [tenisu wa doko de dekimasu ka]

tennis racket テニスラケット [tenisu raketto]
- can you rent tennis rackets? テニスラケットを貸してもらえますか [tenisu raketto o kashite moraemasu ka]

tent テント [tento]
- I'd like to book space for a tent, please テントの場所を予約したいんですが [tento no basho o yoyaku shitai n desu ga]
- can you put up your tent anywhere? テントはどこに張ってもいいですか [tento wa doko ni hatte mo î desu ka]

tent peg テントのくい [tento no kui]
- we're short of tent pegs テントのくいが足りません [tento no kui ga tarimasen]

terminal *(in airport)* ターミナル [tâminaru]
- where is terminal one? 第一ターミナルはどこですか [dai ichi tâminaru wa doko desu ka]
- is there a shuttle between terminals? ターミナルの間にシャトルがありますか [tâminaru no aida ni shatoru ga arimasu ka]

tetanus 破傷風 [hashôfû]
- I've been vaccinated for tetanus 破傷風の予防接種をしてあります [hashôfû no yobô sesshu o shite arimasu]

thank 感謝する [kansha suru] ◆ **thanks** 御礼 [orê]
- I can't thank you enough 御礼の言いようもありません [orê no îyô mo arimasen]
- thanks for everything (you've done) お世話になりました [osewa ni narimashita]

thanking

Thanking people for gifts, favors or kindnesses, not just at the time, but the next time you see or are in contact with them, is an essential part of maintaining good relationships with others.

thank you! ありがとう [arigatô]
- thank you very much! どうもありがとうございます [dômo arigatô gozaimasu]

that *(demonstrative use)* あれ [are] ◆ あの [ano]
- who's that? あれは誰ですか [are wa dare desu ka]
- that's right そうです [sô desu]
- the road that goes to Yokohama 横浜へ行く道 [yokohama e iku michi]
- I'll have that one それにします [sore ni shimasu]

theater *(for plays)* 劇場 [gekijô]
- where is there a theater? 劇場はどこですか [gekijô wa doko desu ka]

theft 盗難 [tônan]
- I'd like to report a theft 盗難の届けを出したいんですが [tônan no todoke o dashitai n desu ga]

then *(at a particular time)* その時 [sono toki]; *(next)* それから [sore kara]; *(in that case)* それでは [sore de wa]
- I'll see you then その時に会いましょう [sono toki ni aimashô]
- I'll see you at six then それでは 6 時に会いましょう [sore de wa roku ji ni aimashô]

there *(in that place)* そこで [soko de]; *(to that place)* そこへ [soko e]
- he's over there あそこにいます [asoko ni imasu]
- there is/are... *(things)* ...があります [...ga arimasu]; *(people, animals)* ...がいます [...ga imasu]

saying thank you

- thank you ありがとう [arigatô]
- thanks, that's very kind of you ご親切に、ありがとう [goshinsetsu ni arigatô]
- thank you for your help 手伝ってもらってありがとう [tetsudatte moratte arigatô]
- I wanted to thank you for inviting me ご招待、ありがとうございます [goshôtai arigatô gozaimasu]

- there's a problem 問題があります [mondai ga arimasu]
- are there any restrooms near here? 近くにトイレはありますか [chikaku ni toire wa arimasu ka]
- there you are *(handing over something)* はい、どうぞ [hai, dôzo]

thermometer 温度計 [ondokê]; *(for person)* 体温計 [taionkê]
- do you have a thermometer? 体温計はありますか [taionkê wa arimasu ka]
- the thermometer shows 18 degrees (Celsius) 温度計は１８度を指しています [ondokê wa jûhachi do o sashite imasu]

thin *(person)* やせている [yasete iru]; *(slice, layer, material)* 薄い [usui]
- isn't that jacket too thin for a cold evening like this? 今夜のように寒い夜には、その上着は薄すぎませんか [kon ya no yô ni samui yoru ni wa sono uwagi wa ususugimasen ka]

thing *(object)* もの [mono]; *(matter)* こと [koto] ◆ **things** *(possessions)* 持ち物 [mochimono]
- what's that thing for? それは何のためですか [sore wa nan no tame desu ka]
- I don't know what the best thing to do is 何をするのが一番いいか分かりません [nani o suru no ga ichiban î ka wakarimasen]
- could you look after my things for a minute? 持ち物をちょっと見ていてもらえませんか [mochimono o chotto mite ite moraemasen ka]

think *(believe)* 思う [omou] ◆ *(use mind)* 考える [kangaeru]
- I think (that)... ...と思います [...to omoimasu]
- I thought service charge was included サービス料は含まれているんだと思っていました [sâbisu ryô wa fukumarete iru n da to omotte imashita]
- I don't think so そうは思いませんが [sô wa omoimasen ga]
- I'll think about it 考えておきます [kangaete okimasu]

third 三番目の [sam bam me no] ◆ *(fraction)* 三分の一 [sam bun no ichi]; *(gear)* 三速 [san soku]
- this is my third time in Japan 日本に来るのは三度目です [nihon ni kuru no wa san do me desu]

thirsty
- to be thirsty のどが渇いた [nodo ga kawaita]
- I'm very thirsty とてものどが渇いています [totemo nodo ga kawaite imasu]

three 三 [san]
- there are three of us 全部で三人です [zembu de san nin desu]

throat のど [nodo]
- I have a fish bone stuck in my throat 魚の骨がのどに刺さっています [sakana no hone ga nodo ni sasatte imasu]

throat lozenge のど飴 [nodo ame]
- I'd like some throat lozenges のど飴がほしいです [nodo ame ga hoshî desu]

train and subway tickets ⓘ

A Japan Railpass, valid for 7, 14, or 21 days, allows standard-class travel on the whole JR network, including all but the fastest bullet trains, and can be very good value. It can only be bought outside Japan. See www.japanrailpass.net. Tickets for long-distance trains are sold at ticket offices, but those for local trains are bought from automatic machines. Basic fare tickets (乗車券 [jôsha ken]) are required for all journeys, but an express supplement (特急券 [tokkyû ken]) also has to be paid for fast trains. Most stations have barriers with machines to check tickets as you go through to the platforms, with a staffed booth at the side. This is where you should show your Japan Railpass. If you don't understand how to use the ticket machines, help will usually be offered by a station employee or a member of the public. Alternatively, if you're not sure where you're going or can't read the price for a destination written in Japanese, you can just buy the cheapest ticket and pay the excess when you arrive. You will not be suspected of trying to cheat if there is an on-train ticket inspection. There are machines at most station exits to collect the tickets, and if you have traveled further than you originally intended, go to the staffed booth to pay the excess. For the subway and local trains, you can get monthly passes (定期 [têki]) to save you having to queue up at the automatic ticket machines. The networks are not divided into zones – a têki is valid from one point to another, on a designated private rail line. When you change from one private line to another, you usually have to pay twice, although companies do have agreements that reduce the cost slightly if you buy a ticket for the whole journey before you set off.

thunderstorm 激しい雷雨 [hageshî raiu]
- will there be a thunderstorm? 激しい雷雨になりそうですか [hageshî raiu ni narisô desu ka]

Thursday 木曜日 [mokuyôbi]
- we're arriving/leaving on Thursday 木曜日に着きます/出ます [mokuyôbi ni tsukimasu/demasu]

ticket チケット [chiketto], 切符 [kippu]
- I'd like a ticket to... ...までの切符がほしいんですが [...made no kippu ga hoshî n desu ga]
- how much is a ticket to...? ...までの切符はいくらですか [...made no kippu wa ikura desu ka]
- I'd like to book a ticket チケットを予約したいんですが [chiketto o yoyaku shitai n desu ga]
- I'd like three tickets for... ...のチケットを３枚お願いします [...no chiketto o sam mai onegai shimasu]

tipping

Tipping is not necessary or expected in Japan.

tide 潮 [shio]
- what time does the tide turn? 何時に潮の流れは変わりますか [nan ji ni shio no nagare wa kawarimasu ka]

tight *(piece of clothing)* きつい [kitsui]
- these pants are too tight このズボンはきつすぎます [kono zubon wa kitsusugimasu]

time 時間 [jikan]; *(occasion)* 機会 [kikai]
- do we have time to visit the town? 町へ行く時間はありますか [machi e iku jikan wa arimasu ka]
- what time is it? 何時ですか [nan ji desu ka]
- what time do you close? 何時に閉まりますか [nan ji ni shimarimasu ka]
- could you tell me if the train from Tokyo is on time? 東京からの列車は時間通りかどうか教えてもらえませんか [tôkyô kara no ressha wa jikan dôri ka dô ka oshiete moraemasen ka]
- maybe some other time また別の機会に [mata betsu no kikai ni]
- three times 三回 [san kai]
- at the same time 同時に [dô ji ni]
- the first time 初めて [hajimete]

timetable 時刻表 [jikokuhyô]
- do you have bus timetables? バスの時刻表はありますか [basu no jikokuhyô wa arimasu ka]

tip チップ [chippu]
- should I leave a tip? チップを置くべきですか [chippu o oku beki desu ka]

tire *(for a vehicle)* タイヤ [taiya]
- the tire's flat タイヤがパンクしました [taiya ga panku shimashita]
- the tire's punctured タイヤがパンクしました [taiya ga panku shimashita]

tired 疲れた [tsukareta]
- I'm very tired とても疲れました [totemo tsukaremashita]

to *(indicating place, direction)* へ [...e]; *(as far as)* まで [...made]
- when is the next train to Kanazawa? 金沢への次の列車は何時ですか [kanazawa e no tsugi no ressha wa nan ji desu ka]
- it's twenty to nine 8時40分です [hachi ji yonjippun desu]

tobacco store タバコ屋 [tabako ya]
- where is the nearest tobacco store? 一番近いタバコ屋はどこですか [ichiban chikai tabako ya wa doko desu ka]

toilets ⓘ

Although western-style toilets are now very common in Japan, you will still find squat ones too. These are set into the floor, sometimes on a platform raised about a foot above the main floor; to use them, squat down, facing the hood. There will sometimes be special slippers to wear, so remember to change back out of these when you leave! Some women's public toilets have buttons to press to play music or make a flushing noise. In smart hotels and in homes, you may find very modern bidet toilets with heated seats, washing and hot air drying functions. Public toilets are quite easy to find in department stores and other large stores, as well as in stations and parks. Many do not have towels or hand-driers, so Japanese carry a handkerchief to dry their hands on instead.

today 今日 [kyô]
- ▶ what's today's date? 今日は何日ですか [kyô wa nan nichi desu ka]

toe 足の指 [ashi no yubi]
- ▶ I think I've broken my toe 足の指を折ったんだと思います [ashi no yubi o otta n da to omoimasu]

together 一緒に [issho ni]
- ▶ let's go together 一緒に行きましょう [issho ni ikimashô]

toilet トイレ [toire]、お手洗い [otearai]
- ▶ I need to go to the toilet お手洗いに行かなければなりません [otearai ni ikanakereba narimasen]

toilet paper トイレットペーパー [toiretto pêpâ]
- ▶ there is no toilet paper トイレットペーパーがありません [toiretto pêpâ ga arimasen]

toll *(for a road, a bridge)* 通行料 [tsûkô ryô]
- ▶ do you have to pay a toll to use the bridge? 橋を渡るのに通行料を払わなければいけませんか [hashi o wataru no ni tsûkô ryô o harawanakereba ikemasen ka]

toll-free *(number, call)* フリーダイアルの [furî daiaru no] ♦ *(to call)* フリーダイアルで [furî daiaru de]
- ▶ there's a toll-free number you can call フリーダイアルの電話があります [furî daiaru no denwa ga arimasu]

tomato トマト [tomato]
- ▶ two tomatoes トマト二個 [tomato ni ko]

tomato juice トマトジュース [tomato jûsu]
- ▶ I'd like a tomato juice トマトジュースがほしいです [tomato jûsu ga hoshî desu]

tomorrow 明日 [ashita]

▸ can you hold my reservation until tomorrow? 明日まで予約をそのままにしておいてくれますか [ashita made yoyaku o sono mama ni shite oite kuremasu ka]

▸ I'm leaving tomorrow morning 明日の朝、出ます [ashita no asa demasu]

▸ see you tomorrow night 明日の晩、会いましょう [ashita no ban aimashô]

tonight 今夜 [kon ya], 今晩 [kom ban]

▸ do you have any rooms available for tonight? 今晩、空いている部屋はありますか [kom ban aite iru heya wa arimasu ka]

too *(also)* も [mo]; *(excessively)* すぎる [sugiru]

▸ enjoy your meal! – you too お食事を楽しんでください–そちらも [oshokuji o tanoshinde kudasai – sochira mo]

▸ I'm too tired to... ...するのには疲れすぎています [...suru no ni wa tsukaresugite imasu]

▸ it's too expensive 高すぎます [takasugimasu]

▸ there are too many people 人が多すぎます [hito ga ôsugimasu]

tooth 歯 [ha]

▸ I've broken a tooth 歯が折れました [ha ga oremashita]

toothache 歯が痛いこと [ha ga itai koto]

▸ I have a toothache 歯が痛いです [ha ga itai desu]

toothbrush 歯ブラシ [haburashi]

▸ I forgot my toothbrush 歯ブラシを忘れました [haburashi o wasuremashita]

toothpaste 歯磨き [hamigaki]

▸ I'd like to buy some toothpaste 歯磨きが買いたいんですが [hamigaki ga kaitai n desu ga]

top *(of a bottle, tube, jar)* ふた [futa]; *(of a mountain)* 頂上 [chôjô] ◆ *(maximum)* 最高で [saikô de]

▸ the car drove away at top speed 車は最高スピードで走り去りました [kuruma wa saikô supîdo de hashiri sarimashita]

tour 旅行 [ryokô]

▸ I'm planning to do a two-week tour of the country 2週間の国内旅行を計画しています [ni shûkan no kokunai ryokô o kêkaku shite imasu]

tourist 観光客 [kankô kyaku] ◆ *(season)* 観光シーズン [kankô shîzun]

▸ do you get many tourists here? ここにはたくさん観光客が来ますか [koko ni wa takusan kankô kyaku ga kimasu ka]

tourist attraction 観光名所 [kankô mêsho]

▸ what are the main tourist attractions in the area? この地域の主な観光名所は何ですか [kono chi-iki no omo na kankô mêsho wa nan desu ka]

tourist guide

Most places of interest do not offer guided tours; instead, visitors can usually hire headsets with commentary in Japanese or English. There is usually an entrance fee, even at temples and shrines. Flash photography is forbidden (フラッシュ禁止 [furasshu kinshi]) in many temples and museums.

tourist class ツーリストクラス [tsûrisuto kurasu]
▸ in tourist class, please ツーリストクラスでお願いします [tsûrisuto kurasu de onegai shimasu]

tourist guide 観光ガイド [kankô gaido]
▸ we have a good tourist guide (book) with a lot of up-to-date information 最新の情報が載っているいい観光ガイドを持っています [saishin no jôhô ga notte iru î kankô gaido o motte imasu]

tourist office 観光案内所 [kankô annaijo]
▸ I'm looking for the tourist office 観光案内所を探しています [kankô annaijo o sagashite imasu]
▸ can I get a map of the town at the tourist office? 町の地図を観光案内所でもらえますか [machi no chizu o kankô annaijo de moraemasu ka]

tow 引っ張る [hipparu]
▸ could you tow me to a garage? 修理工場まで引っ張ってくれませんか [shûri kôjô made hippatte kuremasen ka]

toward (in the direction of) に向かって [...ni mukatte]
▸ we're heading toward Kobe 神戸に向かっています [kôbe ni mukatte imasu]

tow away レッカー車で運ぶ [rekkâ sha de hakobu]
▸ my car's been towed away 車はレッカー車で運ばれてしまいました [kuruma wa rekkâ sha de hakobarete shimaimashita]

towel タオル [taoru]
▸ we don't have any towels タオルがありません [taoru ga arimasen]
▸ could we have more towels? もっとタオルをもらえませんか [motto taoru o moraemasen ka]

tourist office

Tourist information offices are often inside railway stations or nearby, and are open daily from 10 a.m. to 5 p.m. Make sure you pick up plenty of leaflets and a streetmap, as there are few maps on display in towns, and those there are will almost always be in Japanese.

tower 塔 [tô]
▸ can you visit the tower? あの塔へ行けますか [ano tô e ikemasu ka]

town 町 [machi]
▸ to go into town 町の中に入る [machi no naka ni hairu]

town hall 市役所 [shiyakusho]
▸ where is the town hall? 市役所はどこですか [shiyakusho wa doko desu ka]

traditional 伝統的な [dentôteki na]
▸ I'd like to stay in a traditional Japanese inn 伝統的な旅館に泊まりたいんですが [dentôteki na ryokan ni tomaritai n desu ga]

traffic *(vehicles)* 車の量 [kuruma no ryô]
▸ is there a lot of traffic on the freeway? 高速道路は車で混んでいますか [kôsoku dôro wa kuruma de konde imasu ka]

traffic circle ロータリー [rôtarî]
▸ you turn right at the traffic circle ロータリーで右に曲がってください [rôtarî de migi ni magatte kudasai]

traffic jam 交通渋滞 [kôtsû jûtai]
▸ we got stuck in a traffic jam 交通渋滞に巻き込まれました [kôtsû jûtai ni makikomaremashita]

traffic lights 信号（機）[shingô(ki)]
▸ turn left at the traffic lights 信号を左に曲がりなさい [shingô o hidari ni magarinasai]

trail *(path)* 道 [michi]
▸ will this trail take us back to the parking lot? この道は駐車場に戻りますか [kono michi wa chûshajô ni modorimasu ka]

---

getting around town

▸ which bus goes to the airport? どのバスが空港に行きますか [dono basu ga kûkô ni ikimasu ka]
▸ where does the bus to the station leave from? 駅へのバスはどこから出ますか [eki e no basu wa doka kara demasu ka]
▸ I'd like a one-way (ticket) to... ...への片道切符をください [...e no katamichi kippu o kudasai]
▸ could you tell me where I have to get off to go to...? ...へ行くのにはどこで降りたらいいか教えてくれませんか [...e iku no ni wa doko de oritara î ka oshiete kuremasen ka]

trains ⓘ

The Japanese rail network is dense, and concentrated around the Pacific coast cities. The bullet train 新幹線 [shinkansen] links the main cities, while the privatized rail company Japanese Railway (JR), divided into six regions, serves the thousands of small local stations all over the country. There are also many local private rail companies. Trains generally run on time, barring natural disasters, such as earthquakes, typhoons and snowstorms. Train timetables are drawn up in table form with the times running vertically, with a special red timetable for Sundays and holidays. Trains may be super express (特急 [tokkyû]), express (急行 [kyûkô]), semi-express (準急 [junkyû]) or slow (普通 [futsû]). Carriages are divided into first class (グリーン車 [gurîn sha]), second class with reservation (指定席 [shitê seki]) and second class without reservation (自由席 [jiyû seki]). Commuter trains in the big cities are extremely crowded in the morning and early evening. Announcements are made in English on the bullet train, but only in Japanese on other trains.

train 列車 [ressha]

▸ when is the next train to Shibuya? 渋谷に行く次の列車は何時ですか [shibuya ni iku tsugi no ressha wa nan ji desu ka]

▸ which platform does the train for Shinjuku leave from? 新宿行きの列車は何番ホームから出ますか [shinjuku yuki no ressha wa nam ban hômu kara demasu ka]

▸ the train was fifteen minutes late 列車が１５分遅れました [ressha ga jûgo fun okuremashita]

tram 市電 [shiden]

▸ can you buy tickets on the tram? 切符は市電の中で買えますか [kippu wa shiden no naka de kaemasu ka]

▸ which tram line do we have to take? どの市電の線に乗ったらいいんですか [dono shiden no sen ni nottara î n desu ka]

▸ where is the nearest tram stop? 一番近い市電の乗り場はどこですか [ichiban chikai shiden no noriba wa doko desu ka]

transfer (of money) お金を口座から口座に移すこと [okane o kôza kara kôza ni utsusu koto]; (of train, plane) 乗り換え [norikae] ◆ (money) 移す [utsusu]; (train, plane) 乗り換える [norikaeru]

▸ you have to transfer at Nagoya 名古屋で乗り換えなければなりません [nagoya de norikaenakereba narimasen]

travel (movement) 移動 [idô]; (progress) 進行 [shinkô] ◆ 旅行する [ryokô suru]

traveling

Traveling is safe in Japan, and public transportation is well-coordinated and efficient. However, it can be expensive. Trains, buses and subways in the cities are very crowded in the commuter rush-hour periods.

▸ I'd like a window seat facing the direction of travel 進行方向を向いた窓側の席がいいんですが [shinkô hôkô o muita mado gawa no seki ga î n desu ga]
▸ I'm traveling on my own 一人で旅行しています [hitori de ryokô shite imasu]

travel agency 旅行会社 [ryokô gaisha]
▸ I'm looking for a travel agency 旅行会社を探しています [ryokô gaisha o sagashite imasu]

traveler's check トラベラーズチェック [toraberâzu chekku]
▸ do you take traveler's checks? トラベラーズチェックは受け取りますか [toraberâzu chekku wa uketorimasu ka]

tree 木 [ki]
▸ what type of tree is that? あれは何の木ですか [are wa nan no ki desu ka]

trip *(journey)* 旅 [tabi]
▸ have a good trip! 楽しい旅を！ [tanoshî tabi o]

trouble *(difficulty)* 問題 [mondai]; *(nuisance)* 面倒 [mendô]
▸ we didn't have any trouble finding the hotel ホテルを見つけるのに何の問題もありませんでした [hoteru o mitsukeru no ni nan no mondai mo arimasen deshita]
▸ I don't want to be any trouble 面倒をおかけしたくありません [mendô o okake shitaku arimasen]
▸ it's no trouble どういたしまして [dô itashimashite]

trunk トランク [toranku]
▸ my things are in the trunk of the car 持ち物は車のトランクに入っています [mochimono wa kuruma no toranku ni haitte imasu]
▸ I've got two small suitcases and a large trunk 小さなスーツケースが二つに大きなトランクが一つあります [chîsa na sûtsukêsu ga futatsu ni ôki na toranku ga hitotsu arimasu]

try *(attempt)* 試す [tamesu]; *(doing)* てみる [te miru]
▸ I'd like to try the local beer 地ビールを飲んでみたいんですが [ji bîru o nonde mitai n desu ga]

try on *(dress)* 着てみる [kite miru]; *(shoes, pants, skirt)* はいてみる [haite miru]
▸ I'd like to try on the one in the window ショーウィンドーに飾ってあるものを着てみたいんですが [shô windô ni kazatte aru mono o kite mitai n desu ga]

tub (of ice cream) 容器 [yôki]
- do you sell tubs of ice cream to take home? 持ち帰り用の容器に入った アイスクリームは売っていますか [mochikaeri yô no yôki ni haitta aisukurîmu wa utte imasu ka]

Tuesday 火曜日 [kayôbi]
- we're arriving/leaving on Tuesday 火曜日に着きます/出ます [kayôbi ni tsukimasu/demasu]

turn (in a game, order) 順番 [jumban]; (off a road) 曲がり [magari] ◆ (change direction) 曲がる [magaru]
- it's your turn そちらの番です [sochira no ban desu]
- is this the turn for the campground? キャンプ場へ行く道はここで曲が るんですか [kyampu jô e iku michi wa koko de magaru n desu ka]
- turn left at the lights 信号を左に曲がりなさい [shingô o hidari ni magarinasai]
- you have to turn right 右に曲がりなさい [migi ni magarinasai]

turn down (radio, volume, gas) 小さくする [chîsaku suru]
- can we turn the air-conditioning down? エアコンを弱くしてもいいです か [eakon o yowaku shite mo î desu ka]
- how do you turn the volume down? どうやってボリュームを小さくす るんですか [dô yatte boryûmu o chîsaku suru n desu ka]

turn off (light) 消す [kesu]; (appliance) 切る [kiru]
- where do you turn the light off? どこで電気を消しますか [doko de denki o keshimasu ka]
- my cell was turned off 携帯が切ってありました [kêtai ga kitte arimashita]

turn on (light, radio) つける [tsukeru]
- where do I turn this light on? どこで電気をつけますか [doko de denki o tsukemasu ka]
- can you turn on the ignition? エンジンをかけてもらえますか [enjin o kakete moraemasu ka]

turn up (sound, central heating) 強くする [tsuyoku suru]
- how do you turn up the heating? ヒーターはどうやって強くしますか [hîtâ wa dô yatte tsuyoku shimasu ka]

TV (system, set) テレビ [terebi]; (broadcasts) テレビ番組 [terebi bangumi]
- the TV in our room is broken 部屋のテレビは壊れています [heya no terebi wa kowarete imasu]

twelve 十二 [jûni] ◆ (noon) 正午 [shôgo]; (midnight) 真夜中 [mayonaka]
- there are twelve of us 全部で十二人です [zembu de jûni nin desu]
- it's twelve o'clock (noon) 昼の十二時です [hiru no jûni ji desu]; (midnight) 夜中の十二時です [yonaka no jûni ji desu]

typhoons

August and September are the main season for typhoons and tropical storms, and they are given numbers rather than names as in the US.

twice 二度 [ni do]
▸ the ferry runs twice a day フェリーは一日二度出ます [ferî wa ichi nichi ni do demasu]

twin 双子 [futago] ◆ 双子の [futago no]
▸ twin brother 双子の兄弟 [futago no kyôdai]
▸ twin sister 双子の姉妹 [futago no shimai]

twin beds ツインベッド [tsuin beddo]
▸ a room with twin beds ツインベッドの部屋 [tsuin beddo no heya]

twin room ツインルーム [tsuin rûmu]
▸ we'd like a twin room ツインルームがいいんですが [tsuin rûmu ga î n desu ga]

two 二 [ni]
▸ there are two of us 二人です [futari desu]

typhoon 台風 [taifû]
▸ is the typhoon likely to hit here? 台風は上陸しそうですか [taifû wa jôriku shisô desu ka]

umbrella 傘 [kasa]
▸ could you lend me an umbrella? 傘を貸してもらえませんか [kasa o kashite moraemasen ka]

unacceptable 受け入れられない [ukeirerarenai]
▸ it's completely unacceptable! 全く受け入れられません [mattaku ukeireraremasen]

underpass 地下道 [chikadô]
▸ is the underpass safe at night? 地下道は夜も安全ですか [chikadô wa yoru mo anzen desu ka]

understand 分かる [wakaru]
▸ I can understand Japanese, but I can't really speak it 日本語は分かりますが、話せません [nihongo wa wakarimasu ga, hanasemasen]

▸ I understand a little 少しだけ分かります [sukoshi dake wakarimasu]
▸ I don't understand a word 一言も分かりません [hito koto mo wakarimasen]
▸ do you understand? 分かりましたか [wakarimashita ka]

United States (of America)

▸ the United States アメリカ [amerika]
▸ I'm from the United States アメリカからです [amerika kara desu]
▸ I live in the United States アメリカに住んでいます [amerika ni sunde imasu]
▸ have you ever been to the United States? アメリカに行ったことがありますか [amerika ni itta koto ga arimasu ka]

until ...まで [...made]

▸ I'm staying until Sunday 日曜日までいます [nichiyôbi made imasu]
▸ until noon 正午まで [shôgo made]

up (to or in a higher position) 上へ [ue e] ◆ up to ...まで [...made]

▸ what's up? (what's wrong) どうしましたか? (as greeting) やあ [yâ]
▸ what are you up to tonight? 今夜はどうするつもりですか [kon ya wa dô suru tsumori desu ka]
▸ up to now 今まで [ima made]

urgent 急ぎの [isogi no]

▸ it's not urgent 急ぎの用事じゃありません [isogi no yôji ja arimasen]

urgently 急いで [isoide]

▸ I have to see a dentist urgently 急いで歯医者に見てもらわなければなりません [isoide haisha ni mite morawanakereba narimasen]

US(A)

▸ the US アメリカ [amerika]
▸ I'm from the US アメリカからです [amerika kara desu]

---

saying that you have understood/not understood

▸ oh, I see...! ああ、分かりました [â, wakarimashita]
▸ sorry, but I didn't understand すみません、分かりませんでした [sumimasen, wakarimasen deshita]
▸ I'm a little confused... ちょっと混乱しています [chotto konran shite imasu]
▸ I don't understand your question 質問の意味が分かりません [shitsumon no imi ga wakarimasen]
▸ sorry, but I still don't understand すみませんが、まだ分かりません [sumimasen ga, mada wakarimasen]

▸ I live in the US アメリカに住んでいます [amerika ni sunde imasu]

▸ have you ever been to the US? アメリカに行ったことがありますか [amerika ni itta koto ga arimasu ka]

use 使う [tsukau]

▸ could I use your cellphone? 携帯を使わせてもらえませんか [kêtai o tsukawasete moraemasen ka]

vacancy 空き [aki]

▸ do you have any vacancies for tonight? 今晩、空きはありませんか [kom ban aki wa arimasen ka]

vacation 休暇 [kyûka]

▸ are you here on vacation? ここには休暇で来ていますか [koko ni wa kyûka de kite imasu ka]

▸ I'm on vacation 休暇です [kyûka desu]

valid 有効な [yûkô na]

▸ is this ticket valid for the exhibit too? このチケットは展覧会にも有効ですか [kono chiketto wa tenrankai ni mo yûkô desu ka]

▸ how long is this ticket valid for? このチケットの有効期間はどれくらいですか [kono chiketto no yûkô kikan wa dore gurai desu ka]

▸ my passport is still valid パスポートはまだ有効です [pasupôto wa mada yûkô desu]

vegetable 野菜 [yasai]

▸ does it come with vegetables? 野菜も付いてきますか [yasai mo tsuite kimasu ka]

vegetarian 菜食主義の [saishoku shugi no] ◆ 菜食主義者 [saishoku shugisha]

▸ I'm a vegetarian 菜食主義です [saishoku shugi desu]

▸ which dishes are suitable for vegetarians? 菜食主義者が食べられるのはどの料理ですか [saishoku shugisha ga taberareru no wa dono ryôri desu ka]

vending machine 自動販売機 [jidôhambaiki]

▸ the vending machine isn't working 自動販売機が壊れています [jidôhambaiki ga kowarete imasu]

vertigo 高所恐怖症 [kôsho kyôfushô]

▸ I suffer from vertigo 高所恐怖症です [kôsho kyôfushô desu]

very とても [totemo]

▸ I'm very hungry とてもおなかが空きました [totemo onaka ga sukimashita]

vegetables

The large white radish (大根 [daikon]), at least a foot long, is an important vegetable in Japanese cuisine, eaten cooked in miso soup or in slices, or raw in salad, or grated and mixed into soya sauce as a dip. Spinach (ほうれん草 [hôrensô]) is popular, often cooked with soya sauce and other flavorings. Cabbage (キャベツ [kyabetsu]) shredded as a salad is common. Potatoes (ジャガイモ [jagaimo]) feature particularly in a dish beloved of children: カレーライス [karê raisu] (curry rice), which consists of meat, potatoes, and carrots in a thick mild curry sauce, served with rice. Sweet potatoes (さつまいも [satsumaimo]) are traditionally sold by street vendors with carts in the winter.

> very much たいへん [taihen]
> very near とても近い [totemo chikai]

view *(panorama)* 景色 [keshiki], 見晴らし [miharashi]
> I'd prefer a room with an ocean view 海の見える部屋のほうがいいです [umi no mieru heya no hô ga î desu]

villa 貸し別荘 [kashi bessô]
> we'd like to rent a villa for one week 一週間、貸し別荘を借りたいんですが [isshûkan kashi bessô o karitai n desu ga]

virus ウイルス [uirusu]
> I must have picked up a virus どこかでウイルスに感染したようです [doko ka de uirusu ni kansen shita yô desu]

visa ビザ [biza]
> do you need a visa? ビザが必要ですか [biza ga hitsuyô desu ka]

visit 訪問 [hômon] ◆ 訪ねる [tazuneru]
> is this your first visit to Kyoto? 京都には初めて来ましたか [kyôto ni wa hajimete kimashita ka]

vegetarian food

Vegetarianism (菜食主義 [saishoku shugi]) is not common in Japan today, despite the long tradition of Buddhist vegetarian food (精進料理 [shôjin ryôri]). Many Japanese dishes contain small amounts of fish or meat (particularly ham or bacon, which may not be considered as meat), and bonito fish flakes are used in stock for soup and other dishes. You can try asking for a dish without X ([x nashi]).

volcanoes

Situated on the Pacific 'ring of fire,' Japan has a large proportion of the world's volcanoes, with around 80 active ones. Even Mt. Fuji, which has been dormant for almost 300 years, may still erupt again. Volcanoes are often popular tourist areas because of the hot springs they produce in the surrounding area.

▸ I'd like to visit the castle 城を訪ねてみたいんですが [shiro o tazunete mitai n desu ga]

voicemail 留守電 [rusu den]
▸ I need to check my voicemail 留守電をチェックしなければなりません [rusu den o chekku shinakereba narimasen]

volcano 火山 [kazan]
▸ we'd like to visit a volcano 火山に行ってみたいんです が [kazan ni itte mitai n desu ga]

voucher 引換券 [hikikaeken]
▸ I haven't received the voucher 引換券をまだ受け取っていません [hikikaeken o mada uketotte imasen]

waist ウエスト [uêsuto]
▸ it's a little bit tight at the waist ウエストがちょっときついです [uesuto ga chotto kitsui desu]

wait 待つ [matsu]
▸ have you been waiting long? 長く待ちましたか [nagaku machimashita ka]

waiter ウエイター [uêtâ]
▸ waiter, could we have the check, please? ウエイターさん、お勘定お願いします [uêtâ san, okanjô onegai shimasu]

wait for を待つ [...o matsu]
▸ are you waiting for the bus? バスを待っているんですか [basu o matte iru n desu ka]
▸ I'm waiting for them to call back 電話をかけなおしてくれるのを待っています [denwa o kakenaoshite kureru no o matte imasu]
▸ don't wait for me 待たないで先に行ってください [matanaide saki ni itte kudasai]

▸ sorry to have kept you waiting お待たせしました [omatase shimashita]

waiting room 待合室 [machiai shitsu]
▸ is there a waiting room on the platform? ホームに待合室はありますか [hômu ni machiai shitsu wa arimasu ka]

waitress ウエイトレス [uêtoresu]
▸ the waitress has already taken our order ウエイトレスがもう注文は聞いていきました [uêtoresu ga mô chûmon wa kîte ikimashita]

wake 起こす [okosu] ◆ 起きる [okiru]
▸ could you wake me at 6:45? 6時45分に起こしてくれませんか [roku ji yonjûgo fun ni okoshite kuremasen ka]
▸ I always wake early いつも早く起きます [itsumo hayaku okimasu]

wake up 目を覚ます [me o samasu] ◆ 目が覚める [ma ga sameru]
▸ a noise woke me up in the middle of the night 音で夜中に目が覚めました [oto de yonaka ni me ga samemashita]
▸ I have to wake up very early tomorrow to catch the plane 飛行機に乗るために朝早く起きなければなりません [hikôki ni noru tame ni asa hayakau okinakereba narimasen]

walk 散歩 [sampo] ◆ 歩く [aruku]
▸ are there any interesting walks in the area? この地域に散歩するのにおもしろいところはありますか [kono chi-iki ni sampo suru no ni omoshiroi tokoro wa arimasu ka]
▸ let's go for a walk 散歩に行きましょう [sampo ni ikimashô]
▸ how long would it take me to walk there? そこまで歩くとどれぐらいかかりますか [soko made aruku to dore gurai kakarimasu ka]

walking boots ハイキングシューズ [haikingu shûzu]
▸ do you need walking boots? ハイキングシューズはいりますか [haikingu shûzu wa irimasu ka]

wallet 財布 [saifu]
▸ I've lost my wallet 財布を失くしました [saifu o nakushimashita]

want *(wish, desire)* ...たい [...tai]
▸ I want to go to Kyoto 京都に行きたいです [kyôto ni ikitai desu]

warm 暖かい [atatakai]
▸ it's warm 暖かいです [atatakai desu]
▸ where can I buy some warm clothing for the trip? どこで旅行用の暖かい服を買えますか [doko de ryokô yô no atatakai fuku o kaemasu ka]

warn 注意する [chûi suru]
▸ no one warned me about that! 誰もそれについて注意してくれませんでした [dare mo sore ni tsuite chûi shite kuremasen deshita]

water

Tap water is drinkable everywhere in Japan, and bottled water can be bought from stores and vending machines. In cafés and restaurants, you will usually be given a glass of water when you arrive, which will be refilled.

---

wash 洗う [arau]
- where can I wash my hands? 手はどこで洗えますか [te wa doko de araemasu ka]

watch 時計 [tokê] ◆ *(look at)* 見る [miru]; *(guard)* 見張る [miharu]
- my watch has been stolen 時計を盗まれました [tokê o nusumaremashita]
- can you watch my bags for a minute? ちょっと荷物を見ていてくれますか [chotto nimotsu o mite ite kuremasu ka]

water *(cold)* 水 [mizu]; *(hot)* お湯 [oyu]
- could I have some hot water, please? お湯をもらえませんか [oyu o moraemasen ka]
- there's no hot water お湯が出ません [oyu ga demasen]

water ski 水上スキーの板 [suijô sukî no ita]
- can I rent water skis here? ここで水上スキーの板は借りられますか [koko de suijô sukî no ita wa kariraremasu ka]

water skiing 水上スキー [suijô sukî]
- can I go water skiing anywhere around here? この辺で水上スキーはできますか [kono hen de suijô sukî wa dekimasu ka]

---

asking the way

- can you show me where we are on the map? 今どこにいるか、この地図で教えてくれませんか [ima doko ni iru ka kono chizu de oshiete kuremasen ka]
- where is the station/the post office? 駅/郵便局はどこですか [eki/yûbinkyoku wa doko desu ka]
- excuse me, how do you get to the imperial palace? すみませんが、皇居へはどうやって行ったらいいですか [sumimasen ga, kôkyo e wa dô yatte ittara î desu ka]
- is it far? 遠いですか [tôi desu ka]
- is it within walking distance? 歩いていける距離ですか [aruite ikeru kyori desu ka]

weather – climate   *(i)*

The Japanese archipelago stretches from the tip of Hokkaido in the north, at the same latitude as Montreal, to the Ryukyu (Okinawa) islands in the south, at the same latitude as southern Florida. The climate varies correspondingly. Hokkaido has snow for up to five months of the year and a warm but pleasantly fresh summer, while southern Kyushu and southern Shikoku enjoy semi-tropical mild winters. Most of Japan, apart from the high mountainous areas, Hokkaido and the northern parts of Honshu, is hot and humid during the summer. The area between the Japan Alps and the Sea of Japan is known as 'snow country' (雪国 [yuki guni]), and has heavy winter snowfalls of up to 20ft.

wave *(of water)* 波 [nami]
- the waves are very big today 今日は波がとても高いです [kyô wa nami ga totemo takai desu]

way *(means)* 方法 [hôhô]; *(direction)* 方向 [hôhô]; *(route)* 道 [michi]
- what's the best way of getting there? そこへ行く一番いい方法は何ですか [soko e iku ichiban î hôhô wa nan desu ka]
- which way is it to the bus station? バスターミナルに行くのはどちらの道ですか [basu tâminaru ni iku no wa dochira no michi desu ka]
- I went the wrong way 間違った方向に行ってしまいました [machigatta hôhô ni itte shimaimashita]
- is this the right way to the castle? 城に行くのはこの道でいいですか [shiro ni iku no wa kono michi de î desu ka]
- on the way 途中で [tochû de]
- no way! 冗談じゃない！ [jôdan ja nai]

way out 出口 [deguchi]
- where's the way out? 出口はどこですか [deguchi wa doko desu ka]

weak *(person)* 弱い [yowai]; *(drink)* 薄い [usui]
- I feel very weak 力が出ません [chikara ga demasen]
- could I have a very weak coffee? すごく薄いコーヒーをもらえませんか [sugoku usui kôhî o moraemasen ka]

wear *(dress, shirt, jacket)* 着る [kiru]; *(pants, skirt)* はく [haku]; *(hat, cap)* かぶる [kaburu]; *(glasses)* かける [kakeru]
- is what I'm wearing all right? 今、着ているもので大丈夫ですか [ima kite iru mono de daijôbu desu ka]

weather 天気 [tenki]; *(on the TV, the radio)* 天気予報 [tenki yohô]
- what is the weather like today? 今日の天気はどうですか [kyô no tenki wa dô desu ka]

▸ is the weather going to change? 天気は変わりそうですか [tenki wa kawarisô desu ka]

weather forecast 天気予報 [tenki yohô]

▸ what's the weather forecast for tomorrow? 明日の天気について天気予報はなんと言っていましたか [ashita no tenki ni tsuite tenki yohô wa nan to itte imashita ka]

website address ホームページアドレス [hômu pêji adoresu]

▸ can you give me your website address? ホームページアドレスを教えてくれませんか [hômu pêji adoresu o oshiete kuremasen ka]

Wednesday 水曜日 [suiyôbi]

▸ we're arriving/leaving on Wednesday 水曜日に着きます/出ます [suiyôbi ni tsukimasu/demasu]

week *(Sunday to Saturday)* 週 [shû]; *(period)* 週間 [shûkan]

▸ how much is it for a week? 一週間でいくらですか [isshûkan de ikura desu ka]

▸ I'm leaving in a week 一週間後に出ます [isshûkan go ni demasu]

▸ two weeks 二週間 [ni shûkan]

weekly 週の [shû no]

▸ is there a weekly rate? 料金は一週間につきいくらですか [ryôkin wa isshûkan ni tsuki ikura desu ka]

welcome 歓迎される [kangê sareru] ◆ 歓迎 [kangê] ◆ 歓迎する [kangê suru]

▸ welcome! ようこそ！ [yôkoso]

▸ you're welcome *(in reply to thanks)* どういたしまして [dô itashimashite]

▸ you're welcome to join us ご一緒するのは大歓迎です [goissho suru no wa dai kangê desu]

well *(in health)* 元気な [genki na] ◆ よく [yoku]

▸ I'm very well, thank you おかげさまで元気です [okage sama de genki desu]

▸ I'm not feeling very well あまり気分がよくありません [amari kibun ga yoku arimasen]

▸ get well soon! 早くよくなってください [hayaku yoku natte kudasai]

▸ well played よくがんばった [yoku gambatta]

well done *(steak)* ウェルダン [weru dan]

▸ well done, please ウェルダンでお願いします [weru dan de onegai shimasu]

what 何の [nan no], 何 [nan/nani]

▸ what type of tree is that? 何の木ですか？ [nan no ki desu ka]

▸ what? *(asking for repetition)* 何ですって？ [nan desu tte]

▸ what is it? *(what's this thing?)* これは何ですか [kore wa nan desu ka]; *(what's the matter?)* どうしたんですか [dô shita n desu ka]

▸ what's up? *(what's wrong)* どうしましたか？ [dô shimashita ka]; *(as greeting)* やあ [yâ]

- what's your name? お名前は？ [onamae wa]
- what's it called? なんと呼びますか [nan to yobimasu ka]
- what time is it? 何時ですか [nan ji desu ka]
- what day is it? 何日ですか [nan nichi desu ka]
- what desserts do you have? どんなデザートがありますか [donna dezâto ga arimasu ka]

wheel 車輪 [sharin]
- could you help me change the wheel? 車輪を換えるのを手伝ってくれませんか [sharin o kaeru no o tetsudatte kuremasen ka]

when いつ [itsu]
- when was it built? いつ建てられましたか [itsu tateraremashita ka]
- when is the next train to Osaka? 大阪行きの次の列車はいつですか [ôsaka yuki no tsugi no ressha wa itsu desu ka]

where どこ [doko]
- where do you live? どこに住んでいますか [doko ni sunde imasu ka]
- where are you from? どこから来ましたか [doko kara kimashita ka]
- excuse me, where is the nearest bus stop, please? すみませんが、一番近いバス停はどこですか [sumimasen ga, ichiban chikai basu tê wa doko desu ka]

which どちら [dochira]
- which hotel would you recommend for us? どちらのホテルがお薦めですか [dochira no hoteru ga osusume desu ka]
- which way should we go? どちらの道を行ったらいいでしょうか [dochira no michi o ittara î deshô ka]
- which do you prefer? どちらがいいですか [dochira ga î desu ka]

while 間 [aida]
- I'm only planning to stay for a while ちょっとの間だけいるつもりです [chotto no aida dake iru tsumori desu]

white *(in color)* 白い [shiroi]
- I need a white T-shirt 白いTシャツがいります [shiroi tîshatsu ga irimasu]

white wine 白ワイン [shiro wain]
- a glass of white wine, please 白ワインを一杯ください [shiro wain o ippai kudasai]

who 誰 [dare]
- who are you? 誰ですか [dare desu ka]
- who should I speak to about the heating? 暖房については誰に話せばいいですか [dambô ni tsuite wa dare ni hanaseba î desu ka]
- who's calling? どちら様ですか [dochira sama desu ka]

whole 全体の [zentai no] • **on the whole** 全体としては [zentai toshite wa]
- we spent the whole day walking 一日中歩きました [ichi nichi jû arukimashita]

▸ on the whole we had a good time 全体としては楽しかったです [zentai toshite wa tanoshikatta desu]

whole-wheat 全粒粉の [zenryûfun no]
▸ I'd like some whole-wheat bread 全粒粉のパンがほしいんですが [zenryûfun no pan ga hoshî n desu ga]

why 何故 [naze], どうして [dôshite]
▸ why not? 何故だめなの？ [naze dame na no]; *(good idea)* もちろん [mochiron]

wide *(river, road)* 広い [hiroi]
▸ 2 meters wide 幅２メートル [haba ni mêtoru]

will *(to express future tense)* だろう [darô]; *(indicating willingness)* つもりだ [tsumori da]
▸ I'll be arriving at six ６時に着くでしょう [roku ji ni tsuku deshô]

win *(competition, race)* 勝つ [katsu] ◆ *(be ahead)* 勝っている [katte iru]
▸ who's winning? 誰が勝っていますか [dare ga katte imasu ka]

wind 風 [kaze]
▸ there's a strong West wind 強い西の風が吹いています [tsuyoi nishi no kaze ga fuite imasu]

window *(of a building)* 窓 [mado]; *(of a store)* ショーウィンドー [shô windô]; *(at a station, in a post office)* 窓口 [madoguchi]
▸ I can't open the window 窓が開けられません [mado ga akeraremasen]
▸ I'm cold: could you close your window? 寒いです；窓を閉めてくれませんか [samui desu. mado o shimete kuremasen ka]
▸ I'd like to see the dress in the window ショーウィンドーのワンピースが見たいんですが [shô windô no wanpîsu ga mitai n desu ga]
▸ where's the window for buying tickets? チケットの窓口はどこですか [chiketto no madoguchi wa doko desu ka]

window seat 窓側の席 [mado gawa no seki]
▸ I'd like a window seat if possible できれば窓側の席をお願いします [dekireba mado gawa no seki o onegai shimasu]

windshield フロントガラス [furonto garasu]
▸ could you clean the windshield? フロントガラスをきれいにしてくれませんか [furonto garasu o kirê ni shite kuremasen ka]

windsurfing ウインドサーフィン [uindo sâfin]
▸ is there anywhere around here I can go windsurfing? この辺でウインドサーフィンのできるところはありますか [kono hen de uindo sâfin no dekiru tokoro wa arimasu ka]

windy *(day, weather)* 風が強い [kaze ga tsuyoi]
▸ it's windy 風が強いです [kaze ga tsuyoi desu]

wishes and regrets

- I hope it won't be too busy 混んでいないといいんですが [konde inai to î n desu ga]
- it'd be great if you stayed このままいられたらいいのに [kono mama iraretara î no ni]
- if only we had a car! 車さえあったら！ [kuruma sae attara]
- unfortunately, we couldn't get there in time 残念ながら、間に合いませんでした [zannen nagara, ma ni aimasen deshita]
- I'm really sorry you couldn't make it 来られなくて残念です [korarenakute zannen desu]

wine ワイン [wain]
- this wine is not chilled enough このワインはよく冷えていません [kono wain wa yoku hiete imasen]

wine list ワインリスト [wain risuto]
- can I see the wine list, please? ワインリストを見せてください [wain risuto o misete kudasai]

wish 願い [negai] ◆ *(request, hope)* 願う [negau]; *(pray for)* 祈る [inoru]
- we wish you good luck 幸運をお祈りします [kôun o oinori shimasu]

winter 冬 [fuyu]
- in (the) winter 冬に [fuyu ni]

with と一緒に [...to issho ni]
- thanks, but I'm here with my boyfriend ありがとう、でもボーイフレンドと一緒に来ています [arigatô. demo bôifurendo to issho ni kite imasu]

withdraw *(money)* 引きおろす [hikiorosu]
- I'd like to withdraw 10000 yen 一万円引きおろしたいんですが [ichi man en hikioroshitai n desu ga]

wishing someone something

- Happy birthday! 誕生日おめでとう！ [tanjôbi omedetô]
- Merry Christmas! メリークリスマス！ [merî kurisumasu]
- Happy New Year! 新年おめでとう！ [shin nen omedetô]
- enjoy your vacation! 休暇を楽しんでください [kyûka o tanoshinde kudasai]
- enjoy your meal! 食事をお楽しみください [shokuji o o tanoshimi kudasai]
- congratulations! おめでとう！ [omedetô]

without なし [nashi]

- a chicken sandwich without mayonnaise マヨネーズなしのチキンサンド [mayonêzu nashi no chikin sando]

woman 女性 [josê]

- where's the women's changing room? 女性用の更衣室はどこですか [josê yô no kôishitsu wa doko desu ka]

wonderful すばらしい [subarashî]

- that's wonderful! すばらしいです [subarashî desu]
- the weather was wonderful 天気はすばらしかったです [tenki wa subarashikatta desu]

word 言葉 [kotoba]

- I don't know what the word is in Japanese 日本語で何と言うか知りません [nihongo de nan to yû ka shirimasen]
- I don't understand a word 言葉は全然分かりません [kotoba wa zenzen wakarimasen]

work (employment) 仕事 [shigoto] ◆ (do a job) 働く [hataraku]; (function) 動く [ugoku]; (have an effect) 利く [kiku]

- to be out of work 失業する [shitsugyô suru]
- I work in marketing マーケティングの仕事をしています [mâketingu no shigoto o shite imasu]
- the heating's not working 暖房がききません [dambô ga kikimasen]
- how does the shower work? シャワーはどうやって使いますか [shawâ wa dô yatte tsukaimasu ka]

workday 平日 [hêjitsu]

- is tomorrow a workday? 明日は平日ですか [ashita wa hêjitsu desu ka]

world 世界 [sekai]

- people come here from all over the world 世界中からここに人が来ます [sekai jû kara koko ni hito ga kimasu]

worried 心配な [shimpai na]

- I'm worried about his health あの人の健康が心配です [ano hito no kenkô ga shimpai desu]

worry 心配する [shimpai suru]

- don't worry! 心配しないで！ [shimpai shinaide]

worth (in value) 値打ちがある [neuchi ga aru]; (deserving of) 価値がある [kachi ga aru]

- how much is it worth? いくらの値打ちがありますか [ikura no neuchi ga arimasu ka]
- it's well worth a visit 行ってみる価値があります [itte miru kachi ga arimasu]

▶ what's worth seeing in this town? この町で見る価値があるのは何ですか [kono machi de miru kachi ga aru no wa nan desu ka]

wound 傷 [kizu]
▶ I need something for disinfecting a wound 傷を消毒するものが必要です [kizu o shôdoku suru mono ga hitsuyô desu]

wrap (up) 包む [tsutsumu]
▶ can you wrap it (up) for me? 包んでくれますか [tsutsunde kuremasu ka]

wrist 手首 [tekubi]
▶ I've sprained my wrist 手首を捻挫しました [tekubi o nenza shimashita]

write 書く [kaku]
▶ I have some letters to write 手紙を書かなければなりません [tegami o kakanakereba narimasen]

wrong *(incorrect)* 間違っている [machigatte iru]; *(amiss)* 調子が悪い [chôshi ga warui]
▶ to be wrong *(person)* 間違える [machigaeru]
▶ I'm sorry, but I think you're wrong すみませんが、間違いだと思います [sumimasen ga, machigai da to omoimasu]
▶ sorry, I dialed the wrong number すみません、間違えてかけました [sumimasen. machigaete kakemashita]
▶ you've got the wrong number 番号をお間違えだと思います [bangô o omachigae da to omoimasu]
▶ this is the wrong train これは違う列車です [kore wa chigau ressha desu]
▶ what's wrong? どうしたんですか [dô shita n desu ka]
▶ there's something wrong with the switch スイッチの調子が悪いです [suitchi no chôshi ga warui desu]

X-ray レントゲン [rentogen]
▶ do you think I should have an X-ray? レントゲンを撮らなければなりませんか [rentogen o toranakereba narimasen ka]

year *(time)* 年 [toshi/nen]; *(age)* 歳 [sai]
- we came here last year 去年、ここに来ました [kyonen koko ni kimashita]
- I'm 21 years old ２１歳です [nijûissai desu]

yellow 黄色い [kîroi]
- the yellow one 黄色いの [kîroi no]

Yellow Pages® タウンページ® [taun pêji]
- do you have a copy of the Yellow Pages®? タウンページ®はありますか [taun pêji wa arimasu ka]
- why don't you look in the Yellow Pages®? タウンページ®を見てみたらどうですか [taun pêji o mite mitara dô desu ka]

yes *(in agreement)* はい [hai]; *(in disagreement)* いいえ [ie]
- yes, please はい、お願いします [hai, onegai shimasu]
- it doesn't matter – yes it does! 重要なことじゃありません–いいえ、重要です [jûyô na koto ja arimasen – îe, jûyô desu]

yesterday 昨日 [kinô]
- I arrived yesterday 昨日、着きました [kinô tsukimashita]

yet *(up to now)* まだ [mada]; *(at the present time)* 今のところ [ima no tokoro]
- I've not been there yet まだそこには行ったことがありません [mada soko ni wa itta koto ga arimasen]

yogurt ヨーグルト [yôguruto]
- do you have any yogurt? ヨーグルトはありますか [yôguruto wa arimasu ka]

young 若い [wakai]
- I'd like to travel a lot while I'm young 若い時にたくさん旅行したいです [wakai toki ni takusan ryokô shitai desu]

---

yes

The word はい [hai] (yes) is often used just to mean 'yes, I'm listening,' rather than 'yes, I agree with you.' Other verbal and body signals called 相槌 [aizuchi] are also used frequently in conversation to reassure the speaker that one is listening and involved, for example, ê (yeah), sô desu ka or hontô (really?), and nodding. These signals often overlap the speech of the other person and can seem intrusive to a non-native speaker, but a Japanese conversation sounds unnatural without them.

young man 青年 [sênen]
▸ who is that young man? あの青年は誰ですか [ano sênen wa dare desu ka]

young woman 若い女性 [wakai josê]
▸ who is the young woman he's with? 一緒にいる若い女性は誰ですか [issho ni iru wakai josê wa dare desu ka]

youth hostel ユースホステル [yûsu hosuteru]
▸ I'd like to book two beds for three nights in a youth hostel ユースホステルを二人分、三泊、予約したいんですが [yûsu hosuteru o futari bun sam paku yoyaku shitai n desu ga]

Z

zoo 動物園 [dôbutsuen]
▸ is there a zoo nearby? 近くに動物園がありますか [chikaku ni dôbutsuen ga arimasu ka]

Japanese language and culture

Japanese language

Japanese is spoken by the overwhelming majority of Japan's population of around 127 million. It is also spoken in emigrant communities elsewhere, particularly in Brazil, Australia, Peru, California and Hawaii, as well as by older inhabitants of the former Japanese empire in Korea, Taiwan, and some Pacific islands.

The standard language is based on the variety spoken by middle and upper-class speakers in Tokyo, and national broadcasting has helped to spread this variety all over the country. Nevertheless, regional dialects and accents are still strong, particularly among older speakers. These divide roughly into eastern and western Japan, with Tokyo and the Kyoto-Osaka-Kobe area being the two main urban focuses. The dialects that differ most from the standard are found in the parts of the country farthest from Tokyo, particularly Tohoku (northeast Honshu) and Kagoshima (southern Kyushu). The Japanese spoken in Hokkaido, the northernmost of the four main islands, is close to the standard, because the island was only settled by people from other parts of Japan from the nineteenth century onwards. The languages of the Ryukyu (Okinawa) islands are often described as dialects, but in fact they are different enough from mainland Japanese to be recognized as separate languages.

History and development of Japanese

The origins of the Japanese language are unclear, and it is not closely related to any other language spoken today other than those of the Ryukyu (Okinawa) islands. Currently the generally accepted thinking is that Japanese is an Altaic language, like Korean, with which it has some similarities in grammar and honorific language, but that it has also been strongly influenced by Pacific Island languages. Many Chinese words have come into Japanese through the writing system, but the languages are not otherwise related.

Spoken language

Japanese, like any other language, has changed over thousands of years. When Japan began its rapid process of modernization in the late nineteenth century, the need for a standard language understood throughout the whole country was recognized by the country's rulers. This was a practical necessity to facilitate education and thus technical and economic modernization, but also a means to unite the country and develop a sense of nationhood. Language reform was necessary for economic, social, educational and political reforms. A standard spoken language based on the speech of the middle and upper classes of Tokyo was established and promoted, first via the national education system, then, later and more effectively, through radio and television.

Written language

The Japanese writing system is the most complex in the world. It is very time-consuming to learn, even for the Japanese. Its complexity arises from the fact that it was imported from China and had to be adapted greatly for Japanese, which works very differently from Chinese. Chinese words do not change to show grammatical endings, as do Japanese (and English) words, so the writing system had to be adapted to show these grammatical features.

Chinese characters – called 漢字 *kanji* in Japanese – are basically ideographs, characters that represent an element of meaning (an object or concept) as well as having a phonetic (sound) element. The Japanese used these to represent native Japanese words and also took in the Chinese pronunciations of the characters for the words they represent. As a result, most *kanji* have at least two different pronunciations (or readings) today. There are thousands of *kanji*, but official reforms since World War II have simplified the forms of many and restricted the number for general use (in newspapers, etc.) to around 2,000. This is the number of characters to be learned by the end of junior high school.

At first, certain *kanji* were used purely for their sound value; gradually these *kanji* were simplified and became purely phonetic symbols representing syllables. Two separate systems were developed – ひらが な *hiragana* and カタカナ *katakana*. Each syllable can be written in either *hiragana* or *katakana*. Gradually these two systems became differentiated in their usage. Today, *hiragana* are used for grammatical words and endings, and for native Japanese words not written in *kanji*. *Katakana* are used for foreign words, zoological and botanical terms, and to add emphasis. So a page of normal written Japanese today is made up of a mixture of *kanji*, *hiragana*, and *katakana*. Japanese can be written vertically, right to left, or horizontally, left to right.

It is also possible to write Japanese using the roman alphabet, as in the pronunciations given in this book, which are based on one of the most widely used systems of romanization (ローマ字 *rômaji*), the Hepburn system.

Until the late nineteenth century, the written language was based on centuries-old classical Japanese, far removed from the spoken language of the time in terms of grammar and vocabulary. Japan's modernization required mass education and literacy, which in turn required reform of the written language to establish a more accessible style based on the spoken language.

Influence on the English language and US culture

Japanese is now widely taught as a foreign language in US colleges and universities, and the language and culture are no longer as exotic and unfamiliar as they once were.

Japanese words have been taken into the English language since the craze for all things Japanese began when the country opened up to the West in the mid-nineteenth century. Early adoptions include *kimono*, *samurai* (warrior), *harakiri* (ritual suicide, more properly known as *seppuku*), *satsuma* (used to refer to both the citrus fruit and the pottery from southern Kyushu), *geisha* (female artist-performers) and rickshaw (from *jinrikisha*). The Second World War brought *kamikaze* (divine wind) in the form of suicide pilots, while US soldiers during the Occupation brought back the martial arts of *jûdô* and *karate* and words such as *sayonara* (goodbye), honcho (*hanchô* – squadron or group leader) and *sensei* (teacher/master/doctor). The 1960s popularized *zen* Buddhism and *origami* (paper folding). *Haiku* poetry, *ukiyo-e* (wood-block prints) and *Noh* and *kabuki* theater have become well-known in the arts, and *ikebana* (flower arranging), *bonsai* (growing miniature trees) and *sumô* wrestling also have their devotees outside Japan.

The strength of the Japanese economy in the 1980s also began the worldwide spread of Japanese culture that continues to this day, bringing *futon* mattresses, *sushi* and other Japanese cuisine, as well as various forms of popular culture – *karaoke*, *manga* (comic books and graphic novels) and *anime* (animation) – to the US. Recently, the influence of Japanese cinema in US films has grown, both through remakes of Japanese horror films such as *Ring* and in US-made films such as *Kill Bill*. Japanese companies dominate the world of electronic goods and cameras – Sony, Canon, Seiko, Panasonic (Matsushita), Nikon and the rest. The popularity of the Teenage Mutant Ninja Turtles in the mid-1980s brought the word *ninja* into the vocabulary of US children. More sobering borrowings into English include *tsunami* (tidal wave), which sadly became an everyday word after the south Asian disaster of December 2004, and *karōshi* (death from overwork).

Japanese and English: differences and similarities

There are very few similarities between Japanese and English, apart from the large and growing number of English words being taken into Japanese, and the much smaller number of Japanese words traveling in the opposite direction.

Grammar

Japanese grammar works very differently from English in many ways. Here are the main differences:

- The word order in a sentence is very different from English. Most importantly, verbs come at the end of the sentence.

- There is no difference between singular and plural; for example, *hon* can mean "book" or "books," but the context usually makes it clear which is meant.

- There are no definite or indefinite articles ("the" or "a/some").

- Verbs do not change their form according to who is performing the action.

- However, verbs do change their form according to level of politeness and formality, with plain, polite, and honorific forms (see section on politeness and honorific language).

- Personal pronouns (*I, he, she, you, we, they*) are not used much, and overusing them can seem rude or aggressive. Context and the different levels of politeness make it clear who is being referred to.

- Small words called particles, such as *wa, ga, o, to* and *ni*, are used to show the grammatical relationships between different parts of the sentence. Some work like English prepositions, but others have no equivalents in English. They come after the words or phrases they are most closely linked to; for example, *eki e* "to the station." Some particles come at the end of sentences; for example, adding *ka* at the end of a statement changes it into a question.

- There are two kinds of adjectives. One has different forms, like verb forms, to show tense (present or past), affirmative or negative ("new" or "not new"), and level of politeness and formality. They all come before the noun they describe, as in English: *atarashî hon* "'new book."

• There are no relative clauses. Instead, the descriptive phrase is placed before the noun. For example, "The book **that I bought yesterday** is very interesting" becomes "The **I-bought-yesterday** book is very interesting" – *kinô katta hon wa totemo omoshiroi desu*.

Vocabulary

Japanese has a very rich vocabulary. Native Japanese words (known as 大和言葉 *yamato kotoba* or 和語 *wago*) have been supplemented since the sixth century by Chinese vocabulary (漢語 *kango*), either as borrowings directly from China or via Korea, or as new words combining Chinese characters in different ways. Many of the latter were created in Japan in the late nineteenth century to describe new concepts introduced from the West as part of the country's rapid social, political and economic modernization. The Chinese pronunciations changed to fit the Japanese sound system. These Chinese-derived words are seen as being more formal or educated than their native Japanese equivalents, just as words derived from Latin, Greek or French are in English. They form a large proportion of Japanese vocabulary today, particularly in written language.

Japan's early contacts with the West, through Portuguese missionaries and Dutch traders, brought in new words, such as *tabako* (tobacco, used now to mean 'cigarette') and *pan* (bread) from Portuguese, and *bîru* (beer) and *garasu* (window glass) from Dutch. After 200 years of self-imposed seclusion, Japan's re-opening to the outside world in the mid-nineteenth century brought a flood of new words from European languages. Words of German derivation feature a lot in medicine and mountaineering, while French words feature a lot in the fields of food and fashion, and Italian ones in food and music.

However, the overwhelmingly dominant source of foreign loanwords in Japanese today is English. The ultra-nationalistic 1930s and 1940s saw a purge of such words, but the influence of English in the postwar period is immense. Here are some longstanding examples: *kôhî* (coffee), *esukarêtâ* (escalator), *erebêtâ* (elevator), *sûtsukêsu* (suitcase), *takushî* (taxi), and *terebi* (television). As is clear from this short list, the pronunciation changes considerably to fit the more limited set of sounds available in Japanese: "v" becomes "b," "r" and "l" are conflated, "er" becomes *â*, "th" becomes "s," and so on. Consonants must be followed by vowels, which makes the original English words much longer in Japanese. To compensate for this, the resulting words are frequently cut, so that only the beginning or end remains, as in *terebi*, from **televi**sion. This can mean that the resulting word is incomprehensible to native English speakers: for example, *sekuhara* (**sexual hara**ssment), *suto* (**st**rike), *rimokon* (**remo**te **con**trol), *pasokon* (**perso**nal **com**puter), *risutora* (**restru**cturing), *apāto* (**apart**ment), *depāto* (**depart**ment store) and *sūpā* (**super**market).

Moreover, it is common to use English words and to combine them (or parts of them) with other English words and Japanese ones to produce new words and/or concepts, in what is called *wasé égo* (English made in Japan). Such words and phrases are being coined all the time, but here are some established ones: *imēji appu suru* (to improve one's image, from "image + up"), *wanpatān* (repetitive, one-track mind, from "one pattern"), *bakku miraa* (rearview mirror, from "back mirror"), and *sararîman* (office worker, from "salary + man"). At least one such word has been taken back into English: walkman.

English loanwords are also used with different meanings in Japanese: *handoru* means not only "handle" but also "steering wheel"; a *manshon* is an up-market apartment block, not a grand house; and *dorai* means "unsentimental" in addition to its English meanings. Another possibly misleading word is *hōmu*, which is a station platform (shortened from *purattohōmu*), not where you live.

Pronunciation

The range of sounds in Japanese is much more restricted than in English, and pronunciation presents no great difficulties for English speakers, as long as some key points are noted. The most important difference from English is that there is no stress on a particular syllable within a word: each syllable is given equal weight. However, the vowels "i" and "u" are usually whispered so they are barely heard when they occur between any of the consonants k, s, t, h, and p. This is why, for example, the name Yamashita sounds like "Yamashta."

Politeness and honorific language

One important feature of the Japanese language is that politeness and formality are expressed through a complex system of different grammatical forms and vocabulary, as well as in tone of voice, body language and so on, as in English-speaking cultures. The system can be divided broadly into several levels. Within the family and among young people of the same age (classmates, etc.), the friendly familiar level is used, with plain verb endings. When speaking to friends, acquaintances, neighbors and older fellow students, the polite level is used; this is the level used in most of the phrases in this book. The extremely polite level is called 敬語 *kêgo*, also known as honorific language. As well as the polite verb endings, it uses more complex verb forms and some different vocabulary, and has many subtle variations. Honorific language is used when speaking to strangers and distant acquaintances, and by shop assistants, hotel and transportation staff, and others dealing with customers. Deciding which level of language to use depends on hierarchy or relative status (your own and that of the person you are speaking to or about) and familiarity (how well you know the person you are speaking to). This is one reason that business cards, which make clear the status of the person, are so important. The system is difficult to master, and many companies have special *kêgo* training for new employees.

One other point to be aware of is that a higher pitch of voice signals politeness for both men and women. You may therefore hear people answering the phone in a much higher-pitched voice than they would normally use, then dropping back to normal if the caller turns out to be a family member or friend.

Male and female language

Another characteristic of Japanese is that male and female language usage differs significantly in clearly recognized ways. In Japan gender roles have traditionally been clearly defined, at least in the upper and middle classes, and these distinct roles have long been reflected in language. The differences are most obvious in casual, informal speech, but much more limited in formal speech. Male language is characteristically blunt, using less honorific language, more plain verb and adjective forms, and certain particles at the ends of sentences (e.g. *ze, zo*). Female language tends to be gentler and softer overall, with greater use of honorific language (particularly reciprocal usage), more polite forms, and different particles (e.g. *kashira, wa*). The words men and women use to refer to themselves ("I") also differ: while *watakushi* is the most formal and used by both men and women, only men use *boku* or *ore* informally, and women mostly use *watashi*, though young women may also use *atashi* informally.

Modern developments in the language

As Japanese society and culture is changing, so is the language and the way it is used. Honorific language is being used in different ways to meet changing social circumstances, with hierarchy gradually becoming less important. Young women are rejecting the traditional submissive female role and the language that goes with it, and are speaking in a more gender-neutral style; some even use the male personal pronoun *boku*. Vocabulary is constantly being expanded through foreign loanwords. Using foreign words gives an up-to-date, modern image, so youth and fashion magazines and other sections of the media are full of English words written in *katakana*. Similarly, young people are very fond of using English words to create a language of their own that is incomprehensible to older generations. The great majority of these words never become established, but many do. Official bodies also make great use of English words, particularly for concepts that do not exist in Japanese. The vast expansion in foreign loanwords can cause comprehension problems, particularly for older people. The development of computers capable of handling Japanese script has weakened arguments for abandoning Japanese script in favor of romanization, and the Internet and cellphones have allowed new ways of communication to develop, particularly among Japan's youth.

Minority languages

Although Japanese is the official and by far the dominant language of the country, 15 languages are listed internationally; many of them are endangered. Most of these other languages are spoken in the Ryukyu (Okinawa) islands in the far south and are closely related to Japanese. The Ainu language of Hokkaido is quite unrelated to Japanese and is almost extinct today, although efforts to revive it are being made. Korean and Chinese are spoken by the sizeable populations of long-term residents in Japan.

Cultural highlights

Buddhist temples and **Shinto shrines** are easy to find all over Japan, but the former capitals of Kyoto, Nara and Kamakura have the largest concentrations. These range from the world-famous – Kiyomizu and Kinkakuji (Golden Pavilion) temples in Kyoto and the shrines at Ise and on Miyajima island near Hiroshima – to hundreds of other beautiful but relatively little-frequented places. Large shrines and temples are complexes of buildings with extensive landscaped grounds; the setting is as important as the buildings.

Many of the most famous Japanese **gardens** are at temples, such as the stone and raked-gravel garden of Ryôanji in Kyoto, but others are at palaces or the villas of former feudal lords. There are different styles, influenced by Shinto and Buddhist philosophies, but all aim to capture nature and create a quiet place for contemplation. Water, trees, bridges, rocks and plants are all important features.

Tea and rituals for its preparation and drinking were brought from China and developed by the samurai class into the Japanese **tea ceremony** as a ritual based on Zen Buddhist spiritual and aesthetic principles.

Japanese **woodblock prints** (木版画 *mokuhanga*) first became known in the West in the late nineteenth century, and copies of Hokusai's views of Mount Fuji, Hiroshige's landscapes, and Utamaro's 浮世絵 *ukiyo-e*, pictures of the floating world of the entertainment area of Edo (now Tokyo), have become iconic images of Japan.

Ceramics in many different styles, from delicate porcelains to rough and irregular pottery, are produced all over the country. Some of the best-known are Arita-yaki, Bizen-yaki, Hagi-yaki, Seto-yaki and Mashiko-yaki. **Lacquerware** (漆器 *shikki*) bowls, trays, boxes, etc., from Wajima on the Sea of Japan are also world-famous. There are many different kinds of Japanese **dolls** (人形 *ningyô*), from inexpensive *origami* folded paper ones to wooden *kokeshi* and elegant pottery ones. Folding **fans** (扇子 *sensu*) are available in a range of colors and patterns, the larger ones in more subdued colors being for men.

Myths, legends and religion

Japan's myths and legends are closely related to its indigenous faith, **Shinto** (神道 *shintô*), translated as "Way of the Gods." They appear first in written form in the *Kojiki* (Records of Ancient Matters), compiled in 712 AD. According to this chronicle, the Japanese islands were created from the droplets that fell from a jeweled spear with which the brother and sister deities, Izanagi and Izanami, stirred up the ocean of chaos. This and the myths associated with the sun goddess, Amaterasu, daughter of Izanagi, are the most important in Shinto. It is from her that the imperial family claimed descent, until the Emperor Hirohito renounced his divine status after World War II. The Great Shrine of Ise is dedicated to Amaterasu, and is where part of the enthronement ceremony of a new emperor takes place.

Shinto has no formal religious doctrine, consisting rather of a set of ancient folk beliefs, rituals and ceremonies, including lively festivals. It is based on a reverence for nature and the 神 *kami* (gods, deities or spirits) that exist everywhere. Cleanliness and purity are important. In the late nineteenth century, Shinto organizations were divided into state and secular branches, and Shinto was promoted as the national religion. From the 1930s through World War II, state Shinto was used by the militarists to glorify the emperor and promote Japan's military aggression as a divine mission. The postwar constitution strictly separated the state and religious activities.

Buddhism came to Japan via China and Korea in the sixth century, and became established among the ruling elites, spreading only gradually to the masses. Rather than replacing Shinto, it co-existed with it, each meeting different needs. Zen Buddhism spread among the *samurai* warrior class during the medieval period, emphasizing personal enlightenment through meditation and discipline. Various other sects developed over the centuries.

The popular saying "Born Shinto, die Buddhist," refers to the fact that birth rituals are Shinto, as are most marriages, whereas funerals are Buddhist. Most Japanese today claim to be both Buddhist and Shinto. Traditionally, each house has a small Buddhist altar (仏壇 *butsudan*) for veneration of the ancestors. Many also have a miniature Shinto shrine (神棚 *kamidana*) for veneration of the *kami*; these are also found in *dôjô* (martial arts training centers).

Japan's contact with China also brought **Confucianism** into the country. Confucianism is a philosophical and ethical system that emphasizes respect and love for one's family and ancestors, honesty and benevolence, respect for propriety and tradition and loyalty to the state. Its influence is still strong in Japan today.

The Portuguese Jesuit missionary Francis Xavier brought **Christianity** to Japan when he landed on the southern island of Kyushu in 1549. Missionaries continued to proselytize, but opposition from Japan's rulers grew, leading to persecution and executions. The remaining missionaries were expelled from the country in 1641, and the country cut itself off from the outside world for the next two centuries. Small pockets of *kakure kirishitan* (hidden Christians) persisted in remote areas until Japan opened up to the outside world again in the late nineteenth century. Christian-style weddings have become popular in recent years, but this is not necessarily an indication of real belief.

Various so-called **new religions** have evolved since the nineteenth century. These popular religious movements draw on a range of Buddhist, Shinto, Christian and New Age beliefs. The biggest is Sôka Gakkai, a Buddhist sect that is linked to the powerful New Kômeito political party; Tenrikyô is another. The Aum Shinrikyô doomsday cult became infamous worldwide after its sarin gas attack on the Tokyo subway system in 1995.

Traditional music and culture

Music and poetry are closely linked in Japan, and the word 歌 *uta* can mean both "song" and "poem." Influences from China and Korea have mixed with indigenous traditions to create distinctively Japanese forms, as in other areas of the culture. The 琴 *koto* and 三味線 *shamisen* stringed instruments and the long bamboo flute (尺八 *shakuhachi*) are known as typically Japanese, and the Kodo drummers of Sado island have popularized 太鼓 *taiko* drumming outside Japan in recent years.

Music, dance, drama and poetry all combine in the traditional forms of theater, *Noh* (能 *nô*) and 歌舞伎 *kabuki*. In both forms, all the actors are male. *Noh* uses masks, and is highly refined and slow-moving, telling stories of gods, warriors, beautiful women and ghosts. *Kabuki*, while equally stylized, developed as the more down-to-earth theater of the merchant class, with many historical plays. Its heavily made-up actors feature commonly in old woodblock prints. *Bunraku* puppet theater originated in Osaka and is unusual in that the puppeteers, dressed in black, are clearly visible to the audience.

The form of poetry called 俳句 *haiku*, consisting of only 17 syllables, and calligraphy (書道 *shodō*) are other traditional Japanese arts well known in the West.

Japanese dress

The word **kimono** 着物 originally just meant "clothing," literally "wear-thing," but it gradually came to refer to the full-length robe known by the name today. Today, silk *kimono* are only worn by most people for formal occasions, such as weddings, funerals and graduations. A full *kimono* outfit, with 帯 *obi* (sash), 草履 *zōri* (thong sandals), 足袋 *tabi* (ankle-socks divided at the big toe), under-robes and so on is extremely expensive. Both men and women cross the left side of a *kimono* over the right one; the dead are laid out with the right side overlapping the left. Young unmarried women's formal *kimono* are brightly-colored with long sleeves hanging almost to the ground (振袖 *furisode*), while married women wear more sober colors and shorter sleeves (留袖 *tomesode*). Patterned *kimono* frequently bear images of nature appropriate to the season, such as cherry blossom and fall maple leaves. The unlined cotton robes worn at summer festivals and hot-spring resorts (温泉 *onsen*) are called *yukata* 浴衣, worn with 下駄 *geta* (wooden thong sandals). Gauze-lined cotton robes called 寝巻 *nemaki* are used as sleepwear.

Some restaurant chefs, particularly in sushi restaurants, and people participating in festivals often wear short cotton *happi* coats (法被) with the name or symbol of the restaurant or shrine on the back.

Typical traits and habits of Japanese people

Japanese culture and society have been greatly influenced by China, directly or via Korea, over the last two thousand years. The religious and philosophical systems of Buddhism and Confucianism underlie much of Japanese social behavior and values even today, and the complex writing system was adapted over centuries from Chinese ideographs. Contact with Europe began with the Portuguese and Spanish missionaries in the mid-sixteenth century, followed by Dutch traders at the beginning of the seventeenth century. The shogunate (military government) closed Japan to the outside world for two centuries, apart from strictly controlled contacts, until the US forced the country to open up to foreign trade in the mid-nineteenth century.

Since then, the country has modernized at a rapid pace and undergone great social change.

Japan's postwar economic boom concentrated the population in the major cities, and broke down the traditional three-generation households in which the eldest son of the family remained with his parents and his wife became part of that family. Smaller family units of parents and children are now the norm. Men and women are legally equal, but traditional gender role expectations are still strong, with the family and household being considered the responsibility of the wife while the husband works long hours. The falling birthrate and increased life expectancy have resulted in a rapidly aging society today.

Face and personal relations

The concept of "face" (顔 kao) is fundamental in Japanese society, as in other east Asian cultures. It involves one's reputation and image. Embarrassing oneself or others means a loss of face, and people will go to great lengths to avoid this. Direct confrontation is therefore avoided, and maintaining harmony (和 wa) and good personal or human relations (人間関係 ningen kankē) is extremely important.

In the business world, negotiations should be conducted to ensure that everybody you are dealing with maintains face, even if the deal does not conclude successfully. This means bringing negotiations to a close in a manner that will satisfy everyone's superiors. By the same token, it can be difficult to get straight or honest answers in business negotiations. Information that does not present a company in a positive light may simply not be shown. Suggestions for improvements to existing services or systems should be worded carefully, and presented in a positive light if at all possible.

Meeting people and socializing

Greetings are formal, with no kissing or hugging. Among friends and in casual situations, a slight nod of the head is enough, but more obvious bowing is needed in a more formal situation – for example, when meeting older people or new work acquaintances. The greater the formality, the lower the bow and the longer it lasts. You should bow from the waist, keeping your neck and back straight from head to hips. Women should place one hand over the other with their arms held down in front of their bodies, and men should keep their arms at their sides. Japanese people used to meeting foreigners may shake hands instead. It is wise to avoid too much direct eye contact.

When exchanging business cards, you should always give and receive a card with both hands. Look at the card for a moment to show your interest and respect for the person, especially if he or she holds a high position. Then put it away carefully – don't put it in your back pocket!

You should use both hands when somebody gives you something, such as a gift, food or tea. Note that gifts are traditionally not opened in front of the giver, although this custom is changing, particularly among younger people.

Food

Japanese cuisine is well known for being very refined and beautifully presented, but there are also many delicious more down-to-earth dishes. As well as Japanese food, Chinese and Italian restaurants are very popular, and almost any cuisine in the world can be found somewhere in Tokyo. Western food is available in department stores, supermarkets and specialist shops, though it is generally more expensive than Japanese food, and many items are not available in smaller towns and rural areas.

Japan has a long tradition of Buddhist vegetarian food (精進料理 *shôjin ryôri*), and people rarely ate meat until the Meiji period (1868-1912), although they did eat fish and birds. However, vegetarianism (菜食主義 *saishoku shugi*) is not common in Japan today, and many Japanese dishes contain small amounts of fish or meat. Rice is served with almost all Japanese-style meals, and various kinds of noodles are also very popular. Fish and other seafood, a wide range of vegetables, and soy products such as 豆腐 *tôfu* (bean curd) are also important parts of the traditional diet.

Japanese people tend to eat earlier than Americans. Breakfast may be eaten very early because of long commutes. Lunch is usually eaten between noon and 1 p.m., and the evening meal around 6-7 pm.

A traditional Japanese breakfast would include rice (often with a raw egg mixed into it and served with 海苔 *nori* seaweed), 味噌汁 *miso shiru* (miso soup made with fermented soybean paste, seasonal vegetables and tofu), and dried fish. Western-style breakfasts of coffee, bread and jam are becoming increasingly common, and many coffee shops serve モーニングサービス *môningu sâbisu*, a set breakfast of thick white toast with a hard-boiled egg or jam and tea or coffee.

Lunch is often a quick snack in an inexpensive restaurant. The traditional packed lunch known as 弁当 *bentô* is still very popular, whether store-bought or homemade. Families usually get together for a substantial evening meal, but the father may still be working or commuting, so he may eat separately later.

It is not considered rude to make a noise when eating noodles – in fact, slurping shows enjoyment! Lifting up one's rice bowl or soup bowl to eat is considered good manners. If you need to take food from a communal dish with your chopsticks, it is polite to turn them around to do so. You should try not to leave any grains of rice in the bowl when you finish. Never leave chopsticks sticking up in food, or use them to pass food to someone else, as these actions are associated with funerals.

At a restaurant

If you are invited to a meal, the person who invites you will almost always pay the bill. You should offer to pay, but give up after a few attempts. The same should apply in the reverse situation – if you invite people to a meal, you should pay no matter how much your guests protest.

Most Japanese and Chinese restaurants use disposable chopsticks like those often found in the US. These come in a paper packet and are joined together at the top, so you need to split them before use.

It is not considered polite to pour your own drink when you are having a meal with others; if you pour a drink for someone else, he or she will return the favor. Your host will probably ensure that your glass or teacup is always full.

Tipping is not standard or expected in most service businesses, including restaurants.

In a Japanese home

Japanese people tend not to entertain at home much, partly because many apartments are very small. Instead, they meet at restaurants, coffee shops or bars. Although it is common to make vague invitations to visit people's homes, these are generally for politeness' sake, and you should avoid stopping by unannounced. If you are clearly invited for a particular time, be sure to be punctual, and take a gift, such as food, drink or flowers. Japanese distinguish very clearly between inside and outside, and shoes are never worn in the house. There is always a step, even if only a very shallow one, in the entrance (玄関 *genkan*), and this is where you take your shoes off. You will be given slippers to wear on wooden or carpeted floors, but even these need to be removed before walking on 畳 *tatami* matted floors. There may also be special plastic slippers to wear in the bathroom, left just inside the door. Leave your normal slippers outside the bathroom, and be sure to remember to change back when you have finished!

Popular leisure activities

Sports

The most popular spectator sports in Japan are **baseball**, **sumo wrestling** and **soccer**, and **rugby** and **basketball** also have many followers. **Golf**, **skiing**, **hiking**, **camping** and **swimming** are all popular recreational pursuits

There are 12 professional **baseball** (野球 *yakkyū*) teams, the favorites being the Yomiuri Giants (Tokyo), the Chūnichi Dragons (Nagoya) and the Hanshin Tigers (Osaka).

Soccer (サッカー *sakkā*) has become extremely popular among young Japanese since the launch of the professional J.League in 1993, and particularly since 2002, when Japan and Korea hosted the World Cup. The top teams are the Kashima Antlers, Jubilo Iwata and Yokohama F. Marinos.

The ancient sport of **sumo wrestling** (相撲 *sumō*) is associated with Shinto and is full of ritual and ceremony. There are six Grand Sumo Tournaments (本場所 *hombasho*) held in different cities every year; each lasts 15 days.

It used to be extremely expensive to play **golf** (ゴルフ *gorufu*) on an actual course or to join a club, so being a member is a sign of social status. Fees have come down in recent years, and foreigners and other non-members can play on some courses, particularly on weekdays. Large public driving ranges are widely used.

Japan's mountainous terrain and climate make it well-suited for **skiing** and **snow-boarding**. There are hundreds of ski-resorts, but the main ones are concentrated in the Tohoku region (north-east Honshu) and Hokkaido.

For **hiking**, there are many well-made trails, for everything from day hikes to longer treks, in mountainous and rural areas all over the country. The Japan Alps and Hokkaido are particularly well-trodden, but each area has plenty to offer. As well as mountain climbing and walks around hot spring resorts (温泉 *onsen*), following pilgrimage routes around temples (particularly on Shikoku island) is an unusual alternative. The ascent of Mt. Fuji (富士山 *fuji san*) is a long steep hike to the 12,388-foot summit; the official season is July and August, when the mountain huts are open. Many people climb through the night to see the sunrise from the summit.

Camping is becoming popular among students and hikers. There are around 3,000 campgrounds, concentrated in the tourist areas, and mostly run by local municipalities. They can be very busy during students' summer vacation and on weekends. Camping wild is illegal.

Swimmers will have no problem in Japan, with pools in plentiful supply and supported by municipal governments. Swimming in the ocean, lakes and rivers is popular in the summer. **Scuba diving** and **surfing** are also gaining in popularity.

Traditional Japanese games include 将棋 *shōgi* (similar to chess), 囲碁 *igo* (go), 独楽 *koma* (a game played with wooden spinning tops) and 凧 *tako* (kite flying). The American version of **mahjong** was introduced after World War II and is still popular today, particularly in video arcades.

Socializing

Although Japan is a famously hard-working nation, people like to enjoy themselves too. The thousands of lively traditional **festivals** (祭り *matsuri*) that take place all over the country throughout the year are a good opportunity. They range from small community festivals celebrating the local shrine's deity to huge events at major shrines or commemorating particular historical events. The Gion festival in Kyoto, the Nebuta festival in Aomori and the Sapporo Snow Festival are among the best known. Fireworks (花火 *hanabi*) are an essential part of summer festivals.

It is expected for men to go out drinking with colleagues after work often, and young unmarried female workers may join in to a lesser extent. カラオケ *Karaoke* singing features prominently at these gatherings.

Perhaps the most popular leisure activity for men in all age groups is パチンコ *pachinko* (Japanese-style pinball), and they can be seen lining up for the 10 a.m. opening of their favorite pachinko parlors, hoping to win large prizes.

Women of all ages enjoy **eating out.** Taking **classes** in areas such as handicrafts and English conversation are popular, while the traditional

Japanese language and culture

Japanese arts of calligraphy, tea ceremony and *ikebana*, flower-arranging, are now mainly practiced by older women. Group excursions are also popular.

Shopping is a major leisure activity, particularly for young people, who also enjoy visiting **video arcades** (ゲー（ム）セン（ター）*gê(mu) sen (tâ)*) and going out.

Japanese–English dictionary

signs in public places

入口
[iriguchi]
entrance

出口
[deguchi]
exit

非常口
[hijôguchi]
emergency exit

無料
[muryô]
free

駐車禁止
[chûsha kinshi]
no parking

禁煙
[kin'en]
no smoking

オープン/営業中
[ôpun/êgyô chû]
open

故障中
[koshô chû]
out of order

予約席
[yoyaku seki]
reserved

お手洗い/トイレ
[otearai/toire]
toilets

男性用 トイレ
[dansê yô toire]
gents' toilets

女性用 トイレ
[josê yô toire]
ladies' toilets

立入禁止
[tachi-iri kinshi]
no entry

押す
[osu]
push

引く
[hiku]
pull

案内
[annai]
information

注意
[chûi]
attention

...禁止
[kinshi]
do not ...

落し物/遺失物
[otoshimono/ishitsubutsu]
lost property

ホテル
[hoteru]
hotel

銀行
[ginkô]
bank

郵便局
[yûbinkyoku]
post office

湯．
[yu]
public bath-house (literally 'hot water')

at the airport

空港
[kûkô]
airport

到着
[tôchaku]
arrivals

出発
[shuppatsu]
departures

飛行機
[hikôki]
plane

便
[bin]
flight

キャンセル/中止
[kyanseru/chûshi]
cancelled

乗り換え
[norikae]
connections/transfers

遅延
[chien]
delayed

案内
[annai]
information

切符/チケット
[kippu/chiketto]
tickets

荷物受取所
[nimotsu uketorijo]
baggage claim

パスポート
[pasupôto]
passport

入国審査
[nyûkoku shinsa]
passport control

税関
[zêkan]
customs

申告が必要なもの
[shinkoku ga hitsuyô na mono]
goods to declare

申告するものがない
[shinkoku suru mono ga nai]
nothing to declare

両替
[ryôgae]
foreign currency exchange

チェックイン
[chekku-in]
check-in

搭乗券
[tôjôken]
boarding pass

出発ロビー
[shuppatsu robî]
departure lounge

国内線
[kokunai sen]
domestic flights

免税
[menzê]
duty-free shops

すぐに搭乗
[sugu ni tôjô]
immediate boarding

シャトルバス
[shatoru basu]
shuttle bus

...番ゲートにお進みください。
[...ban gêto ni osusumi kudasai]
please proceed to gate number ...

...様、最後のお呼び出しでございます。
[...sama, saigo no oyobidashi de gozaimasu]
this is a final call for ...

finding your way

左
[hidari]
left

右
[migi]
right

まっすぐ
[massugu]
straight ahead

曲がる
[magaru]
to turn

降りる/下る
[oriru/kudaru]
go down

上る/上がる
[noboru/agaru]
go up

そのまま行く
[sono mama iku]
keep going

交差点
[kôsaten]
crossroads

歩いて
[aruite]
on foot

橋
[hashi]
bridge

道路
[dôro]
road

川
[kawa]
river

通り
[tôri]
street

信号
[shingô]
signal/traffic lights

going out

映画館
[êgakan]
movie theater

祭
[matsuri]
festival

劇場
[gekijô]
theater

切符売場
[kippu uriba]
box office

博物館
[hakubutsukan]
museum

予約
[yoyaku]
bookings

公園
[kôen]
park

携帯品一時預かり所
[kêtaihin ichiji azukarijo]
cloakroom

喫茶店
[kissaten]
coffee shop

入口
[iriguchi]
entrance

バー /スナック
[bâ/sunakku]
bar (a bâ has hostesses and can be
very expensive; a sunakku is more
like an American bar)

出口
[deguchi]
exit

非常口
[hijôguchi]
emergency exit

携帯電話の電源をお切りくださ
い
[kêtai denwa no dengen o okiri kudasai]
please turn off your cellphones

public transportation

駅
[eki]
station

バスターミナル
[basu tâminaru]
bus station

バス停
[basu tê]
bus stop

地下鉄の駅
[chikatetsu no eki]
subway station

切符売り場
[kippu uriba]
ticket office

予約
[yoyaku]
bookings

大人
[otona]
adult

小人
[kodomo]
child

改札口
[kaisatsuguchi]
ticket barrier

手荷物預かり所
[tenimotsu azukarijo]
left-luggage (office)

コインロッカー□
[koin rokkâ]
left luggage lockers

新幹線
[shinkansen]
bullet train

特急
[tokkyû]
super express (train)

急行
[kyûkô]
express (train)

準急
[junkyû]
semi-express (train)

普通
[futsû]
slow

グリーン車
[gurîn sha]
first-class train carriage

時刻表
[jikokuhyô]
timetable

乗車券
[jôsha ken]
(ordinary) train ticket

車/自動車
[kuruma/jidôsha]
car

特急券
[tokkyû ken]
express supplement

高速道路
[kôsoku dôro]
freeway

地下鉄
[chikatetsu]
subway

指定席
[shitê seki]
reserved carriage/seats

タクシー
[takushî]
taxis

自由席
[jiyû seki]
unreserved carriage/seats

フェリー
[ferî]
ferry

ホーム
[hômu]
platform

路面電車
[romen densha]
(in some cities) streetcar/tram

弱冷房
[jaku rêbô]
mild air conditioning

市電
[shiden]
(in some cities) streetcar/tram

...で乗り換えてください。
[...de norikaete kudasai]
you'll have to change at ...

... 行き
[...yuki]
bound for ...

...番のバスにお乗りください。
[...ban no basu ni onori kudasai]
you need to take the number ... bus

at the hospital

病院
[byôin]
hospital

医者
[isha]
doctor

歯医者
[haisha]
dentist

眼科医
[ganka-i]
ophthalmologist/optician

診療所/医院
[shinryôjo/i-in]
doctor's office

救急病院
[kyûkyû byôin]
emergency room

外科
[geka]
surgical department

内科
[naika]
internal medicine department

眼科
[ganka]
ophthalmology department

耳鼻咽喉科
[jibi-inkôka]
ear, nose and throat department

産婦人科
[sanfujinka]
obstetrics and gynecology department

受付け
[uketsuke]
reception desk

処方箋
[shohôsen]
prescription

レントゲン
[rentogen]
x-ray

待合室でお待ちください。
[machiaishitsu de omachi kudasai]
please take a seat in the waiting room

どこが痛みますか。
[doko ga itamimasu ka]
where does it hurt?

深く息をしてください。
[fukaku iki o shite kudasai]
take a deep breath

横になってください。
[yoko ni natte kudasai]
lie down, please

…にアレルギーがありますか。
[…ni arerugî ga arimasu ka]
are you allergic to …?

他に薬を飲んでいますか。
[hoka ni kusuri o nonde imasu ka]
are you taking any other medication?

in the pharmacy

薬局/薬屋
[yakkyoku/kusuriya]
pharmacy

塗る
[nuru]
apply

禁忌
[kinki]
contra-indications

クリーム
[kurîmu]
cream

軟膏
[nankô]
ointment

副作用の可能性
[fukusayô no kanôsê]
possible side effects

粉薬
[konagusuri]
powder

錠剤
[jôzai]
tablet

食前/食後/食間
[shoku zen/shoku go/shokkan]
before/after/between meals

official offices

大使館
[taishikan]
embassy

米国大使館
[bêkoku taishikan]
US Embassy

英国大使館
[êkoku taishikan]
British Embassy

領事館
[ryôjikan]
consulate

警察署
[kêsatsusho]
police station

姓/名字
[sê/myôji]
family name

名/名前
[mê/namae]
given name

住所
[jûsho]
address

郵便番号
[yûbin bangô]
zip code

国
[kuni]
country

国籍
[kokuseki]
nationality

生年月日
[sênengappi]
date of birth

出生地
[shussê chi]
place of birth

年齢
[nenrê]
age

性別
[sêbetsu]
sex

滞在期間
[taizai kikan]
duration of stay

入国/出国日
[nyûkoku/shukkoku bi]
arrival/departure date

職業
[shokugyô]
occupation

旅券番号
[ryoken bangô]
passport number

at the restaurant/coffee shop

朝食/朝ごはん
[chôshoku/asagohan]
breakfast

昼食/昼ごはん
[chûshoku/hirugohan]
lunch

夕食/夕飯/晩ごはん
[yûshoku/yûhan/bangohan]
dinner/evening meal

前菜
[zensai]
starter

メインコース
[mên kôsu]
main course

デザート
[dezâto]
dessert

飲み物
[nomimono]
drink

予約席
[yoyaku seki]
reserved

準備中
[jumbi chû]
closed

メニュー
[menyû]
menu

注文
[chûmon]
(noun) order

予約
[yoyaku]
reservation

勘定書き
[kanjôgaki]
check

禁煙
[kin'en]
non-smoking

サービス
[sâbisu]
service

定食
[têshoku]
fixed-price menu

サービス料込み
[sâbisu ryô komi]
service included

会計 /勘定
[kaikê/kanjô]
check

おしぼり
[oshibori]
small moistened towel to wipe hands on

はし
[hashi]
chopsticks

お持ち帰り
[omochikaeri]
take out

food and drink

水
[mizu]
water

ビール
[bîru]
beer

酒
[sake]
rice wine

ワイン
[wain]
wine

白ワイン
[shiro wain]
white wine

鍋
[nabe]
one-pot stew

赤ワイン
[aka wain]
red wine

冷たい
[tsumetai]
cold, chilled

コーラ
[kôra]
Coke®

辛い
[karai]
hot, spicy

フルーツジュース
[furûtsu jûsu]
fruit juice

甘い
[amai]
sweet

ミネラルウォーター
[mineraru uôtâ]
mineral water

塩辛い/しょっぱい
[shiokarai/shoppai]
salty

コーヒー
[kôhî]
coffee

レアの
[rea no]
(steak) rare

お茶
[ocha]
green tea

ミディアムの
[midiamu no]
(steak) medium

紅茶
[kôcha]
black tea

ウェルダンの
[werudan no]
(steak) well done

ゆでた
[yudeta]
boiled

おいしい
[oishî]
delicious

揚げた
[ageta]
deep-fried

精進料理
[shôjin ryôri]
Buddhist monks' vegetarian cuisine

炒めた
[itameta]
stir-fried

肉
[niku]
meat

...の肉
[...no niku]
... meat

牛肉/ ビーフ
[gyûniku/bîfu]
beef

松阪牛
[matsuzaka gyû]
high quality beef, known abroad as Kobe beef

豚肉/ ポーク
[butaniku/pôku]
pork

鶏肉/ チキン
[toriniku/chikin]
chicken

ハム
[hamu]
ham

ベーコン
[bêkon]
bacon

焼き鳥
[yakitori]
grilled chicken on a skewer

焼き肉
[yakiniku]
grilled meat

串カツ
[kushikatsu]
pieces of pork and vegetables, breaded and deep-fried, served on a skewer (specialty of Osaka)

ミートボール
[mîto bôru]
meatballs

すき焼き
[sukiyaki]
beef, tofu (bean curd) and vegetables cooked fondue-style at the table and dipped in beaten raw egg

しゃぶしゃぶ
[shabushabu]
thinly sliced beef and vegetables cooked fondue-style at the table in a fish and seaweed stock and dipped in a sauce based on soya sauce, and flavored with citrus juice, sesame seeds and other flavorings

刺身
[sashimi]
slices of raw fish dipped in soya sauce flavored with wasabi (hot green horseradish sauce)

にぎり寿司
[nigirizushi (sushi)]
slices of fish, seafood, omelet on small blocks of lightly vinegared rice

巻き寿司
[makizushi]
rice filled with fish, omelet, mushrooms etc., wrapped in nori seaweed and sliced

ちらし寿司
[chirashi zushi]
scattered sushi (cold, lightly vinegared rice with carrots, cucumber, mushrooms, fish, strips of omelet, nori seaweed etc. scattered on top)

マグロ
[maguro]
tuna

赤身
[akami]
least fatty (and cheapest) piece of tuna

トロ
[toro]
fatty part of tuna

鮭
[sake]
salmon

タイ
[tai]
sea bream

エビ
[ebi]
prawn

イカ
[ika]
squid

タコ
[tako]
octopus

鯖
[saba]
mackerel

鰻
[unagi]
eel

ウニ
[uni]
sea urchin

アワビ
[awabi]
abalone

牡蠣
[kaki]
oyster

ホタテ貝
[hotate gai]
scallop

タラコ
[tarako]
cod roe

イクラ
[ikura]
salmon roe

ししゃも
[shishamo]
small dried fish

クラゲ
[kurage]
jellyfish

ご飯
[gohan]
boiled white rice

玄米
[gemmai]
brown rice

おにぎり
[onigiri]
rice ball wrapped in nori seaweed and containing various fillings, such as a pickled plum, salmon, or seaweed

弁当
[bentô]
lunchbox with rice and a variety of other foods

丼ぶり
[domburi]
large bowl of rice with various toppings

カツ丼
[katsudon]
large bowl of rice topped with breaded deep-fried pork cutlet

牛丼
[gyûdon]
large bowl of rice topped with fine slices of beef with soya sauce

天丼
[tendon]
large bowl of rice topped with tempura (battered and deep-fried vegetables, fish and prawns)

親子丼
[oyakodon]
large bowl of rice topped with chicken and lightly scrambled egg

卵丼
[tamagodon]
large bowl of rice topped with lightly scrambled egg and vegetables

五目ご飯
[gomoku gohan]
warm rice mixed with shredded vegetables, eggs, etc.

チャーハン
[châhan]
fried rice, usually containing meat and vegetables

お茶漬け
[ochazuke]
rice on which hot green tea is poured

オムライス
[omuraisu]
rice with tomato ketchup wrapped in an omelet

もち
[mochi]
sticky rice cakes eaten either with soya sauce or with sweetened azuki bean paste

そば
[soba]
buckwheat noodles, served hot in broth or chilled on a bamboo tray topped with nori seaweed and then dipped in soya sauce

うどん
[udon]
thick white wheat noodles, served in broth with meat and vegetables

きつねうどん
[kitsune udon]
thick white wheat noodles topped with deep-fried sweetened bean curd and spring onions

ラーメン
[râmen]
Chinese noodles served in broth

そうめん
[sômen]
thin white wheat noodles, served cold in summer

焼そば
[yaki soba]
fried noodles with meat and vegetables and a special sauce

餃子
[gyôza]
Chinese crescent-shaped steamed or fried dumplings containing minced pork, cabbage, spring onions, and seasonings, served with a dipping sauce based on soya sauce and vinegar

お好み焼□
[okonomiyaki]
cross between a large pancake and a pizza covered with cabbage and other vegetables, bacon or shrimps, and noodles, cooked on a hot plate, topped with a thick sweet and spicy sauce (specialty of Hiroshima and Osaka)

おでん□
[oden]
winter stew with hard-boiled eggs, deep-fried tôfu, konnyaku (devil's tongue jelly), kamaboko (somewhat rubbery fish cake) etc.

鍋料理
[nabe ryôri]
stew with vegetables, pork or beef, fish or shellfish

ちゃんこ鍋
[chanko nabe]
hearty stew of meat and vegetables, famous for being served to sumo wrestlers

のり
[nori]
type of seaweed dried and used to wrap sushi or shredded on top of rice dishes

わかめ
[wakame]
type of seaweed mainly used in miso soup, nabe dishes, or served with râmen (Chinese noodles)

昆布
[kombu]
type of seaweed used to make stock, along with bonito fish flakes

しょう油
[shôyu]
soya sauce

味噌
[miso]
fermented soya bean paste, used particularly in soup

味噌汁
[miso shiru]
miso soup

豆腐
[tôfu]
tofu, bean curd

冷や奴
[hiyayakko]
cold bean curd

揚げ出し豆腐
[agedashidôfu]
deep-fried bean curd

納豆
[nattô]
fermented soya beans

もやし
[moyashi]
bean sprouts

枝豆
[edamame]
fresh green soya beans boiled and lightly salted and served with beer (to be removed from their pods)

豆乳
[tônyû]
soya milk

卵
[tamago]
egg

生卵
[nama tamago]
raw egg

ゆで卵
[yude tamago]
hard-boiled egg

半熟卵
[hanjuku tamago]
soft-boiled egg

卵焼き
[tamago yaki]
slices of rolled sweet omelet flavored with soya sauce, served on sushi and in bento lunchboxes

目玉焼き
[medama yaki]
fried egg

オムレツ
[omuretsu]
omelet

茶碗蒸し
[chawan mushi]
savory egg custard with vegetables, quail's egg, mushrooms etc. served in a small lidded bowl

天ぷら
[tempura]
battered and deep-fried fish, prawns and vegetables

トンカツ
[tonkatsu]
breaded pork cutlet

エビフライ
[ebi furai]
breaded and deep-fried prawns

カキフライ
[kaki furai]
breaded and deep-fried oysters

会席料理
[kaiseki ryôri]
high-class formal seasonal Japanese cuisine, consisting of many different courses of small dishes

ウナギ
[unagi]
grilled eel

フグ
[fugu]
globe-fish/blowfish/puffer-fish

伊勢エビ
[ise ebi]
lobster

カニ
[kani]
crab

スッポン
[suppon]
softshell turtle

クジラ
[kujira]
whale

ナマズ
[namazu]
catfish

生き造り
[ikizukuri]
fish served whole and alive, with slices of flesh having been cut and put back in place

野菜
[yasai]
vegetables

大根
[daikon]
white radish

ニンジン
[ninjin]
carrot

タマネギ
[tamanegi]
onion

長ネギ
[naganegi]
spring onion

ゴボウ
[gobô]
burdock

ジャガイモ
[jagaimo]
potato

サツマイモ
[satsumaimo]
sweet potato

キャベツ
[kyabetsu]
cabbage

白菜
[hakusai]
Chinese leaves

ナス
[nasu]
eggplant

キュウリ
[kyûri]
cucumber

ほうれん草
[hôrensô]
spinach

カボチャ
[kabocha]
pumpkin

竹の子
[takenoko]
bamboo shoots

キノコ
[kinoko]
mushroom

椎茸
[shîtake]
Japanese brown mushroom with strong taste, commonly available dried

松茸
[matsutake]
pine mushroom, much sought-after and very expensive

栗
[kuri]
chestnut

果物/フルーツ
[kudamono/furûtsu]
fruit

トマト
[tomato]
tomato

レモン
[remon]
lemon

オレンジ
[orenji]
orange

ミカン
[mikan]
satsuma/clementine/mandarin

グレープフルーツ
[gurêpufurûtsu]
grapefruit

ブドウ
[budô]
grape

リンゴ
[ringo]
apple

梨
[nashi]
Japanese pear

柿
[kaki]
persimmon

メロン
[meron]
melon

イチゴ
[ichigo]
strawberry

梅
[ume]
plum

塩
[shio]
salt

コショウ
[koshô]
pepper

醤油
[shôyu]
soya sauce

ゴマ
[goma]
sesame

ワサビ
[wasabi]
*Japanese horseradish mustard –
bright green and very hot!*

パン
[pan]
bread

漬け物
[tsukemono]
pickles

チーズ
[chîzu]
cheese

紅しょうが
[beni shôga]
*sliced ginger pickled in vinegar
(bright red-pink)*

バター
[batâ]
butter

梅干
[umeboshi]
pickled plum

ジャム
[jamu]
jelly

shopping

店
[mise]
store

...時から...時まで営業
[...ji kara ...ji made êgyô]
open from ... to ...

デパート
[depâto]
department store

日曜日営業
[nichiyôbi êgyô]
open Sundays

スーパー
[sûpâ]
supermarket

営業中
[êgyô chû]
open

商店街
[shôtengai]
shopping district/center/mall

準備中
[jumbi chû]
closed

自動販売機
[jidôhambaiki]
vending machine

休日
[kyûjitsu]
holiday

酒屋
[sakaya]
liquor store

特別奉仕
[tokubetsu hôshi]
special offer

セール
[sêru]
sales

試着室
[shichaku shitsu]
changing rooms

婦人服
[fujin fuku]
ladieswear

紳士服
[shinshi fuku]
menswear

子供服
[kodomo fuku]
children's clothes

下着/ランジェリー
[shitagi/ranjerî]
lingerie

いらっしゃいませ。何にいたしましょう。
[irasshaimase. nan ni itashimashô]
hello, can I help you?

手造り
[tezukuri]
handmade

... 名物
[...mêbutsu]
specialty of ...

地方の特産品/名物
[chihô no tokusanhin/mêbutsu]
local specialties

自家製
[jika sê]
homemade

賞味期限
[shômi kigen]
best before ...

何か他にお入用ですか。
[nani ka hoka ni o iriyô desu ka]
will there be anything else?

レジでお支払いください。
[reji de oshiharai kudasai]
please pay at the counter

何でお支払いになりますか。
[nan de oshiharai ni narimasu ka]
how would you like to pay?

ここに署名/サインをお願いします。
[koko ni shomê/sain o onegai shimasu]
could you sign here, please?

numbers

Japanese numbers

ひとつ
[hitotsu]
one

ふたつ
[futatsu]
two

みっつ
[mittsu]
three

よっつ
[yottsu]
four

いつつ
[itsutsu]
five

むっつ
[muttsu]
six

ななつ
[nanatsu]
seven

やっつ
[yattsu]
eight

ここのつ
[kokonotsu]
nine

とお
[tô]
ten

Chinese-based numbers

ゼロ/零
[zero/rê]
zero

一
[ichi]
one

二
[ni]
two

三
[san]
three

四
[yon/shi]
four

五
[go]
five

六
[roku]
six

七
[shichi/nana]
seven

八
[hachi]
eight

九
[kyû/ku]
nine

十
[jû]
ten

十一
[jûichi]
eleven

十二
[jûni]
twelve

十三
[jûsan]
thirteen

十四
[jûyon/jûshi]
fourteen

十五
[jûgo]
fifteen

十六
[jûroku]
sixteen

十七
[jûshichi/jûnana]
seventeen

十八
[jûhachi]
eighteen

十九
[jûkyû/jûku]
nineteen

二十
[nijû]
twenty

二十一
[nijûichi]
twenty-one

二十二
[nijûni]
twenty-two

三十
[sanjû]
thirty

三十五
[sanjûgo]
thirty-five

四十
[yonjû]
forty

五十
[gojû]
fifty

六十
[rokujû]
sixty

七十
[nanajû]
seventy

八十
[hachijû]
eighty

九十
[kyûjû]
ninety

百
[hyaku]
one hundred

百一
[hyakuichi]
one hundred and one

二百
[nihyaku]
two hundred

三百
[sambyaku]
three hundred

五百
[gohyaku]
five hundred

六百
[roppyaku]
six hundred

七百
[nanahyaku]
seven hundred

八百
[happyaku]
eight hundred

九百
[kyûhyaku]
nine hundred

千
[sen]
one thousand

二千
[nisen]
two thousand

三千
[sanzen]
three thousand

一万
[ichiman]
ten thousand

十万
[jûman]
one hundred thousand

百万
[hyakuman]
one million

Notes